THE TEAM HANDBOOK

Second Edition

Peter R. Scholtes
Brian L. Joiner
Barbara J. Streibel

The Team Handbook
Second Edition

3800 Regent St.   P.O. Box 5445   Madison WI 53705-0445   USA
PH: (800) 669-8326 (U.S. only) or (608) 238-8134 FAX: (608) 238-2908

First Printing June 1996

Production and Administrative Staff:

Barbara Streibel Subject Matter Expert, Project Leader
John Roderick Clark Writer
Jan Harris Desktop Publisher
Dawn Rolli Desktop Publisher
Jennifer Schilling Proofreader
David Charbonneau Proofreader
Dale Mann Cartoonist
Laura Moss Gottlieb Indexer

Brian Joiner Subject Matter Expert
Kevin Kelleher Subject Matter Expert
Lynda Finn Subject Matter Expert
Gordon Myers Subject Matter Expert
Casey Garhart Developer
Deb Simon Marketing
Angela Schoeneck Marketing
Vickie Benchlikha Production
Kelly E. See Intern
William Lawton Market Research

Production Notes:

Printing and binding were done at Straus Printing Company (Madison, WI). Lamination was done at Plastics Unlimited.

About Joiner Associates Inc.

Founded by Dr. Brian Joiner in 1983, Joiner Associates Inc. has specialized in helping organizations around the world improve effectiveness, reduce waste, and compete better in the marketplace. Our unique understanding of how to develop and implement strategic efforts built around customer needs and organizational strengths has allowed our customers to change better, faster, and more effectively than their competitors.

We offer a wide range of learning resources, training, and consulting services that can support your efforts to develop leadership skills, use teams more effectively, manage change, improve decision making, eliminate problems, improve processes—and much more.

Call today to discover how Joiner can help you unleash your potential.

ISBN 1-884731-11-2

Acknowledgments

We'd like to recognize the efforts of the people involved in the development of the first edition of *The Team Handbook*: Peter Scholtes, Brian Joiner, Gretchen Brant, Bill Braswell, Lynda Finn, Warren Gaskill, Heero Hacquebord, Kevin Little, Deb Mies, Sue Reynard, Barbara Streibel, Molly Rose Teuke, and Lonnie Weiss. It is the hard work and dedication that this team of people put into the first edition that we are building upon with the second edition.

We want to thank our reader panel for agreeing to review the second edition. They gave us many hours of their valuable time providing us with feedback on our ideas and writings.

Joseph Abelson
Philadelphia College of Textiles & Science
Business School

Brian Blecke
EDS

Eric Budd
EDS

Kathryn Christiansen
Rush Home Care Network
Rush-Presbyterian-St.Luke's Medical Center

Ann H. Dodd
The University of North Carolina at Chapel Hill

Janet B. Forton
EDS

Constance Green
Benjamin Moore & Company

Mary Haymore
Allergan, Inc.

Donna Long
DML Training & Consulting

Lynette Pedrosa
Forum Corporation

Diane Primozic
Northwestern Medical Faculty Foundation

Jim Quillen
Express Personnel Systems

Pat Roam
Mount Carmel Health System

Peter R. Scholtes
Scholtes Seminars & Consulting

Greg Sengstock
Pulte Home Corporation, Illinois Division

Mary Ann Mings-Tennant
Suncast Corporation

Jame L. Todd, P.E.
Bureau of Reclamation

Tommy Williams
Louisiana Blood Center and Blood Center of Southeast Texas

Lori Yokich
EDS

We'd like to thank the following people and companies for sharing their time to help us better understand how they use teams in their organizations.

EDS
A team of many who gave their valuable time and input

Wilson Sporting Goods, Golf Division
Lynn Shemmer and a group of Wilson team leaders

Meriter Health Systems
Eileen Hankerson, James E. Tracy

S&B Engineers & Constructors, Ltd.
Ralph Miller, Carolyn Dortch, Don Smith

Foreword

The original edition of *The Team Handbook,* published in 1988, was written over a period of two or three years. It reflected what we knew then about Teams and Quality and what our customers taught us about what was useful.

That was then. Since that time, we have learned more about quality, teams, and customer needs. It is therefore time for a new edition of *The Team Handbook.*

There's been another change since 1988. I am no longer an employee of Joiner Associates. I have been on my own since February of 1994. This 2nd edition was developed by my Joiner Associate friends and former colleagues. I salute their effort. This 2nd edition has several important new practical contributions that will lead to the success of your teams.

The 1st edition of *The Team Handbook* focused on cross-functional teams engaged in improvement projects. While these teams are still well-served in this new edition, there is a broadening of focus. The 2nd edition of *The Team Handbook* includes useful approaches for management teams, new product development teams, natural work groups, and others. This new edition includes some new team strategies and tools and new approaches to the old strategies and tools.

When we set out to develop *The Team Handbook* about ten years ago, we wanted to make it "useful" and "friendly," sort of like having your favorite older brother or sister standing by your side giving you some good practical advice. Our customers have told us that we succeeded. This new edition maintains that same character of a knowledgeable and friendly advisor.

I have one more bit of advice. The importance and popularity of teams have escalated dramatically in the last several years. As someone who perhaps helped to contribute a bit to that trend, I feel a need to offer a caution: teams are *not* a panacea. Teams are one vehicle for getting work done. Teams will not always be the best vehicle. A given team may not be able to deal with the causes of the problem or the needs of the system. There is no substitute for leadership, good planning, well-functioning systems, excellent services, well-designed and executed products, and an environment of trust and collaboration. Some managers seem to want to proliferate teams, the more the better. But teams need to be part of larger contexts and larger systems: systems that select priorities, systems and processes for providing goods and services to the customers, systems for training and educating the workforce. Without purpose, Dr. Deming has told us, there can be no system. And without purpose and systems, there can be no team. Leaders, therefore, must focus on their organization's mission, purpose, and the systems needed to successfully accomplish that mission and purpose. Then they may be better able to decide where, when, and how to use teams.

May *The Team Handbook* continue to be your guide.

Peter R. Scholtes
April 1996
Madison, WI

Dedication

This book is dedicated to all of you who used the first edition of *The Team Handbook* over the past eight years. It is you who have made teams successful, and in doing so have made *The Team Handbook* a success. You have given the concepts in this book meaning through their application, improving the quality of your organizations and the value you deliver to customers. It is also you who have provided us with the feedback and suggestions to make this second edition an even more valuable resource for your teams and their important work.

Introduction

A New Edition

Welcome to the second edition of *The Team Handbook*. We believe that new readers will find this volume the finest handbook on working with teams available today. For those of you who have enjoyed working with the first edition of *The Team Handbook*, we believe this new edition will have everything you liked about the original, and a lot more.

The original handbook created in 1988 has become standard reading for people working with teams in the United States and around the world. Since then, however, the world in which teams function has changed dramatically. The fundamental tenets of the "quality revolution" are now widely practiced in a diversity of forms and contexts. The arrival of the information age and many new technologies has increased the need for teams of all kinds. For example, today some customers are applying team concepts and tools found in the original handbook to ongoing work teams or management teams. At the same time, many people are using the handbook for project teams and quality improvement work.

Over the years many of you have called and talked to us about the handbook. We've listened to your comments and questions. We also interviewed a number of you to learn more about how we might better meet your needs. We heard you asking for a new edition that was easier for ongoing teams to use and that offered more support for managers who sponsor teams. Since many of you use the handbook as a reference, we wanted to streamline the information flow in the new edition, making it more user friendly, with a format that would help you find the information you need more quickly and easily. In creating the new handbook, we strove to retain what worked for you in the original (in some cases sharpening those strategies), as well as add new ideas in form and content.

> ➤ **Tip**

How to Use This Book

People use *The Team Handbook* in different ways. You may:

- Read it cover to cover

- Use it as a reference

Those of you familiar with the first edition will note that the order of the chapters in this book is basically the same, so you don't have to relearn where to find things.

Those of you new to *The Team Handbook* may want to review the table of contents or look up your specific topic in the index before plunging in.

What's New in This Edition

Chapter 1 has been substantially rewritten in order to focus on the widening context for teams in today's complex and ever changing competitive environment, while at the same time retaining a strong interest in quality issues. Additional detailed information on Quality Leadership can be found in Appendix A. Users who are starting a quality initiative are encouraged to read Appendix A early in your work.

In **Chapter 2** the information on the scientific method has been updated and reorganized. New information on how to use the tools in problem-solving has been added. Whether you want to plunge into hands-on applications and try out a few tools to see how they work, or whether you want to ground yourself in the big picture first, you will find this chapter suited to your needs.

Information of particular interest to managers who sponsor teams has been pulled together into **Chapter 3**. New information on how to review projects has been added here as well.

Even more information on how to handle effective meetings, discussions, decisions, and team closure has been added to **Chapter 4**.

Chapter 5 now reveals how two approaches to improvement—the *Joiner 7 Step Method*™ and the *5 Step Plan for Process Improvement*—help implement improvement strategies. We have also added two strategies of particular use to ongoing work teams.

Chapter 6 focuses on understanding the stages of team development. The stages of team growth and the recipe for a successful team, which many of you used and loved in the first edition, are still here. We moved the 10 common group problems to the new Chapter 7 so that we could expand the material on conflict.

The new **Chapter 7** now includes material on the 10 common group problems. We have also added new information on groupthink and managing conflict to this chapter.

Appendix A contains information about Quality Leadership.

Appendix B has an example of a storyboard summarizing a team's problem-solving efforts.

Appendix C includes many of the warm-up activities and exercises that were in Chapter 7 in the first edition. The exercises can be used to develop team members' meeting skills or agreements around roles and responsibilities, and to learn more about the process under study.

Appendix D contains references for additional reading.

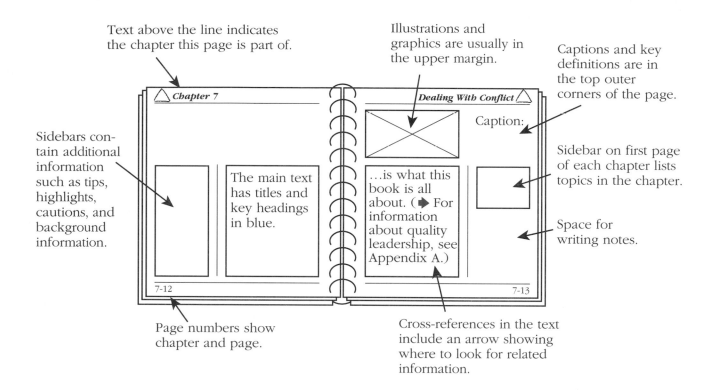

Text above the line indicates the chapter this page is part of.

Illustrations and graphics are usually in the upper margin.

Captions and key definitions are in the top outer corners of the page.

△ *Chapter 7*

Dealing With Conflict △

Caption:

Sidebars contain additional information such as tips, highlights, cautions, and background information.

The main text has titles and key headings in blue.

...is what this book is all about. (➡ For information about quality leadership, see Appendix A.)

Sidebar on first page of each chapter lists topics in the chapter.

Space for writing notes.

7-12

7-13

Page numbers show chapter and page.

Cross-references in the text include an arrow showing where to look for related information.

Background Information

Background information is additional information that adds depth or an interesting sidelight to the main text. Sometimes this information will be in a sidebar, and other times it will need a full page of its own. In either case, it will always be on a gray background with a line around it to help you separate it from the rest of the text.

Updates in the Format

If you're familiar with the first edition of *The Team Handbook*, this edition will look very familiar. We still have the cartoons and lots of white space where you can make your own notes. We still use blue to highlight important information. And we still have sidebar information separated out for ease of use.

But we have made a few changes that are designed to help you move through the book and find what you are looking for. (See the diagram of a typical page above.) When we cross-reference information, we have included an arrow to help you find the reference easily, indicating whether you need to look ahead or turn back.

Definitions...

Can usually be found in the upper corner of a page. This space is also reserved for captions of cartoons or other graphics.

We have also identified different types of sidebar information. On the first page of each chapter we have a sidebar that summarizes the content of that chapter. And in some chapters we also include sidebars titled "For Ongoing Teams."

Other specialized sidebars include Background Information, Cautions, Tips, Highlights, and Definitions. You can see examples of each on these two pages.

Like many of you we are constantly striving to improve our products and services. We hope the second edition of *The Team Handbook* meets with your approval. Lct us know how it works for you. There is a form in the back of the book for you to use to give us feedback.

➤ Tip

These are helpful hints on what to do or what not to do. They will always have the blue arrow head and Tip title to make them easy to find.

 Caution!

The caution sidebars signal things to watch out for, pitfalls, or common problems to avoid. When you see the caution sign you know to beware.

 Highlights

These sidebars summarize the main points of the text. They may be paragraphs, like this one, or bulleted lists. In either case, the lighthouse indicates a summary of the adjacent text.

Table of

Contents

Chapter 5

Building an Improvement Plan

Chapter 6

Learning to Work Together

Chapter 7

Dealing With Conflict

Appendices

> **For help finding information on a specific topic,
> see the Index at the back of the book.**

Chapter 1

Using Teams to Meet Today's Challenges

I t used to be that an organization could reasonably expect to experience periods of change alternating with periods of stability.

Today we have entered an environment in which turbulence seems the norm and change is the only constant. Many factors are forcing organizations to look for new ways to meet market demands quickly and efficiently. These factors include: the need for speed, the need to respond to vast technological change, the trend toward globalization, and increased market pressures.

Why We Need Teams More Than Ever

To succeed in this new environment, the knowledge, skills, experience, and perspectives of a wide range of people must be brought together. Only then can an organization hope to solve many-faceted problems, make good decisions, and deliver solutions to customers. Thus the growing need for teams. Teams create environments in which participants can keep up with needed changes, learn more about the business, and gain skills in collaboration. Teams outperform individuals when:

- The task is complex
- Creativity is needed
- The path forward is unclear
- More efficient use of resources is required
- Fast learning is necessary
- High commitment is desirable
- The implementation of a plan requires the cooperation of others
- The task or process is cross-functional

What You Will Find Here

In this chapter we explore:

Chapter 1

As more and more tasks fit this description, organizations are creating teams to meet these challenges.

Companies are increasingly relying on teams as they discover that traditional methods of problem solving, decision making, communication, and implementation are not fast or flexible enough to respond to the challenges of the times. The teams they use take many forms: management teams, ongoing work teams, improvement teams, and self-directed work teams, to name a few.

Organizations are using teams to accomplish a wide variety of purposes: reduce lead times, decrease cycle time, cut service errors, do daily work, increase the rate of transactions, operate business units, redesign systems, understand customer needs, and the list goes on.

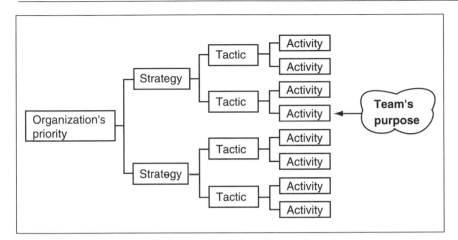

Linking the Team and the Organization

It is important to know how a team's work links to the organization's key strategies.

I. What Has to Be in Place for Teams to Work Well

Teams are being used because organizations have a growing need to achieve complex goals swiftly and efficiently and often with fewer resources. To be effective, teams must stay in touch with these needs. It is important to remember that teams are not the solution to every problem, nor should they be created as ends in themselves—that wastes resources. Here's a short list of what teams must have in order to do what they do best.

Teams Must Have Clearly Defined Purposes and Goals That Serve the Organization

Teams need to understand what they are trying to accomplish and why. Team purposes and goals must be clearly linked to larger organizational missions, goals, and strategies that deliver added value to customers and to the operations of the organization. Team goals should be focused and have a workable scope. When the team is working on something that is clearly important to the organization, people are more likely to feel that they are doing the necessary work of the organization and that their time is being well spent. Purpose is a vital ingredient of a successful team. It gives a team focus and direction.

Checking the Link Between Team Purpose and Organization Priorities

If you use a tree diagram, like the one above, to check the relationship between a team's purpose and the organization's key goals or priorities, the following questions are helpful:

- Ask of any goal or strategy (going left to right), "What will it take to successfully accomplish this priority?" Each priority should have the necessary and sufficient sub-activities. Some of these activities might be the focus of a team's work.

- Ask of any activity (moving right to left), "What is the purpose of this activity and how is it linked to some larger objective?"

Teams Need Clearly Defined Parameters Within Which to Work

Early on, the sponsor of the team needs to define the importance of the team's task in the larger context of the organization. The sponsor must explain what the relative importance of the task is, what the parameters are, what the expectations of the organization are, what the timeline is, what the budget and available resources are, and what kinds of decisions the team is empowered to make. (Ongoing teams, of course, will have already established many of these points.)

Teams Need to Be Able to Communicate Within the Organization

The sponsor should define how the team is connected to other teams, departments, and customers. It's vital for teams to know how to communicate with the organization, with whom to communicate, and how often. If the team leader is responsible for all communication with the organization, that individual must make special efforts to make sure that all necessary communication channels to the organization are open and operative. Key questions must be dealt with: How does the team get the data it needs? How does the team let the organization know what they are doing? How does the team take advantage of technology to get its work done?

Teams Need to Know How to Do Their Tasks

A team should be able to identify the steps it will take to complete its work.

Teams Need to Have People With the Necessary Knowledge and Skills to Accomplish Their Tasks

Teams need to have the right human resources to complete the work assigned them. They often need access to people with diverse talents and points of view. For example, they may need people with skills in planning, applying logic and data in problem solving, decision making, running effective meetings, communicating, documenting, or conflict management. Team sponsors have the responsibility to make sure that the needed skills are "on board," and that people have the time available to accomplish the tasks assigned within the structure of their work schedules. If vital skills are lacking, new players should be recruited or training should be provided to fill the gap.

Teams Need to Know How They Are Going to Accomplish Their Tasks

Teams work best when they have a detailed understanding of how their work will proceed and how the team will accomplish its tasks.

A team should be able to clearly identify the steps it will take to complete its work. Several outlines for solving problems and creating improvements can be found in Chapter 5.

Chapter 1

The Joiner Triangle

We use the triangle to symbolize the relationship that quality, a scientific approach, and a feeling of "all one team" must have if an organization is to be successful. Taken together, these three elements are extremely powerful.

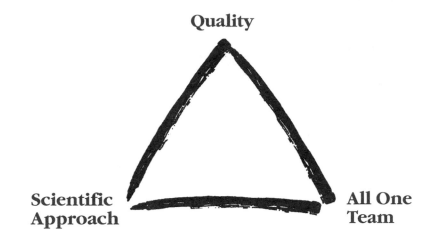

II. Key Elements of a Successful Business Strategy

Organizations are using a variety of approaches to steer through the turbulent "whitewater" of today's business environment. These approaches include 4th Generation Management, reengineering, continuous quality improvement, continuous learning, quality leadership, and many more. Today, teams are being widely and successfully used in all of these approaches.

The Joiner Triangle

We use the Joiner Triangle to represent three key elements that are prevalent in many of today's business strategies:

- A dedication to quality and customer value
- A scientific approach to continuous improvement
- An environment of teamwork and cooperation

These three elements all work together. None of them is fully effective without the others, but together they are enormously powerful. Note that the apex is quality as defined by the customer. Note that the base of the triangle is defined by a data-based scientific approach to learning coupled with an aligned all-one-team culture. Only by applying a scientific approach to the analysis of the way in which all products and services are delivered to the customer, and aligning all of the company's energies to meet the challenges that the analysis presents, can a company continuously improve what it does and delight the customer.

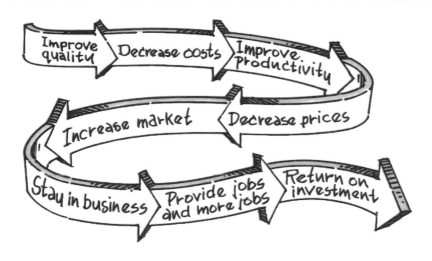

The Chain Reaction

With each improvement, processes and systems run better and better. Productivity increases as waste goes down. Customers get better products, which ultimately expands the market and provides better return on investments. Dr. W. Edwards Deming developed this chain reaction. It is often called the Deming Chain Reaction.

These key elements have become a part of the practices and philosophy of most companies, even those who have not formally adopted a "quality" approach. Today, more decisions are being made on the basis of data instead of guesswork. More organizations are placing a priority on quality "as perceived by the customer," or "as defined by our mission." More organizations are putting new emphasis on continuous improvement, abandoning old axioms like "leave well enough alone" and "if it ain't broke, don't fix it." There is an increased focus on how work gets done, as well as on what is done. And, of course, there is much greater emphasis on tapping the potential of all employees, which is what this book is all about. (➧For more information on quality leadership, see Appendix A.)

W. Edwards Deming (1902-1993)

W. Edwards Deming, pioneering statistician, lecturer, author, and consultant, emphasized a systems and leadership approach to improving quality. He taught that quality is achieved by studying and constantly improving processes and systems so that the final product or service delights the customer. In other words, understanding customer needs and customer use of services and products is the means of defining quality. For example, if you are asked to clean off a table, knowing how to do it well depends upon whether the table is to be used for eating or for surgery.

Deming taught managers the importance of understanding organizations as systems, and of responding appropriately to the variation in their processes. He developed his 14 Points which identify the principles of management that leaders need to implement as part of their responsibility to improve corporate systems. (➧For more information about Dr. Deming and the 14 points, see Appendix A.)

Chapter 1

III. The Challenge of Alignment

The increased pace of change, as well as the new emphasis on the improvement of whole systems and entire processes, has increased the importance of teams. Increasingly, the problems to be solved require more than one set of skills and the alignment of a number of systems and processes. There is also a growing need to take cross-functional approaches to problem solving. Companies have come to realize that it is easier to develop and improve systems and processes by working collaboratively within the organization. Whatever your organization's business strategy, chances are it will rely heavily on teams to carry it out.

Challenges for Team Sponsors

Team sponsors are playing an increasingly important role to assure team productivity and effectiveness. The sponsor helps to make sure the team is connected to the business strategy and, on occasion, runs interference for the team and represents the team to the larger organization. If you are a team sponsor, therefore, major responsibilities have been placed in your hands. It is not enough to help gather a team, support a leader to get the team rolling, and then sit back. There are a number of things you will need to do to ensure success. Most of all, you will need to monitor and support the team's progress around three particular challenges or tasks:

1. Developing the team's charter—we call this PURPOSE

2. Establishing ways of relating—we call this PARTNERSHIP

3. Generating methods to achieve goals—we call this PROCESS

A Sponsor's Task

A team's sponsor should make sure the team is lined up with the organization's purpose.

In focusing upon these three primary tasks, it is necessary for the team sponsor to:

- Work closely with the team leader
- Ensure that the team's purpose and the organization's purposes are aligned
- Make sure the right people are on the team
- See that team members are clear about and committed to their roles and responsibilities, as well as the limits of their authority
- Support the team in constructing and using communication channels to interact with other groups and individuals within the organization
- Review and guide the team in developing and using work methods and plans

Teams that are vague about their purpose, lack ways of relating with others, or have no agreed upon methods for solving problems don't function well. It is confusing to work inside these teams and difficult for others in the organization to work with them. Consider the following example:

> An insurance organization set up an ongoing cross-functional team to serve as a "knowledge resource" for salespeople in the field. This group of lawyers, accountants, insurance statisticians, and marketers were to help salespeople customize large sales contracts in a timely way. Shortly after establishing the team, the team's sponsor, a VP for marketing, was told that some team members did not want to remain on the team. Others never really became part of the team at all. They always seemed to have some reason why they could not attend meetings.

The sponsor worked closely with the team's leader to find out what was going on. After analyzing the situation, it became clear that the team's purpose was vague, roles weren't clearly defined, and the team's existence had not been connected to the business strategy of the company. In addition, rewards and recognition were based on individual performance, not team results. No wonder commitment was low and team members confused.

The team sponsor and team leader met with the team for a full day plus 90 minutes a day for an additional week. During that time, team members gained clarity and commitment to their roles and to the team's identity. They also worked out channels of communication between the team and salespeople in the field and other groups and departments within the larger organization. The sponsor played a key role in helping the team understand its limits of authority. In a brief period of time, the team leader helped the team formulate agreements concerning how decisions were to be made and implemented.

Failure to be clear about purpose, to connect with others in the organization, and to make decisions can cause serious breakdowns in performance and morale. Once purpose, partnership, and process tasks were addressed, the team portrayed in our example experienced a dramatic improvement in morale; team membership was no longer in question. For further information, refer to the Team Development Model on the next page.

Team Development Model

In order to keep individuals, teams, and the organization as a whole aligned, it may be helpful to think in terms of the model below. This model shows the three dimensions of the organization as columns: Organization, Team, and Individual Members. For each dimension there are three primary tasks: Purpose, Partnership, and Process. These issues are the three horizontal slices.

Dimensions

	Organization	Team	Individual Members
Purpose (why, what)	Mission	Charter and goals	Roles and responsibilities
Partnership (with whom)	Values & beliefs	Norms and communication channels	Interpersonal skills
Process (how)	Management systems and reviews	Methods and procedures	Problem solving & planning skills

Primary Tasks (left-side label)

The Purpose is the reason behind the work being done. At the organizational level, this is the mission. At the team level, it is the goal. And at the individual level, it is each person's role. In order to maintain alignment it is critical that the team's goals line up with the organization's mission, and that the individuals' roles line up with both the mission and the team goals. It is equally important that everyone in the organization understands *how* these purposes line up with one another.

The second task of the model deals with Partnership, or how people relate to one another. The organization has certain values and beliefs that are represented by the corporate culture. Teams have norms for how to work together and channels for communicating with management and other teams. Individual team members have interpersonal skills. Like purposes, it is important that these three dimensions of partnership line up with one another. Although we may make an effort to line up mission, goals, and roles, it is often the case that we forget about lining up organizational values, team norms, and individual skills. We create new team norms without considering how they fit with the organizational culture or the interpersonal skills we have been rewarding in the past.

Finally, the third task of the model considers Process, or how people get the work done. The organization has systems of work and management reviews; teams have procedures; and individuals have their own problem solving and planning skills. Once again, if we change one of these without changing the others we are setting ourselves up for failure. And even if we do change all three, it is critical that everyone understands the new alignment. Too often we change the management review system to match new team procedures without making any changes to the entrenched work habits of the individuals.

Chapter 1

IV. Teams and Change

As organizations discover the benefits of having people at all levels work together in teams, organizational cultures are undergoing a change from only valuing individual contributions to valuing both individual and team contributions.

Most teamwork involves change, and change is seldom easy. It is unlikely that anyone will figure out how to change an organization without asking its people to change as well. Therefore we must all be sensitive to the problems that people will have with any change that affects them.

Keep in mind some of the "laws" of organizational change:

People don't resist change; they resist being changed

> The best way to get people to dig in their heels is to give them an arbitrary mandate to change. To ensure their cooperation, it is vital to involve people in every step of a change effort: clearly identifying the need for a change, planning and implementing the change, monitoring and acting on the results. Ask for their opinions. What do they fear? What do they hope will happen? What suggestions can they make to ensure the success of the effort?

Things are the way they are simply because they got that way

> Somebody, sometime, had to write the outdated policy or create the problem-plagued methods that you are working with. Remember that there were probably good reasons for doing things that way when the system was established. Therefore, it helps to understand the history behind any problem before you attempt to change it.

Unless things change, they are likely to remain the same

As long as people continue to do things the way they've always done them, you'll continue to get the results you've always gotten. If you want improvement, people will need to change the way they work. An exception to this law is that things left unattended or unimproved will change—for the worse. However, do not mistake attention and improvement for tampering. Tampering is worse than inattention. The methods described in this book will help you decide when you are improving a process and when you are just tampering with it. Pay attention to systems; improve them, but don't tamper with them.

Change would be easy if it weren't for all the people

There are other versions of this law. "Management would be easy if it weren't for all the employees," and "Business would be easy if it weren't for all the customers." The message in the irony of these statements is that people are the organization; and the organization is there for the customers. Therefore: Pay attention to the people as well as the systems. Listen to them. Listening to employees and customers before problems arise makes any change go more smoothly.

Break Down Barriers

There are several common problems you will run into when attempting to change an organization. People will often be afraid of having their security or position put at risk. The following guidelines will help you surface, identify, and overcome these barriers as the process unfolds.

Feeling like a "lonely little petunia in an onion patch"?

Onion Patch Strategy

What do you do if no one will listen, if you're having trouble getting the attention of the people on high, feeling like a "lonely little petunia in an onion patch"?

Our advice: Think big but stay close to your roots.

Select change efforts within your control. Make certain they will capture the attention of people at least two links up the chain of command. Look for opportunities with big dollar implications, such as reduced waste or increased revenue. Focus on getting results that others, even skeptics, will respect. Involve fellow workers in your efforts, sharing credit for a successful job. Slowly build a network of supporters.

Be patient. Be persistent. When someone expresses interest, be prepared to provide more information and detail about the implications. Identify the most common questions or objections and have the answers at hand. Communicate success stories.

Identify informal networks

Imagine your company as a small town. Along with its official work system, it has a social system—a loose network of small groups of people. These groups offer their members support and friendship. Loyalty to these groups may be stronger than loyalty to the company.

Informal groups have their own leaders and "rules" that can determine, for example, the pace of work or the relationship with the boss. If the informal organization and its leaders accept a proposed change, events will proceed more smoothly; if they are opposed, change may be nearly impossible. Identify the informal leaders. Get to know them. Spend time listening to them. When you understand their needs and concerns, you will understand how the changes you seek might be fashioned.

Build a critical mass

To get any idea rolling, you need to build understanding and enthusiasm. When the idea is supported by a sufficient number of diverse people, it reaches a "critical mass." It takes off under its own steam, giving the impression of a growing movement and a sense of momentum. The size of the critical mass can vary from just a few key people to the whole company. In the early stages of change, the critical mass builds as key opinion leaders shift from neutral positions to more supportive ones, or from resistance to neutrality.

When planning a change, identify these key opinion leaders—both in the formal and informal networks. Find out how you can sway their opinions: What are their concerns? If they see a risk, what is the source of the risk? Find out what their needs are, and how their needs

can be met and incorporated into the implementation plan. Do they need to see an idea in action? Do they need to see data you have already collected? Do they need to talk to the people involved in the change?

Create emotional acceptance

Since people resist being changed, any organizational change is a campaign for their hearts as well as their minds. Even when there is a lot of detailed planning and communication, very little actually happens as a result of a solely rational, logical process. Change happens because people as a group commit to it.

You will need creative, thinking people to successfully implement a major change. Talk to the people who will be involved in or affected by a change. Include them in decisions about the change whenever possible. Help them to understand the need to change. They need a clear picture of what the future will be like, and an answer to the question: "How will work be different?" Listen and respond to their needs, fears, desires, and concerns about change. Make accommodations as necessary.

Treat change like a courtship

Approach any change as you would a courtship, slowly and with a sense of surprise.

"Woo" the people. Listen to them. Be responsive to their concerns. When change represents a new lifestyle for people, they need time to warm up to and experiment with it. Permit them to be inelegant and to make mistakes. Help the organization stretch itself, but not too much at a time. An idea approached as an experiment may be accepted more readily than one imposed as a permanent change.

Anchor the change

The individuals or groups on the cutting edge of change will often feel isolated or inadequate. Combat such feelings by providing support and guidance. Help them feel anchored to the direction and mainstream activities of the company. With a well-connected network of activity, the people implementing change will become part of a common effort to learn and change. If a group falters, let it know that help is at hand.

Summary

In this chapter we have defined some of the contexts in which the work of teams takes place. We recommend, as you carry forward the work of teams, that you refer to this chapter, and the appendices cited in it, to gain a deeper understanding of the team's relationship to the organization. In the remainder of this book, the larger context for teams will be put aside as we focus on the very important work that goes on within the team. In particular, we will be concentrating on how to create teams to achieve the goals of our organizations and delight our customers. In the following pages, we will describe the tools, techniques, and attitudes that will make teamwork successful in your organization. Like people, teams need time to develop. Many organizations are a long way from the kind of alignment necessary to create an all-one-team culture, but the process has begun. Much learning and collaboration lies ahead of us. The task is difficult, but the rewards are great.

Chapter 2

Getting Started: Learning the Tools

Everyone uses teams, and everyone wants the teams they have to be good at solving problems. Whether your team is managing part of a business, or building a customer data base, or coordinating work in the accounting department, or implementing a merger with another organization, it's likely that you will also be improving processes or solving problems. To do this, you will need good data—and to get good data, understand what it means, and use it properly, you will need a scientific approach and some of the tools described in this chapter.

So What's Your Problem?

To some of us it may seem obvious what the problems are, but our hunches are often inaccurate. Symptoms can often disguise themselves as causes. The real culprits may in fact be very different from those that appear on the surface. Misdiagnosis can waste time and resources. That's why it helps to gather and analyze data in a scientific fashion. In this chapter we will introduce a variety of tools that will help you gather data and help you discover what the data has to tell you. Whatever the tasks of your team, these tools are sure to be valuable.

Problems Teams Encounter

Teams often encounter problems when doing their work. Whether they are doing a special project or participating in an ongoing effort to improve a process, teams may have to grapple with some of the following: *mistakes, delays,* and *inefficiencies.*

What You Will Find Here

In this chapter we explore:

Handling Mistakes

Too many organizations still concentrate their efforts on fixing mistakes instead of preventing them.

1. Mistakes

When mistakes or errors occur, work has to be repeated and extra steps added to correct the error or dispose of the damage. Many companies call this "scraping burnt toast," that is, fixing up the product rather than preventing the problem.

Examples:

1. When a packaging machine dents boxes, employees have to inspect all the boxes and replace those that are damaged.

2. When a patient's ID number is incorrectly written down, the staff has to recheck many records to locate and verify the correct ID.

These steps add no value to the product or service. The solution lies in finding ways to error-proof the process, preventing errors or defects in the first place.

2. Delays/Breakdowns

Sometimes even when services or products are not harmed, supply or production systems break down and real work is put on hold. Efforts are then diverted to repair work.

Examples:

1. A poorly maintained copy machine keeps breaking down. This causes delays all along the process, and much confusion as people try to keep track of exactly where everything was before the copier stopped.

2. Key information is missing for a report, so it is started based on available information—and then put aside, to await the missing pieces. This report is handled many times to add the missing

information as it comes in. Each time, the draft has to be located, missing information has to be entered in the correct places, inconsistencies have to be fixed, and on and on.

3. Someone wants to notify people of an upcoming meeting, but the list of telephone numbers and addresses is incomplete. Many calls are needed to get the information.

3. Inefficiencies

Even when products and services aren't defective, nor the work flow interrupted, more time, material, and movement than necessary are often used. Often the inefficiency arose originally because something happened that upset the system and extra steps were added. But the effects have remained long after the problem was gone. In these cases, there is a clear reason why the system was established the way it was. At other times, there is no way of knowing how the inefficient system began.

Example:

By tracing their movements on a floor plan of their work area, employees discovered they crisscrossed their paths many times to get all the material they needed. No one was sure exactly how the floor plan got the way it was. A redesigned layout eliminated a lot of unnecessary movement and complexity. (➡See work-flow diagrams on p. 2-15.)

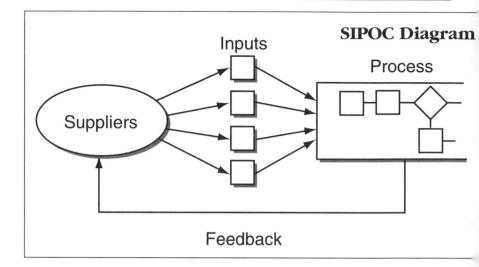

SIPOC Diagram

Inputs

Process

Suppliers

Feedback

Process for Filling an Order

1
Receive purchase order

↓

2
Open customer file

↓

3
Update information

↓

4
Enter order information

↓

5
Send information to Shipping and Billing

↓

6
Pack and ship order

I. Processes and Systems

We tend to think of organizations as places where countless tasks get done: putting labels on envelopes, x-raying a patient, tightening the screws on a component, calling customers, and on and on. Teams often struggle to understand how the tasks which are part of their jobs fall into a sequence of steps, or a process.

A process can be represented by the SIPOC (**S**uppliers, **I**nputs, **P**rocess, **O**utputs, **C**ustomers) diagram above. Processes consist of a sequence of steps which transform some input (envelopes, information, components, etc.) from suppliers into a final output (letters mailed, report written, components assembled) which goes to customers. The steps in the following tasks are all examples of processes:

- Producing a product
- Delivering a service
- Opening a bank account
- Giving a medication
- Hiring or training a new employee
- Performing a surgical procedure
- Filling an order (see illustration on left)
- Processing payroll

Almost every word that ends in "ing" is a process. In this light, we begin to see that every task can be part of a process, and there are thousands upon thousands of processes in every organization.

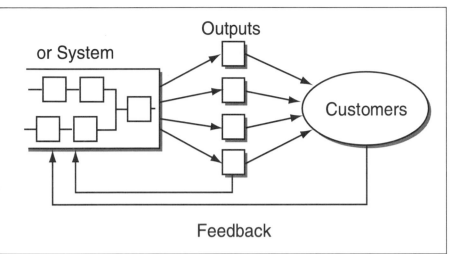

or System

Outputs

Customers

Feedback

SIPOC Diagrams...

Show suppliers, inputs, process steps, outputs, and customers—the key elements of a process.

Thinking in terms of processes is perhaps the most profound change that occurs when you begin to see tasks as related series of activities. You start to see how jobs throughout your organization are related. Since your organization works through processes, you can only improve your work by improving processes. Better processes mean better quality, which means greater productivity.

When employees begin to look at processes, they will, often for the first time, develop a common understanding of what their jobs are and how they are linked. Someone can talk about specific steps in a process and everyone will understand where those steps fit into the larger picture. They will then be able to improve the effectiveness of this collection of tasks by asking questions such as:

- What is the purpose of this process?
- What do we have coming into the process?
- What must we do to get from one step to the next?
- Which steps are unnecessary?
- Where do we run into problems?

If a series of related tasks can be called a process, a group of related processes can then be seen as a system. Selling a product, for example, is a system that may involve dozens of interrelated processes. If a team feels overwhelmed at first, perhaps it is trying to study a system instead of a process. Unless such a team narrows its focus, it stands a good chance of getting mired down and not making progress.

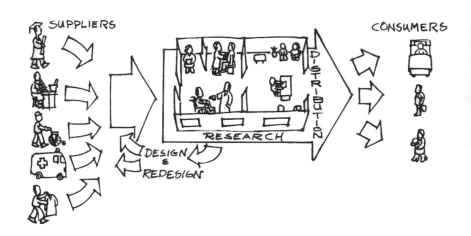

Organization as a System

Organizations are systems designed to serve customers. Processes and tasks are linked together and affect one another. To excel at meeting customer needs, an organization must constantly improve processes.

Questions to Ask Customers

- What are you getting that you need?
- What are you still unable to accomplish?
- What are you getting that you don't need?

Customers and Suppliers

The concepts of customers and suppliers follow readily once you understand the nature of a process. The people or organizations who provide inputs to the series of tasks you identify as a process are suppliers. Those who use the product or service are customers.

External customers purchase the product or service, financially supporting the organization. Obviously it is important to satisfy these people. It is useful to understand your relationship to your customers in terms of what they are trying to accomplish, rather than in terms of the product or service they receive. For example, customers want:

- The ability to take photographs, not just purchase cameras
- The ability to transfer funds quickly and safely, not just use credit cards
- The knowledge and skills to get a job they will enjoy, not just get a diploma

Often when we look at customers, we see a "chain" of customers. For example, a company makes paper, which it sells to a paper merchant, who sells the paper to a printer, who uses the paper to print a magazine for a publisher, who sells the magazine to a subscriber, who reads it, and then disposes of it in conformance with the community's recycling regulations. All of the people in the chain are customers for the paper company. The paper company's challenge is to find ways to maintain awareness of the needs, concerns, and opportunities related to each customer in the chain. If a team is trying to understand problems customers are having with their paper, it helps to know which customers are having which problems.

Chapter 2

Value

If customers are the people who receive your work, they are the ones you need to be in touch with to understand what they want and how they want it. Providing highly valued products and services at competitive prices requires you to know what is important.

Target characteristics

Are you doing the right things? Understanding what features of your product or service your customers value helps you do the right things. Are customers getting what they need, precisely when and how they need it? A goal of high quality means choosing target characteristics based on the needs, wants, and capabilities of your customers.

Quality of execution

Are you doing things right? How efficient are the processes used to design, produce, deliver, and support your products and services? Improving the way you do things can improve quality *and* reduce your cost.

Sources of Customer Information

The following are some useful sources of customer information:

- Customer complaints or suggestions
- Customer visits
- Feedback through salespeople
- Feedback through technical support or service providers
- Market research
- Customer observations
- Trading places (working at customer sites using your own products)

II. Scientific Approach

The scientific approach is really just a systematic way for individuals and teams to solve problems and improve processes. It means seeking to make decisions based on data rather than hunches, to look for root causes of problems rather than react to superficial symptoms, to seek lasting solutions rather than just rely on quick fixes.

The heart of the scientific approach is collecting and using data to guide your thinking. Usually that does not involve sophisticated statistics and experiments. Simple graphical tools like bar charts and time plots can help to find lasting improvements that help us go beyond band-aids that merely cover up problems.

The following pages describe the tools most commonly used to improve processes and solve problems. If you want to plunge ahead into the scientific method and take a look at some useful tools, maybe trying a few out on some of your tasks—keep reading. If, on the other hand, you want to look at the bigger picture of problem solving before looking at tools, take a look at the Joiner 7 Step Method™ on p. 2-28 first, and check out the tools below later. For more detailed information on all of the tools and methods in this chapter, see the *Plain & Simple* books listed on p. D-1.

Value of Using Data

Many of us have spent years at work without using data. We came up with ideas for improvement simply through the experience of trying to work on a process or by talking with customers. As problems arose, we used our experience and knowledge to come up with solutions. Sometimes the problem would disappear, sometimes not.

There is nothing wrong with using knowledge, experience, insight, or even intuition to come up with improvement ideas or to solve problems. So why is there an increasing emphasis on using data? The reason is simply that use of data is a powerful tool we can add to our toolkit. It does not replace experience or knowledge. But experience and knowledge are not always enough. When confronted with a new problem, we form theories about what is happening based on past experiences. This is normal. Unfortunately, we are likely to see only the similarities between the past and present. We are likely not to notice important differences.

Using data can help us avoid these pitfalls. It can help us understand at a deeper level what is really going on with a process, service, or product. It can help us focus our attention on the factors that really do make a difference. In short, using data helps us use our time, energies, and resources most effectively.

Tools like Pareto charts, time plots, and scatter plots help us see patterns in the data. These patterns help us identify and understand the problem better and choose better solutions. However, the output of each of the tools is only as good as the data that goes into it. Too often people discover that the data they collected cannot help them do what they wanted to do. They may have the wrong kind of data, or not enough data, or they may be missing key information that would help them understand the problem better.

It's worth spending time making sure the data you collect will be meaningful and appropriate for your needs. Some concepts and tools to help you collect useful data are: *operational definitions, stratification, checksheets,* and *work-flow diagrams.*

> ## Data Can Help You
>
> - Separate what you think is happening from what is really happening
> - Establish a baseline so you can measure improvement
> - Avoid putting expensive solutions in place that don't solve the problem

Operational Definitions...

Are precise definitions that tell how to get a numerical value for the characteristic you are trying to measure.

Operational Definitions

An operational definition describes what something is and how it is measured. For example, an operational definition of "bath temperature" could be: the average of three temperature readings from Vat #7B104, one taken three inches above the bottom near the left side, one taken three inches below the top, six inches in from the side, and one taken one foot below the surface in the middle. An operational definition of "on-time departure" for airlines could be when the doors to the jetway are closed no more than 10 minutes after the scheduled departure time.

Each team must discuss what quality characteristics or other quantities it will be measuring, and decide how these will be measured. The goal is to get a definition that all team members agree to, and that gives consistent results no matter who does the measuring. Having these common definitions is critical for gathering meaningful data. To be useful, they must represent a consensus on precisely what criteria everyone will use in studying or measuring a problem, what procedures and instruments will be used, and so forth.

This issue arises because we tolerate a lot of imprecision in our everyday conversation—"When I'm out too late I feel lousy the next day!" What does this person mean by "out," "too late," or "feel lousy?" Would these words mean the same thing to everyone? Or even to the same person on different days?

To collect meaningful data we must know precisely what to observe and how to measure it. In a business context, what do we mean by "fresh," "on-time," "soft," "fast," "strong," "user-friendly," "outside the limits," or "easy to assemble"?

Suppose you go to a shopping mall to count the number of adults accompanied by children. Sounds clear enough, doesn't it? But then you see a woman chasing a five-year-old. Does that count as "accompanied by"? What if you see a man in his fifties talking to a twenty-year-old man holding a small child. Is the twenty-year-old a "child" of the older man? Does "talking to" count as "accompanied by"? Is the older man accompanied by the small child? You have no way of knowing unless you have operational definitions of these terms.

To avoid these problems when your team collects data, have people envision or walk through the procedures they will use. Discuss similarities and differences between different data collectors. Decide exactly what everyone will measure, how they will measure it, how far off something can be and still be counted, what equipment or criteria will be used, and so forth. Even if one procedure does not stand out as clearly superior, choose one that everyone agrees is useful for present purposes.

Run trials where everyone taking data will measure or categorize the same items. Compare results, discuss differences, and continue to run trials until there is agreement regularly. If customers or suppliers will be involved in data collection, include them in these trials.

All these considerations are part of an operational definition.

(For more about operational definitions, see *Data Collection: Plain & Simple*, listed on p. D-1.)

> ## Operational Definitions
>
> - Identify what to measure
> - Identify how to measure it
> - Help ensure that no matter who does the measuring, the results are essentially the same

Stratification...

Helps pinpoint a problem by uncovering where it does and does not occur. Helps teams focus their efforts.

Stratification

Another key to collecting useful data is the concept of stratification. Stratification means dividing data into categories to see which factors have the most impact on a problem. To stratify data, make a list of the things you think could cause systematic differences in your results. For example, might western districts differ from eastern districts? Are mistakes made by new employees different from ones made by experienced employees? Are employees in one department more dissatisfied than in other departments? Is the output on Monday different from the rest of the week? Design your data collection form to include the information you will need later to analyze your data. For example, include the day of the week on the form so you can later see if results were different on different days of the week.

Checksheet of Reasons Guests Return to Hotel Front Desk Immediately After Checking In			

Collected by_____ During week of _____

	North Wing	South Wing	East Wing	West Wing
Room not serviced	II	II	I	III
Room has bad odor	II	||||||| (7 groups of 5)	I	I
Noisy location				||||| (5 groups of 5)
Furniture or carpet stained	||| (3 groups of 5)			
Room occupied	I		I	
Key doesn't work	||||| (5 groups of 5)	||||| (5 groups of 5)	||| III (3 groups of 5 + III)	|||| III (4 groups of 5 + III)

Additional comments:

Chapter 2

Checksheets...

Are structured forms that make it easy to record and analyze data.

III. Tools for Collecting Data

The tools in this section are used to collect data. Data collection often comes first when solving problems. Without good data, the rest of the tools aren't very helpful. And as each tool helps narrow the problem, more data may need to be collected.

Checksheets

A checksheet is a simple data collection form on which you make tally marks to indicate how often something occurs. At the end of the data collection period, the tally marks are counted up to get a total. With some planning ahead of time, you can design a checksheet to include information that can later be used to stratify the data. For example, a hospital could use one checksheet per surgical team per patient to gather data to help them understand the costs of various procedures. If the checksheet has a place to list the type of procedure, the patient classification, the surgical team, and the date, the hospital can later stratify the data by these factors to look for patterns that might help them understand their costs.

(For more information about checksheets, see *Data Collection: Plain & Simple*, listed on p. D-1.)

➤ Tip
Effective Checksheets

Here are some hints to make your checksheets more effective:

- Keep the form simple to use and understand.

- Include only information you intend to use.

- Make sure people interpret the categories in the same way, using agreed-upon operational definitions. (If they don't, the data will probably be useless.)

- Keep separate checksheets for different days, different people, and so on. That way you can look for patterns related to those factors. (In the checksheet above, look for patterns in type of problem and hotel wing.)

- If a sequence of steps is being checked, make sure the sequence on the checksheet is the same as the process being followed.

- Try out the form before you use it full-scale. Make changes if necessary.

Concentration Diagrams...

Are data collection forms where you write directly on a picture of the object. They let you quickly see where problems cluster.

Concentration Diagram of Traffic Accidents
Map Quadrant C-8   Anywhere City, USA
1 July 1995 – 31 December 1995

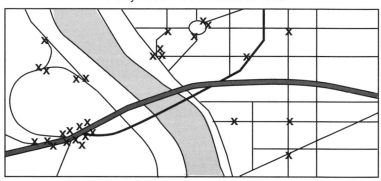

Concentration Diagrams

A concentration diagram is a pictorial checksheet on which you mark what type of problems occur and where they occur. You mark your information directly on a picture of the object. This method of data collection lets you quickly see where problems occur and how they cluster. For example, in the diagram above you can quickly see where the accidents cluster. The advantages to this form are that it is easy to fill out and doesn't need a lot of words. The disadvantages are that it can only be used with a physical object such as a product, form, or picture, and it can become cluttered.

(For more information about concentration diagrams, see *Data Collection: Plain & Simple*, listed on p. D-1.)

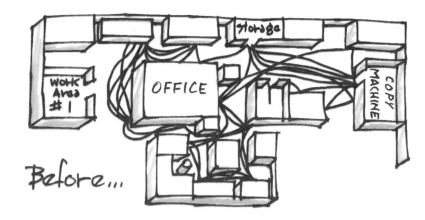

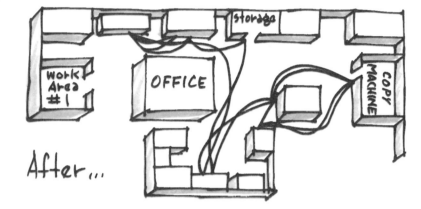

Work-flow Diagrams...

Show the flow or movement of materials, people, or information within any space.

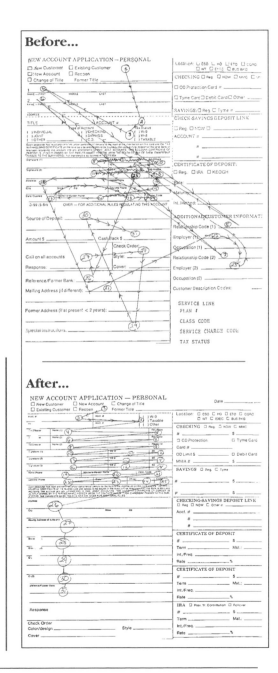

Work-flow Diagrams

A work-flow diagram is a picture of the movements of people, materials, documents, or information in a process. It is created by tracing these movements on a sketch of the floor plan or some similar map of the work space. The power of these sketches lies in illustrating a system's inefficiency in a clear picture. Places where work can be simplified will jump off the page. The example above shows how people were able to redesign the workspace to minimize movements.

For example, employees can draw lines on a floor plan to show how they move around during a normal work day; data-entry specialists can similarly mark copies of forms they use to see whether information is arranged in a logical sequence; billing clerks can track the flow of invoices through their department. In each case, the interest lies in whether there is excessive or unnecessary movement. If so, have the people involved think about what an ideal layout would be, then see if the work space or forms can be rearranged to eliminate the problem.

(For more information on work-flow diagrams, see *Data Collection: Plain & Simple*, listed on p. D-1.)

Detailed Flowcharts...

Describe most or all of the steps in a process. The purpose or intended use of the flowchart will help decide which level of detail is most appropriate.

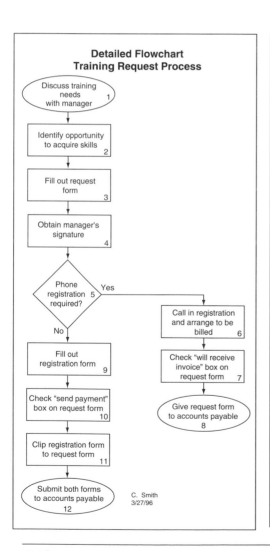

**Detailed Flowchart
Training Request Process**

1. Discuss training needs with manager
2. Identify opportunity to acquire skills
3. Fill out request form
4. Obtain manager's signature
5. Phone registration required?
   - Yes → 6. Call in registration and arrange to be billed → 7. Check "will receive invoice" box on request form → 8. Give request form to accounts payable
   - No → 9. Fill out registration form → 10. Check "send payment" box on request form → 11. Clip registration form to request form → 12. Submit both forms to accounts payable

C. Smith
3/27/96

IV. Tools for Mapping Processes

The tools in this section are used to describe the steps in a process. Different types of flowcharts are useful in different situations.

Flowcharts

A flowchart is a picture of the sequence of steps in a process. Different steps or actions are represented by boxes or other symbols. These step-by-step pictures can be used to plan a project, describe a process, or to document a standard method for doing a job. They can help team members understand what is happening now in a process, and can also help them agree on the order of activities in a new, improved process.

Before people start to flowchart a process, they should be clear about the purpose of the process. This means identifying the output (the product or service) that the work process is designed to produce, and who receives the outputs, as well as understanding what happens to inputs (e.g., materials, information, or documents) as they are transformed into the output. It is often useful to be clear about what is flowing through the process and to trace that flow with a flowchart. (◀ For more on processes, see pp. 2-4 to 2-7.)

Today many different kinds of flowcharts are used. Five particularly useful types are: basic, top-down, detailed, deployment, and opportunity flowcharts. Each highlights different aspects of a process or task.

Basic and Detailed Flowcharts

A basic flowchart just outlines the major steps in a process. It is useful when an overview is sufficient. For example, a hospital brochure might use a basic flowchart to show the main steps a patient goes through to receive care at a clinic.

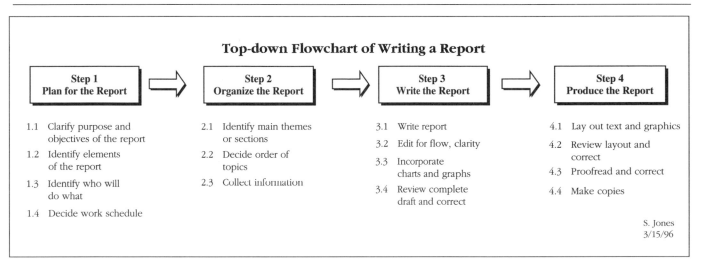

Top-down Flowchart of Writing a Report

| Step 1
Plan for the Report | Step 2
Organize the Report | Step 3
Write the Report | Step 4
Produce the Report |

1.1 Clarify purpose and objectives of the report
1.2 Identify elements of the report
1.3 Identify who will do what
1.4 Decide work schedule

2.1 Identify main themes or sections
2.2 Decide order of topics
2.3 Collect information

3.1 Write report
3.2 Edit for flow, clarity
3.3 Incorporate charts and graphs
3.4 Review complete draft and correct

4.1 Lay out text and graphics
4.2 Review layout and correct
4.3 Proofread and correct
4.4 Make copies

S. Jones
3/15/96

Chapter 2

However, if you want to standardize or improve a process, you will need to spend time capturing the details of at least some parts of the process. For example, a flowchart used to train someone to set up a machine will require some detail. The more detail you capture, the more information you have about how the process actually works. Capturing that detail has a cost however, so you should be sure you need it. The purpose or intended use of the flowchart will help decide which level of detail is most appropriate. For example, the flowchart on p. 2-16 is used by employees who request training. If you are unsure about how much detail you need, start with less detail. It is relatively easy to add more detail later.

Top-down Flowcharts

A top-down flowchart shows both the major steps in a process and the next level of substeps. If people have trouble thinking of the steps in a process, a top-down flowchart can sometimes help them see how to break a process into steps without getting into too much detail too soon.

To construct a top-down flowchart, first identify the major steps in the process (this is just like a basic flowchart). There should be no more than 6 or 7 major steps. Draw these steps in a simple flow of boxes across the top of the page. Then list the main substeps beneath each major step. This is the sequence of activities in more detail. In top-down flowcharts, the substeps are sometimes not in rectangles. They are just listed under the major steps. When the flowchart is complete, you will notice that the major steps serve as headings for the substeps listed underneath them. For example, in the flowchart for writing a report (above), the flow of work at the substep level goes from step 1.4 to 2.1.

(For more information about flowcharts, see *Flowcharts: Plain & Simple*, listed on p. D-1.)

Top-down Flowcharts...

Show both the few major steps in a process and the next level of substeps.

Deployment Flowcharts...

Show both the flow of a process and which people or groups are involved at each step.

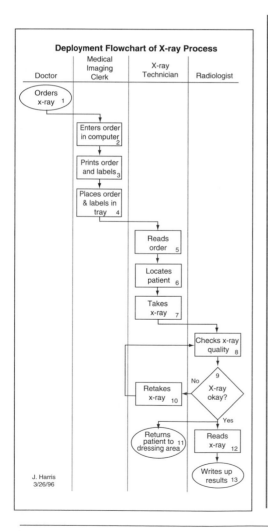

Deployment Flowchart of X-ray Process

J. Harris
3/26/96

Deployment Flowcharts

A deployment flowchart shows both the detailed steps in a process and which people are involved in each step. This flowchart is particularly useful in processes with many handoffs, where information or material is passed back and forth among people or groups. When people who carry out different steps in a process get together to create a flowchart, their discussion often uncovers unclear responsibilities, missing information, and unshared expectations which contribute to problems.

To construct a deployment flowchart, list each of the individuals or groups involved across the top of the chart. Then arrange the steps in the columns of the people who carry them out. Place each step lower on the chart than the step that precedes it. In this flowchart, the work flows down the page.

When the steps are connected with flowlines, the flowline will cross from one column to another as the work moves from one individual or group to another. Each time a flowline crosses a column, that is a handoff. Hand-off areas are prone to errors and confusion. People may not know when they should get involved, when to expect to receive something from another group, and so on. Making the handoffs clear is a key benefit of using a deployment flowchart instead of some other chart. Hand-off points are good places to collect data to determine how often problems occur and which problems occur most often.

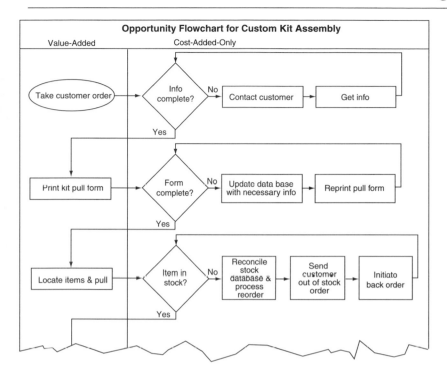

Opportunity Flowchart for Custom Kit Assembly

Opportunity Flowcharts...

Highlight opportunities for improvement by separating value-added steps from cost-added-only steps.

Opportunity Flowcharts

Opportunity flowcharts are a variation of detailed flowcharts. They get their name because they highlight opportunities for improvement. Like all flowcharts, they make the process visible. But they take this idea one step further by separating value-added steps (those essential for making the product or delivering the service) from cost-added-only steps (those that are included only to check for or fix problems). This flowchart is useful where the cost of redoing work, scrapping components, or waiting for information or parts is a major concern, or where complexity—work that makes a process more complicated without adding value—is present.

The opportunity flowchart is created by rearranging a detailed flowchart. The steps that are needed if everything works perfectly should flow down the left side of the chart. Steps that exist because of problems and inefficiencies flow across the right side of the chart.

Once the two kinds of steps are separated, people can use the opportunity flowchart to collect data on which cost-added-only loops occur most frequently. This will help focus improvement efforts. When cost-added-only steps occur frequently, it may be important to eliminate the need for these steps by making the value-added steps work right every time.

 Caution!

Labeling steps "cost-added-only" can be volatile. Some jobs consist mainly of cost-added-only activities. For example, the need to expedite orders or handle customer complaints exists because of problems. People in these jobs need to know how they will be affected if the "cost-added-only" steps are eliminated.

Pareto Charts...

Help to focus improvement efforts by ranking problems or their causes.

V. Tools for Looking at Data Relationships

The tools in this section help you see relationships between data. Understanding these relationships can help you narrow a problem, detect a change, select an improvement strategy, identify potential causes, or show results.

Pareto Charts

A Pareto chart is a series of bars whose heights reflect the frequency or impact of problems. The bars are arranged in descending order of height from left to right. This means the categories represented by the tall bars on the left are relatively more important than those on the right. The name of the chart derives from the Pareto Principle ("80% of the trouble comes from 20% of the problems"). Though the percentages will never be that exact, teams usually find that most trouble comes from only a few problems.

Pareto charts are useful throughout problem solving: early on to identify which problem should be studied, later to narrow down which causes of the problem to address first. Since they draw everyone's attention to the "vital few" important factors where the payback is likely to be greatest, Pareto charts can be used to build consensus in a group. In general, teams should focus their attention first on the biggest problems— those with the highest bars.

(For more information about Pareto charts, see *Pareto Charts: Plain & Simple* listed on p. D-1.)

**Pareto Chart of Errors on Patient Bills
Jan. 9 - Jan. 23**

Number of Occurrences: 125, 100, 75, 50, 25, 0
Right axis: 100%, 80%, 60%, 40%, 20%, 0%

Categories: Missing Procedures, Wrong Procedures, Address Incorrect, Duplicate Entries, Other

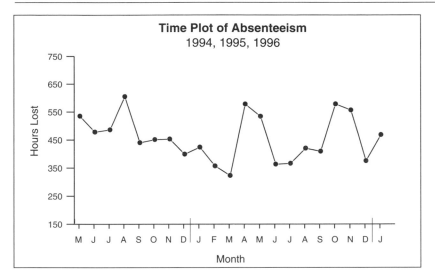

Time Plot of Absenteeism
1994, 1995, 1996

Time Plots

Many factors that affect a process change over time: ingredients decay, new employees are hired, tools and equipment wear down, suppliers make changes from time to time. Any of these changes can affect data you collect from a process over time. Detecting these time-related shifts, trends, or patterns is an essential step in making long-lasting improvements. And the best way to detect the effect of these types of changes is to plot your data in time order. A time plot, also known as a run chart, is a graph of data in time order.

Time plots are often kept to help identify if and when problems appear. However, they can also be used to see trends over time (e.g., in sales data). By collecting data, plotting it regularly, and noting process changes on the graph, we can see when shifts and changes occur. This allows us to take timely action—to stop problems before they get worse, or to capture and preserve good changes. Time plots also help identify whether the variation in a process is due to common causes or special causes. Knowing what kind of variation there is in a process helps us choose effective ways of reducing the variation. Reacting inappropriately can waste resources, or even make the variation worse. There are specific tests to use to tell whether the patterns in the data are due to common causes, or are the more distinctive shifts and trends indicating special causes. The presence of a shift or trend is important to note. A shift can invalidate other forms of data analysis such as frequency plots.

(For more information about creating and interpreting time plots, see *Time Plots: Plain & Simple,* listed on p. D-1.)

Time Plots...

Are used to examine data for trends or other patterns that occur over time. A time plot is a graph of data points plotted in time order.

Variation

If you had your choice of working with a process that was predictable, consistent, and had minimal waste, or one whose performance was erratic, whose quality was high one day and low the next, which would you choose? It's not hard to recognize the benefits of having a process whose capability and performance are consistent and well understood.

One of the main culprits working to make processes unreliable or erratic is variation. Every process has variation in its outputs because it has variation in its inputs. In fact, there are a vast number of potential causes of variation in every process. And that means that no two outputs—be they components, reports, services—will ever be the same. If, for example, your job is to serve food in the cafeteria and you are to serve equal portions to each customer, there will always be some inconsistencies. There will be at least a trace more or less than the prescribed amount, no matter how well you do your job.

Though we cannot hope to eliminate all the variation in a process, we have tools such as time plots and control charts that help us understand the kind of variation present and decide how to reduce it.

Control Charts...

Are used to monitor a process to see whether it is in statistical control. The UCL and LCL—or upper and lower control limits, respectively—indicate how much variation is typical for the process. Points that fall outside the limits or into particular patterns indicate the presence of a special cause of variation, a cause that deserves investigation.

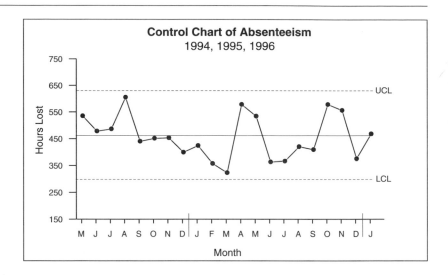

Types of Variation

To know if your process is truly consistent and predictable, it is helpful to understand the difference between "common causes" and "special causes" of variation.

Common cause variation is typically due to a large number of small sources of variation. The sum of these small causes may result in a high level of variation or a large number of defects or mistakes. For example, common causes of variation in the arrival time of a bus might include: the amount of traffic, the weather, and how long it takes passengers to board the bus at each stop. It is the sum of the common causes that determines the inherent variation of the process and thus determines its limits and its capability as it is currently operated.

Special causes of variation are not part of the process all the time. They arise because of specific circumstances. For example, having a new employee who didn't know the standard procedure could lead to increased errors.

Dealing with each type of cause requires different approaches. You should track down and eliminate a special cause, but common causes are often reduced only by hard detective work.

Control Charts

A control chart is a time plot with one extra feature: it also indicates the range of variation built into the system. The boundaries of this range are marked by upper and lower statistical control limits. These limits are calculated according to statistical formulas from data collected on the process. These limits allow you to quickly detect shifts of a single point or more, in contrast to the time plot which can detect shifts only after a number of data points have fallen into a particular pattern.

Control charts help you distinguish between variation inherent in a process (variation from "common causes" as illustrated in the control chart above) and variation arising from sources that come and go unpredictably ("special causes"). The same tests for special causes (shifts and trends) that apply to time plots also apply to control charts. In addition, one or more points that occur outside the control limits are signals of special causes of variation.

It is important to remember that control limits are not the same as specification limits. They are not related to budgets, targets, or customer requirements. Control limits say nothing about how a process is supposed to perform or what managers hope it can achieve. They only indicate what the process is capable of doing.

(For more information on how to construct and interpret control charts, see *Fourth Generation Management: The New Business Consciousness* by Brian Joiner; *Individuals Charts: Plain & Simple*, and the *Fundamentals of Fourth Generation Management* video series, listed on pp. D-1 and D-2.)

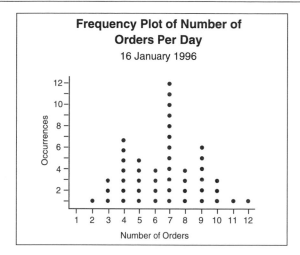

Frequency Plot of Number of Orders Per Day

16 January 1996

Frequency Plots...

Show the shape, or distribution, of the data by showing how often different values occur.

Frequency Plots

A frequency plot, or histogram, starts as a line marked off in units corresponding to the data. A dot is then placed above a value for each time that value appears in the data. Frequency plots are easily constructed, display all the data points, and readily convey information. A quick look at one tells you right away the range of measurements, roughly where the center of the data is, and how data points are distributed around the average (whether they are symmetric or straggle out to one side). Sometimes they are used to get a quick look at data before further analysis. Any data plotted on a time plot that doesn't show time-related patterns is usually then plotted on a frequency plot to look at the distribution (spread of points).

In many cases, the plotted points will fall into the outline of a bell, a shape familiar to statisticians. The bell is formed by a natural tendency in data points to cluster about a central value (the "average") and taper off symmetrically on both sides. Other times they may show abnormal data patterns such as those caused by a mistake or by inspector bias.

Frequency plots are a key tool in stratification analysis. (◀For more information on stratification, see p. 2-12.)

(For more information on frequency plots, see *Frequency Plots: Plain & Simple*, listed on p. D-1.)

 Caution!

Do not make a frequency plot of data that shows time-related patterns. It's much more confusing than helpful.

Cause-and-Effect Diagrams...

Organize potential causes of problems into chains of cause-and-effect relationships. This allows you to see the relationships among potential causes.

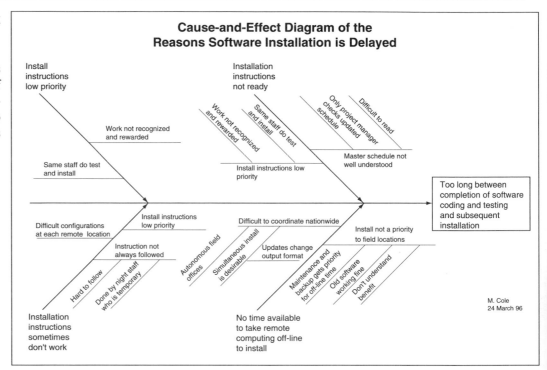

Cause-and-Effect Diagram of the Reasons Software Installation is Delayed

Too long between completion of software coding and testing and subsequent installation

M. Cole
24 March 96

Cause-and-Effect Diagrams

A cause-and-effect diagram is a tool for identifying and organizing the possible causes of a problem in a structured format. It is sometimes called an "Ishikawa diagram" after Kaoru Ishikawa who developed this tool. It is also referred to as a "fishbone diagram" because it looks like the skeleton of a fish, with a head, spine, and bones. Unlike the other tools in this section, cause-and-effect diagrams do not analyze data. They help people organize their ideas and theories about causes. These theories need to be verified later with data.

This diagram is a kind of map showing possible cause-and-effect relationships.

- The focused problem under investigation is described in a box at the head of the diagram.

- A long spine with an arrow pointing towards the head forms the backbone of the "fish." The direction of the arrow indicates that the items that feed into the spine *might cause* the problem described in the head.

- A few large bones feed into the spine. These large bones represent the main categories of potential causes of the problem. Again, the arrows represent the direction of the action: the items on the larger bones are thought to cause the problem in the head.

- The smaller bones represent deeper causes of the larger bones they are attached to. Each bone is a link in a cause-and-effect chain that leads from the deepest causes to the targeted problem.

One of the biggest challenges in creating a cause-and-effect diagram is to have the bones show cause-and-effect relationships.

Remember that cause-and-effect diagrams identify only potential causes. Before taking action, you need to verify which potential causes are actual causes. Once you have confirmed the actual causes with data, the next step is developing solutions to address those causes.

(For more information on cause-and-effect diagrams, see *Cause-and-Effect Diagrams: Plain & Simple*, listed on p. D-1.)

➤ Tip

How to Identify Causes

People often use the "4 M's" (Man, Materials, Methods, and Machinery) or the "4 P's" (People, Procedures, Policies, and Plant) when creating cause-and-effect diagrams. These categories can be useful when initially brainstorming possible causes, or when checking to see if an important cause has been overlooked.

However, it is important to realize that these categories are not causes. Too often people will list all the machines in the area, or the procedures, or the people involved, on the diagram. These lists do not show cause-and-effect relationships.

You can turn items like these into causes by asking, "What is it about people, or about procedures, which might cause the problem?" A cause might be "people not following procedures" or "procedures not clear."

Scatter Plots...

Display the relationship between two characteristics.

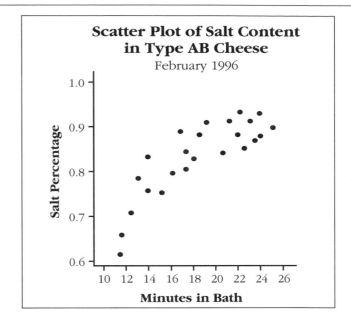

Scatter Plot of Salt Content in Type AB Cheese
February 1996

 Caution!

Finding a relationship between two factors does not prove one causes the other. For example, there is a strong positive relationship between increasing shoe size and increasing reading ability in children.

Scatter Plots

Whereas a frequency plot allows you to look at only one characteristic at a time, a scatter plot lets you look at the relationship between two characteristics. It can be used to check whether one variable is related to another variable, and is an effective way to communicate the relationship you find.

A scatter plot shows one variable along the vertical axis and another variable along the horizontal axis. Each data point represents a pair of measurements. The resulting pattern shows how the two measurements are related.

For example, suppose the salt content of cheese is an important quality characteristic. You can use a scatter plot to see whether the time the cheese stayed in a salt bath influenced its salt content. For each piece of cheese, there are a pair of measurements: salt content and time in the bath. You can plot time in the bath along the horizontal axis (sometimes called the X axis) and salt content along the vertical axis (sometimes called the Y axis). You place points where the values of each pair intersect. For example, the lowest dot in the example above was in the bath for 11.5 minutes and had a salt content of 0.61.

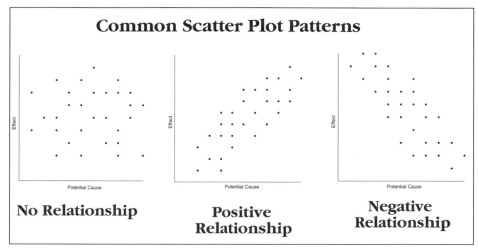

Common Scatter Plot Patterns

No Relationship

Positive Relationship

Negative Relationship

Common Scatter Plot Patterns

If the factors being plotted are not related, the points will be scattered on the graph as in the far left example. If higher values of one factor are associated with higher values of the other, the pattern will resemble the middle example. If larger values of one factor are associated with smaller values of the other, the pattern will resemble the example on the right.

The shape of the scatter of points tells you if the two factors are related. As you can see in the examples above, if they are unrelated, the points will be randomly scattered around the graph. If larger values of one factor occur with larger values of the other, the points will group around a line running from lower left to upper right; if larger values of one are associated with smaller values of the other, the points will cluster around a line running from upper left to lower right.

In the case on page 2-26, salt content is greatly influenced by time in the bath up to a certain point (somewhere in the 16 to 20 minute range). Letting the cheese sit any longer in the bath has very little effect.

(For more information on scatter plots, see *Scatter Plots: Plain & Simple*, listed on p. D-1.)

The Joiner 7 Step Method™...

Provides a structured approach to problem solving.

| Step 1 Project | Step 2 Current Situation | Step 3 Cause Analysis | Step 4 Solutions | Step 5 Results | Step 6 Standard-ization | Step 7 Future Plans |

VI. The Joiner 7 Step Method™

The Joiner 7 Step Method is a scientific approach to problem solving that involves collecting data and testing theories. Too often we jump directly from identifying a problem to implementing a solution. For complex problems, this often leaves us playing a sort of guessing game. It is only after we have implemented our solutions that we learn whether or not we guessed correctly.

The Joiner 7 Step Method is designed to help you narrow down your definition of a problem and analyze its causes in a systematic way. You will notice that the solutions step comes in the middle of the process. Before developing a solution, you study what is currently happening and look for what might cause the current problem. When you come up with a solution, you try it on a small scale and check the results. Then, after implementing the solution, you again evaluate the results. If it works, you take steps to ensure that your solution stays in place by standardization. Finally you document your learnings and look to the future.

One of the benefits of using a structured problem-solving method is that it provides teams with a roadmap to follow. It helps them ask the right questions at the right time. This roadmap also helps teams know when to use which tools for data collection and analysis. The chart on the next page shows which tools are often used in each of the seven steps.

Tool / Step	Data Collection Tools	Flow-charts	Pareto Charts	Time Plots	Control Charts	Frequency Plots	Cause-and-Effect Diagrams	Scatter Plots
1. Project	X	X	X	X	X			
2. Current Situation	X	X	X	X	X	X		X
3. Cause Analysis	X					X	X	X
4. Solutions	X	X						
5. Results	X		X	X	X	X		
6. Standardization	X	X		X	X			
7. Future Plans	X		X	X	X			

When to Use the Tools

The matrix above shows when different tools are most likely to be used in the Joiner 7 Step Method for problem solving. The matrix should be used as a guide to help you choose the most appropriate tools. All the tools indicated do not need to be used in each step. There is no set sequence for using each of the tools in problem solving. The nature of the problem, as well as the type of data collected, will help determine which tools are used in what sequence.

Chapter 2

The Joiner 7 Step Method™

The following is an outline of the Joiner 7 Step Method. Most data-based problem-solving methods include some variation on the following steps. Some have more steps. Some have fewer. But most follow the same basic sequence. (➡For more detail on the Joiner 7 Step Method, see Chapter 5, pp. 5-15 to 5-24.)

Step 1: Project

Goal: Define the project's purpose and scope—what problem or opportunity is being addressed, why it is important, and how much progress or improvement is expected.

Output: A clear statement of the intended improvement and how it is to be measured.

Step 2: Current Situation

Goal: Focus the improvement effort by gathering information on the current situation.

Output: A focused problem statement.

Step 3: Cause Analysis

Goal: Identify deep causes and confirm them with data in order to pave the way for effective solutions.

Output: A theory that has been tested and confirmed.

Chapter 2

Step 4: Solutions

Goal: Develop, try out, and implement solutions that address deep causes.

Output: Planned, tested actions which should eliminate or reduce the impact of the causes identified in Step 3.

Step 5: Results

Goal: Use data to evaluate both the solutions and the plans used to carry them out.

Output: Data which shows how well the goals were met and the plan was followed.

Step 6: Standardization

Goal: Maintain the gains by implementing the new work methods or processes consistently throughout the organization.

Output: Documentation of the new method. Training in the new method. A system for monitoring its consistent use and for checking the results.

Step 7: Future Plans

Goal: Anticipate future improvements and preserve the lessons from this effort.

Output: Completed documentation and communication of results, learnings, and recommendations.

Chapter 2

Summary

Every kind of team has challenges to face and problems to solve. While our hunches, instincts, and experiences may provide valuable insights into the problems to be solved, a scientific approach helps avoid misdiagnosis and the resulting waste of time and resources. The scientific approach is based on data gathering and analysis, not hunches. Data can help you separate what you think is happening from what is really happening. It can establish a baseline so that you can measure improvement and avoid putting expensive solutions in place that don't solve problems. In this chapter we introduced you to a variety of useful techniques and tools that can help you and your team gather and analyze data to solve problems.

In our next chapter, we will talk about the tasks teams should complete before taking on a project.

Chapter 3

Supporting Successful Projects

Many different kinds of teams work on projects. Ongoing teams often engage in projects as part of their work together. For example, a management team might spend some of its time designing or improving a key system, such as a patient admissions system. An ongoing work team might focus its attention on solving a problem or making a needed improvement, such as a work team of customer service employees redesigning the way they handle orders.

On the other hand, some teams are put together just for the project. When the project is complete, they disband. For example, a cross-functional team working on improving the purchasing process might work together for some months until the improvements are implemented. Members might then move on to new projects with new team members.

The first part of this chapter focuses on the planning and prework needed to ensure that improvement or problem-solving projects are likely to be successful, regardless of what kind of team is doing the work. Since much of the planning and prework for project teams is done by the sponsors of those teams, this chapter is particularly useful to those who are responsible for defining the project and assembling the team.

The chapter also outlines sponsor or guidance team responsibilities in starting and sustaining the team, as well as in following up on the changes after the team has moved on.

What You Will Find Here

In this chapter we explore:

Team Sponsors...

Are individual managers who identify projects and review and support teams.

Terminology

Many functions need to be filled for a team to be successful. We divide these tasks among the team sponsor (or guidance team), the team coach (or quality advisor), and the team leader. Your organization may use different labels for these roles. For example, often there is no sponsor or guidance team. Those responsibilities are filled by the area manager as part of his or her daily work. Or the team's coach may be called a facilitator or an internal consultant. Or the coaching may be done by a supervisor or the team leader.

How the roles are structured and what they are called is less important than making sure someone is doing what's necessary for team success.

I. Responsibilities of the Sponsor or Guidance Team

Enthusiastic, hard-working team members contribute most to the success of a project. But they must be given an effective team system within which to work. The success of that system depends both on the people who assign the project and regularly review the team's work, and on those who guide and coach the team.

The following discussion describes the functions that need to be filled for a successful project. We divide these responsibilities among the team sponsor (or guidance team), the team coach (or quality advisor), and the team leader. Some organizations have one or two people take on all the responsibilities. Others disperse the responsibilities among half a dozen people. The particular structure or set of roles is less important than having someone responsible for doing what's necessary for team success.

Team Sponsor

In most organizations there is a system for identifying work priorities and projects, and assigning them to individuals or teams. Individual managers often review and support these team efforts. These managers may be called team sponsors. In some organizations the role of sponsor is limited to overseeing cross-functional project teams. In others it expands to include the daily management of teams within an individual manager's span of control.

Guidance Teams...

Are groups of two or three managers who oversee and support the activities of one or more project teams.

Guidance Team

A guidance team is a group of managers and other key leaders who oversee and support the activities of one or more teams. Typically, these are the same managers who chose the projects and appointed the teams in the first place, but other people may also be involved.

The guidance team has two or three members

- With diverse skills and resources
- Who have a stake in the chosen process or problem
- With authority to make changes in the process under study
- With clout and courage

One or two members of the guidance team will likely be managers who have established authority and responsibility regarding the problem or process they want studied. For some managers, membership on a guidance team carries an additional challenge: letting go of some responsibilities. A project team may need to conduct tests and experiments on a process, and eventually will want to make changes. An improvement project is a perfect opportunity for these managers and supervisors to learn to delegate control and pass some decision making to those closer to the process.

Sponsors or guidance team members do not conduct the actual project; they guide and support the efforts of the team. They may appoint the team leader, and together with that leader determine the project's boundaries and select the team members. They make certain the project team has the resources it needs to be successful.

For Ongoing Teams

If you are an ongoing work team without a sponsor or guidance team, here's how to use this chapter:

- To select a problem or process to work on, read pp. 3-5 to 3-9.
- To understand your team leader's role, read pp. 3-14 to 3-16.
- To understand your team member responsibilities, read pp. 3-21 to 3-22.
- To decide whether expertise in meeting skills or improvement methods would help you, review the coach's role on pp. 3-18 to 3-20.
- To understand the benefits of having a manager review your efforts, read pp. 3-25 to 3-30.

Chapter 3

The duties of the guidance team or sponsor occur in three phases:

1. Before the project, the sponsor or guidance team
- Selects the project
- Defines the project
- Identifies needed resources
- Selects the team leader
- Assigns a quality advisor or coach
- Selects the team members

Each of these activities is described in detail starting on p. 3-5.

2. During the project, the sponsor or guidance team
- Orients the team
- Meets regularly with the project team to review progress
- When necessary, "runs interference" for the team, representing its interests to the rest of the company

3. After the project, the sponsor or guidance team
- Ensures that changes made by the team are monitored; implements changes the team is not authorized to make
- Feeds data and learnings from the project into a system for future improvements

The remainder of this chapter offers more detail on these three phases of the sponsor's or guidance team's tasks.

Selecting a Project

Select a problem or process that is important to the organization and its customers.

II. Responsibilities Before the Project Begins

Before asking either an ongoing team or a project team to work on improving something, or solving a problem, the sponsor or guidance team must be absolutely clear about *what* the team should work on and *why* the work is important.

Having a clear statement of purpose helps a team understand what it is supposed to do and why. The team will use this statement to stay focused, to establish boundaries for what is and is not included in its work, and to define success.

Select an Improvement Project

If you are selecting a process to improve, the guidelines below will increase your chances for a successful project.

Select a process that:

- Is important to the organization and its customers.
- Is in an area where the managers, supervisors, and employees will cooperate in the improvement efforts.
- Is not already undergoing major changes or being studied by another group (unless the project is to study how to make the change).
- Is relatively simple, with clearly defined starting and ending points. Even if you would rather target a large or complex system—such as the accounting system—for most teams it is best to break it down into smaller components.
- Completes a cycle once a day or so. The effects of changes you make will then likely show up within a few weeks.

 **Early Responsibilities**

The following key things should be done before the project starts:
- Select an improvement project
- Define the project
  - Determine the resources
  - Select the team leader
  - Assign the coach or quality advisor
  - Select team members

➤ Tip
Identifying an Improvement Project

If you do not already have a focused project, start by finding out what is important to your customers.

Strategy 5: Identify Customer Needs, p. 5-39, leads a team through the steps designed to get reliable and useful information about customer concerns. This strategy is especially effective in departments that have not been in close contact with their customers.

Chapter 3

If the project is one of your organization's first improvement efforts, it should be important and clearly focused so there is a high likelihood of success. That makes it likely that people outside the department will notice both how the work is done and the results achieved. In this way, early improvement efforts can serve as models for how teams can effectively solve problems. (➤For more information on how to use project teams to educate others about improvement, see Appendix A, pp. A-7 to A-8.)

The Project Selection Checklist can help managers and others select improvement projects with a good chance for success. (➤Also see Common Errors in Selecting Projects, p. 3-8.)

Project Selection Checklist

Instructions: If you have selected and defined an appropriate project, you should be able to check most, if not all, items listed below. If you can't check all of these items, you may want to reevaluate your choice.

____ 1. The process or project is related to key business issues.

____ 2. The problem or process targeted for improvement will benefit the organization's external customers.

____ 3. All managers concerned with this process or problem agree that it is important to work on.

____ 4. Enough managers, supervisors, and employees in the area will cooperate to make this project a success.

____ 5. This process is not currently being changed in any way, nor is it scheduled to be overhauled in the near future. (This criterion does not apply if the team is being commissioned to study how the change might occur.)

____ 6. This process is not being studied by another group.

____ 7. If the project is to improve a process, there are easily identified starting and ending points. If the project is to solve a problem, it is clearly defined and focused.

____ 8. One cycle of the process is completed each day or two. (That is, there is quick turnaround time. This is not as important for management teams who may tackle longer, more complex processes.)

____ 9. The charter or mission statement for this project describes a problem to be studied, or an improvement opportunity, not a solution to be tried. (This criterion does not apply if the problem has already been studied and this team is to implement the selected solution.)

Common Errors in Selecting Projects

Organizations commonly make mistakes in selecting improvement projects, including:

- **Selecting a problem that no one is really interested in**. A common error in selecting projects is picking one neither management nor the team cares about. As a result, the effort is likely to die from inattention. Improving a process or solving a problem takes time and hard work, and sometimes the effort is sustained only by being a priority.

- **Selecting a solution to implement rather than a problem to investigate.** Sometimes managers think they already know what improvements need to be made. For example, they might say, "Computerize the process for ordering lab tests," instead of, "Improve the turnaround time for lab tests." Asking a team to implement a solution may be appropriate if the problem has been sufficiently studied before the solution was selected. Often, however, a team investigating a problem will discover new information about the nature of the problem. This, in turn, can lead to better solutions than were thought of before the study.

- **Selecting a process in transition.** Asking a team to improve a process that is, or soon will be, undergoing transition will only waste resources. For example, avoid studying the current scheduling process if someone else is independently computerizing it.

- **Selecting a system to study, not a process.** Sometimes the project selected is too ambitious for the team. Instead of selecting a single process, a system is selected that consists of many smaller processes (e.g., hiring new employees). Designing or improving a system might be appropriate for a management team. However, ongoing work teams have a better chance for success if they focus on a smaller process, such as maintaining updated job descriptions.

Define the Project

Once the problem or improvement opportunity has been selected by the sponsor and the guidance team, important new issues must be considered. One of the first orders of business is to clearly define the project.

Prepare a charter or mission statement

A charter or mission statement enables a team to understand their boundaries on the project, know what is and isn't within their jurisdiction, understand where the project fits in the organization's overall improvement efforts or business strategy, and have a clear idea of where they should begin.

The statement should tell the team:

- What process or problem to study

- Why it is important to customers and to the organization

- What boundaries or limitations there are, including limits on time and money

- What magnitude of improvements they are expected to make

- When they are scheduled to begin the project and, if appropriate, the target date for completion

- What authority they have to call in coworkers or outside experts, request information normally inaccessible to them, and make changes to the process

Localizing Problems

One way to define a problem is to pinpoint when and where the problem occurs. This is called "localizing." You will use your energies best if you localize a problem before plunging deep into a project. The more information you have, the better you will be able to focus on the real source of problems.

Often the problem we observe may only be a symptom of other problems upstream in the process. For example, errors that appear with calling up a computer record could be caused upstream when the information is entered into the computer; mistakes in a customer's bill may result from mistakes in the original order or any steps in-between. Localizing directs the team to the part of the process that really needs improvement.

At other times a problem may appear to be widespread—"it happens all the time"—when it is actually limited to one place. For example, a hotel manager thought that noise was a problem for guests throughout the hotel. After collecting data she discovered complaints were limited to one floor in one wing. By localizing the problem early, time and effort was saved.

Sometimes it is best for the sponsor or guidance team to investigate and narrow the problem before giving it to a team to pursue. In other cases it will be best for the team to start by gathering data to focus their work. What's important is that the sponsor or guidance team work closely with the project team to define the project. (➡For more information, see Localize Recurring Problems, p. 5-43.)

Determine the resources

Once a draft of the charter or mission statement is complete, and the goals of the project have been generally defined, the sponsor or guidance team must determine what resources the team needs to be successful.

What training is needed? Budget? Equipment? Which in-house or external specialists will be needed to advise the team? How much time must be allotted so team members will be able to complete the project? How will their normal work get done? By whom?

Select the team leader

The team leader is often the manager or supervisor responsible for the unit where most of the changes are likely to occur. This person should be someone interested in solving the problems that prompted this project, and someone reasonably good at working with individuals and groups. (➤Further details are provided on pp. 3-14 to 3-16.)

Assign the coach or quality advisor

The sponsor or guidance team should assign a coach or quality advisor to work with the team leader and the team. The coach is someone experienced in working with groups, who knows and can teach others the basic scientific tools. The coach and team leader will review the charter and orchestrate the project's development. (➤See Balancing Roles, p. 3-20.)

Select the team members

The sponsor or guidance team should collaborate with the team leader and quality advisor to determine what disciplines, work units, or job classifications should be represented on the team. Ideally, team members should represent each area affected by the improvements and each level of employees affected.

Typically, teams should have no more than five members in addition to the team leader and quality advisor. Do not let the team get too large. Not everybody who could contribute something worthwhile need be on the team, and project team members can always consult with experts, operators, or other advisors as the project unfolds.

For similar reasons, project team membership does not have to represent different levels of the organization. Even when the nature of the project requires a slice of the hierarchy, be cautious. High-level managers on a team may intimidate lower-level managers, supervisors, and line workers. However, managers and supervisors in some companies have found that mixing levels is an effective way to improve communication and leadership methods.

Don't expect team members to take on the project work as additional work; adjust workloads to make time for the project.

On the following pages there is a worksheet that will help guide managers, sponsors, quality advisors, and/or team leaders through the issues they need to address to set up a project team. Use the questions to stimulate discussion of these topics.

Worksheet for Project Team Groundwork

Instructions: Use these questions to spur discussion of the purpose for having a project. Record the answers and use your notes to generate a charter or mission statement for the team. Attach any relevant documentation to your notes. If the project has not yet been selected, use the Project Selection Checklist (p. 3-7) as a guide.

Step 1: Determine the nature of the project (outcomes, expectations).

1.1. What process or problem will the team study? What are the boundaries of the team's work (e.g., what parts of this process or problem should the team NOT study)?
Note: A flowchart is useful for describing the process or system and showing which parts the teams should target. (See p. 2-16)

1.2 Why is the project important? What needs of customers, the organization, or the work area will be addressed? What data was collected to verify the choice and focus of the project? If you have no data, what kinds should you collect to verify your choice?

1.3 What are the goals or desired outcomes of this project? What magnitude of improvement is the team expected to make? What changes are expected to result from this project?

Step 2: Settle team membership and logistics.

2.1 If there is a guidance team, who is on it?

2.2 Who will be the team leader?

2.3 If there is a coach or quality advisor, who will it be?

2.4 Who will be members of the team? What work areas or technical specialties must be represented for the team to accomplish its mission?
Note: Do not let the team get too large. Team members can consult with experts, operators, or others as the project unfolds.

2.5 When, where, how often, and for how long will the team meet?

2.6 How often do you expect the team to meet with the sponsor or guidance team?   What is the date of the first joint meeting?

Step 3: Describe the expectations and support the team will have.

3.1 When will the project begin? What is the target date for completion?

3.2 Will the team need financial resources? What department(s) or division(s) will provide this support? What limitations are there on budgets? Can the team request additional financial support? From whom?

3.3 What decision-making authority will the team have? What authority will the team have to call in coworkers or outside experts, request equipment or information normally inaccessible to them, and make changes to the process?

3.4 What training will team members need? In what skills? Who will provide the training?

3.5 What in-house or external specialists may be needed to provide support on technical matters?

3.6 How will team members' normal work get done while they are involved in the project?

3.7 Are there other resources (technical support, equipment, supplies, personnel) that this team will need?

Project Roles

Understanding the following roles and relationships is vital for project success:
- Team leader
- Coach or quality advisor
- Team members

III. Project Roles and Relationships

No orchestra can play music together without careful planning and cooperation. Understanding the various roles and relationships within the team structure and how all the players can work together effectively is vital if you are going to make beautiful music together!

Team Leader

The team leader is the person who manages the team: calling and facilitating meetings, handling or assigning administrative details, orchestrating all team activities, and overseeing preparations for reports and presentations. The team leader should have a strong interest in solving the problems that prompted this project and be reasonably good at working with individuals and groups. Ultimately it is the leader's responsibility to create and maintain channels that enable team members to do their work.

Ordinarily team leaders are supervisors or managers in the project area. Their closeness to the process means they will be better able to guide team members. It also means they must take extra precautions to avoid dominating the group during meetings. The leader leaves rank outside the meeting room, facilitating discussions and only occasionally actively participating in the content.

Effective leaders share their responsibilities with other team members and give team members a chance to try new skills on their own. They understand the value of learning from experience.

Team Leaders...

Orchestrate team activities, maintain team records, and serve as a communication link with the rest of the organization.

Responsibilities of the team leader

- Serve as the contact point for communication between the team and the rest of the organization, including the guidance team. Develop ways of updating others who might be affected by the team's work. If a team member has trouble finding time to work on the project in between meetings, the team leader may talk with other supervisors or managers to resolve the problem or may seek help from the sponsor or guidance team. When necessary, the leader meets with the sponsor or guidance team in between scheduled meetings with the whole project team.

- Keep the official team records, including copies of correspondence; records of meetings and presentations; meeting minutes and agendas; and charts, graphs, and other data related to the project. Others involved in the project may also keep their own records, but the team leader is responsible for documenting the project. (➨Examples of documentation are described in Chapter 4 on pp. 4-7 to 4-8, and 4-26 to 4-28.)

- Participate as a full-fledged team member. As such, the team leader's duties also include attending meetings, carrying out assignments between meetings, and generally sharing in the team's work. The only exception, as described previously, is that the team leader may want to restrain his or her participation in discussions so that other team members may be more active.

- Retain authority as a manager or supervisor. The leader can immediately implement changes recommended by the team that are within the bounds of this authority. Changes beyond these bounds must be referred to the guidance team or other appropriate level of management.

Chapter 3

- Help the team resolve its problems. Team leaders often need to remember that most problems are caused by faulty processes and systems, not by individuals. Team problems are usually not solved by blaming someone, but by finding and improving the inadequate process or system.

(➡For more information on how to handle team problems, see Chapter 7.)

Coaches or Quality Advisors...

Understand the tools and concepts of improvement, including approaches that help a team have effective, productive meetings. The coach or quality advisor is there to help facilitate the team's work—coaching team members in needed skills and tools—but not to do the team's work for them.

Coach or Quality Advisor

Many organizations may not have employees who have skills in project management, group process, data collection and analysis, problem solving, and process improvement. Some organizations select a few people to receive extra training in these skills. These employees then coach and teach others to use these skills in their work. These consultants or coaches are sometimes called "quality advisors." It doesn't matter whether this coaching and teaching is done by internal consultants, team leaders, managers, or supervisors. It only matters that the support is there to help the team be successful.

If your organization has coaches or internal consultants to help improvement efforts, this section will tell them how to work with teams. If your organization does not have these resources, then the team leader or supervisor may fulfill these responsibilities.

How coaches or quality advisors work with teams

Coaches attend team meetings but are neither leaders nor team members. They are outsiders to the team in many ways, and can maintain a neutral position. One of their most important jobs is to observe the team's progress and to help the team function more effectively.

A coach or quality advisor's second major focus is teaching team members the scientific tools and helping to guide the team's effort when technical expertise is needed.

Coaches or quality advisors rarely run meetings, handle administrative or logistical details, or carry out between-meeting assignments such as

---

Chapter 3

data gathering. Except when teaching the team about the scientific tools or helping the team get unstuck during a meeting, the coach works primarily before and after the team meeting, in conference with the team leader. That is when the two discuss the team's progress and try to find ways to improve how the team works.

It is important that coaches observe first-hand the process or problem under study so they can understand the challenges facing the team.

Responsibilities of the coach or quality advisor

- Focus on the team's process more than its product. Be concerned more with how decisions are made than what decisions are reached.

- Assist the team leader in structuring or breaking down tasks into individual assignments to be done in between meetings.

- Work with the team leader between meetings to plan for upcoming meetings. Help structure discussions and decisions so the team can work effectively. Help revise plans in response to suggestions from team members, the sponsor, or daily experience on the project.

- Help team members become more comfortable with statistics and with the scientific approach. Teach data collection and analysis techniques to the team, showing what conclusions may or may not be drawn from the data.

- Help team members learn to graph data in ways that make the message clear, particularly to people outside the team. Encourage the team to seek the causes of problems before identifying solutions and to distrust decisions unsupported by data.

- Help the team decide what data will be useful and how best to gather that data. Work with team members and those outside the team who may be gathering and recording data to develop appropriate forms for data collection.

- Continually develop personal skills in facilitation and planning. Learn a variety of techniques to encourage reluctant participants, control digressive, difficult, or dominating participants, and resolve conflict among participants. Learn when and how to employ these interventions and how to teach such skills to team members. (➧Some helpful hints are explained in Chapter 6, pp. 6-23 to 6-31.)

- Help project teams prepare and, on occasion, rehearse presentations to management.

Finding people with the proper qualifications for becoming coaches or quality advisors can be difficult. We provide some hints (right).

Selecting and Training Coaches or Quality Advisors

The ideal coach or quality advisor has a combination of people, technical, and training skills—talents seldom found together. Some of the skills a quality advisor should have or be willing to acquire are:

- **People skills**

  Has interpersonal communication, group process, and meeting skills; knows how to form groups, build teams, listen, resolve conflict, and give feedback.

- **Technical skills**

  Understands basic scientific tools, statistics, and the use of data; can organize and plan a project; understands the technical aspects of the project; is customer focused; can ask good questions.

- **Teaching skills**

  Can teach others the skills described above.

As you select people to develop these skills, either as coaches or leaders, look for people who are inclined toward all three areas. Look among engineers or other technicians who demonstrate caring and sensitivity toward people. Look also for those with proven people skills who seem capable of learning the data analysis and scientific skills.

(For information about training programs for coaches or quality advisors, contact Joiner Associates Inc.)

Chapter 3

Balancing Roles

Continuum of Power-Sharing between a Team Leader and Coach

Amount of Active Leadership by Coach or Quality Advisor

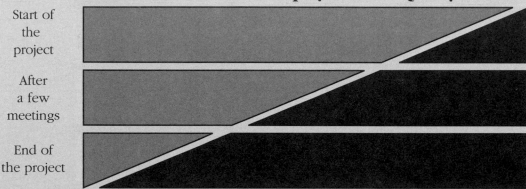

Start of
the
project

After
a few
meetings

End of
the project

**Amount of Active Leadership by Team Leader
(may be shared with others)**

When organizations have coaches or quality advisors available to help teams and team leaders learn new skills, the coach and team leader may need to spend time agreeing how best to work together with the team. If team problem solving or process improvement is new for both the team leader and the team, the coach or quality advisor may be very active during the team's initial meetings. In this circumstance, the challenge will be for the coach to remain, as much as possible, the outside consultant to the team.

The diagram (above) illustrates how the proportions of active leadership taken on by the team leader and coach can vary throughout a project. The coach or quality advisor, trained in meeting skills, may run parts of the first team meetings, but the team leader

gradually assumes more of these duties. Throughout a project, the team leader may also choose to share responsibility from time to time with other team members.

While it would be most efficient to have a team leader who also could coach the team and teach them new skills—combining two roles in one person—the two roles are kept separate if the team leader does not yet have the knowledge and experience to train the team. Also, teams and team leaders can benefit from the outside, objective view that a coach or quality advisor offers—and, in times of crisis, the coach is available to step in and temporarily take over more responsibility.

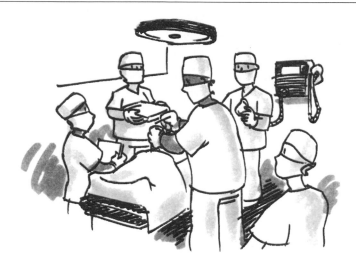

Team Members...

Carry out the team's work, sharing their knowledge and experience, listening to others, and completing assignments.

Team Members

Team members—typically up to five per project—are the people who do the work on the project.

They are appointed by the sponsor or guidance team in consultation with the team leader. The nature of the project dictates who they are. Usually they work closely with some aspect of the process under study, often representing different stages of the process. Sometimes they represent groups likely to be affected by the project. They can be of various ranks, professions, trades, classifications, shifts, or work areas (if the project cuts across departmental boundaries, so should team membership). Sometimes project teams need subject matter expertise. However, the subject matter experts don't have to be team members. They can consult with the team during key phases of the project.

Responsibilities of team members

- Consider the team's work a priority, not an intrusion on their real jobs. The project is now part of the members' real jobs.

- Contribute fully to the project; share knowledge and expertise; participate in meetings and discussions. They should not be shy about asking what might seem like dumb questions. Each has a right to clearly understand all aspects of the problem or process under study.

- Listen to others and be open to their ideas. The success of a team often depends on how well members reach a common understanding of the issues. Listening to understand others is at the heart of teamwork.

Chapter 3

- Carry out assignments between meetings: interviewing custom-ers, observing processes, gathering data, charting the data, writing reports, and so on. These tasks will be selected and planned at team meetings.

(For more information about team member responsibilities, see *The Team Memory Jogger™*, listed on p. D-1.)

Roles and Responsibilities for Improvement Projects

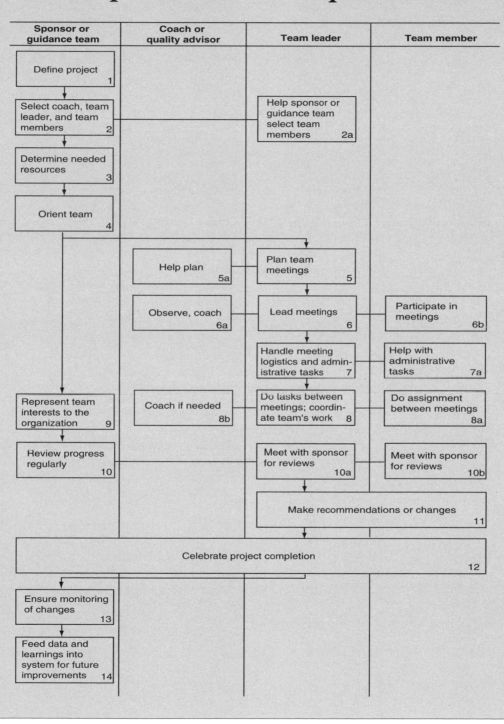

Sponsor or guidance team	Coach or quality advisor	Team leader	Team member
Define project **1**			
Select coach, team leader, and team members **2**		Help sponsor or guidance team select team members **2a**	
Determine needed resources **3**			
Orient team **4**			
	Help plan **5a**	Plan team meetings **5**	
	Observe, coach **6a**	Lead meetings **6**	Participate in meetings **6b**
		Handle meeting logistics and administrative tasks **7**	Help with administrative tasks **7a**
Represent team interests to the organization **9**	Coach if needed **8b**	Do tasks between meetings; coordinate team's work **8**	Do assignment between meetings **8a**
Review progress regularly **10**		Meet with sponsor for reviews **10a**	Meet with sponsor for reviews **10b**
		Make recommendations or changes **11**	
Celebrate project completion **12**			
Ensure monitoring of changes **13**			
Feed data and learnings into system for future improvements **14**			

Chapter 3

Chapter 3

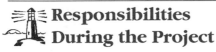 **Responsibilities During the Project**

Sponsor or guidance team responsibilities continue as the project gets under way. These responsibilities include:
- Orienting the team
- Reviewing progress

IV. Responsibilities During the Project

Once the project is selected and defined, the players chosen, and the groundwork done, the sponsor or guidance team has additional responsibilities in starting and supporting the team. They need to orient the team to the project and regularly review the team's progress.

Orienting the Team

Once team members are ready to go to work, the sponsor or guidance team should meet with them to review the project definition. This includes discussing the focus of the project, why it is important, what the boundaries are, and the schedule for the work. The team will need to know what resources are available and how to obtain them. It is also useful to discuss limits of authority (which decisions the team can make, which decisions the team and sponsor make together, and which decisions belong to the sponsor or to others in the organization). Since it is important that the team and its work not be isolated from the rest of the organization, the team will need to know how to communicate with others, especially those likely to be affected by their work. The orientation meeting is also a good time to discuss how the sponsor or guidance team will review project team progress.

Reviewing Progress

Joint meetings between the project team and its sponsor or guidance team greatly increase the project's chances of success.

Reviewing Progress

It is vital that a project team and its sponsor or guidance team stay in touch with one another. Open communication between them at joint meetings can greatly increase the chances of success. These review meetings can be used to discuss problems the project team encounters, revise the work plan, and celebrate progress. The review meeting also helps sponsors and guidance teams fulfill their responsibilities to:

- Keep the project on track and focused

- Encourage the team to use logic and data

- Offer support and boost team morale

- Help the team overcome roadblocks

At first, these joint meetings will probably focus on ironing out controversial or unclear portions of the charter or mission, which is ordinarily written by the sponsor. After that, the two teams should hold meetings regularly—at least every four to six weeks. You may call additional meetings to address urgent issues, something that happens a lot in a project's early stages. The meetings serve several purposes. They allow:

- The project team to update the sponsor or guidance team on progress made since the last joint meeting

- The project team to ask for help overcoming barriers to the project's success

- Members of both teams to iron out unclear or controversial issues

- The sponsor or guidance team to reinforce priorities

- The sponsor or guidance team to show support for improvement efforts

Chapter 3

It's a good idea to keep these joint meetings informal, with the emphasis on discussion, and questions and answers, rather than formal presentations. Hold them at a regular time and place. Do not change them except in case of emergencies. A team leader may be tempted to cancel or postpone this meeting when "we have nothing to report"—but these meetings are intended to keep communication lines open with managers, not to impress them. So hold the joint meeting (though it might be briefer than usual) even when there has been little apparent progress.

If sponsors or guidance teams are overseeing several improvement projects, they should meet periodically by themselves to discuss any common issues or concerns being raised during the reviews of the teams.

Review Structure

The following structure works well for review meetings.

Before the review

- Project team members agree on what to present and who will be prepared to discuss which topics. They also prepare handouts summarizing their work so far.

- Materials summarizing the team's work should be sent to reviewers 2 to 3 days before the meeting.

- Reviewers read the material, looking for the team's logic and the data which supports their logic.

Part 1 of the review

- The project's sponsor or guidance team leader opens the meeting and reviews the agenda.

- The project team presents the highlights of their work. (This takes 20 minutes. Reviewers listen and take notes.)

- Reviewers ask questions for clarification, note strengths in the team's use of logic and data, and offer suggestions and help to the project team.

- The project team asks questions and responds to reviewers' questions with more detail and data.

- The sponsor closes this part of the meeting and reviews what happens next.

Part 2 of the review

There are separate concurrent meetings of reviewers and presenters. Reviewers meet and discuss:

- – What were the main messages we sent to the project team?
- – What do we wish we had said?
- – How could we improve this review?

Presenters meet and discuss:

- – What did we hear as the sponsor's or guidance team's main points?
- – How will we address these main points?
- – How could we improve this review?

Part 3 of the review

Reviewers and project team members reconvene. They discuss:

– The main messages sent and received
– Any modifications to those messages
– The project team's plans for their next steps
– How to improve the next review

The structure of the review meeting described above has proven very useful for both project teams and their sponsors. The structure allows the reviewers to hear the full logic of the team's work before commenting on it. It provides time to delve into details at points selected by the reviewers. It allows the team to receive clear messages about the logic of their approach and the appropriateness of their data, while receiving guidance on the next steps. And it allows both the team and the reviewers to check their understanding of what was said before the team departs and continues to work.

Review Notes

Instructions: Fill out this form at the end of each joint review meeting between the project team and its sponsor or guidance team. These notes can then be used to guide the project team's work, remind the sponsor of barriers to be addressed, and improve the reviews themselves.

Project: _____

Review Date: _____ Review Number: _____

Brief status of project at this review:

Key messages from reviewers at this review:

Next steps planned for project at this time:

Suggestions for improving the next review:

Issues/concerns raised during review:

Chapter 3

Sample Agenda for Final Project Review

Instructions: At the end of the project it is important to capture the lessons learned while they are still fresh in everyone's minds. This can occur at a joint meeting between the project team and its sponsor or guidance team. The meeting's purpose is to identify and understand what worked and what didn't work, and to apply these learnings to future projects. The outcome of the meeting is a list of recommendations for future efforts.

Project:

Charter:

1. Review purpose of the meeting and agenda.

2. Silently reflect on the following questions:
   a. In your area, what went so exceptionally well that you want to repeat it in future projects?

      In the project as a whole, what went so exceptionally well that you want to repeat it in future projects?

   b. In your area, what superb contributions do you want to acknowledge?

      In the project as a whole, what superb contributions do you want to acknowledge?

   c. In your area, what new "experiments" were tried, and what were the results?

      In the project as a whole, what new "experiments" were tried, and what were the results?

   d. In your area, what went wrong, and how could this problem have been prevented?

      In the project as a whole, what went wrong and how could this problem have been prevented?

3. Share responses to each of the questions in number 2.
   Write main ideas on flipcharts. Do not discuss ideas; only ask questions for clarification.

4. Narrow the list from number 3 to a few specific, important things that can be acted upon to improve future efforts. Decide who will do what by when.

5. Evaluate this meeting.

V. Responsibilities After the Project

After the project is completed, the sponsor or guidance team is responsible for communicating the team's results and ensuring that any changes made by the team become part of the daily work methods in the area. Sponsors are also responsible for implementing changes that the team itself is not authorized to make.

In addition to monitoring the improvements, the sponsor or guidance team should review information collected during the project about systems issues or barriers which the team encountered during its work. It may be important to address these barriers for future projects to be successful.

If there were several improvement efforts underway, the sponsors of those efforts should review data gathered across all efforts in order to assess patterns. For example:

- What percentage of teams is providing adequate data to back up claims? Is the data displayed graphically so that the patterns are clear? Are the conclusions drawn warranted by the data analysis?

- What percentage of teams is adequately analyzing causes?

- What percentage of teams reports problems getting access to data?

- What percentage of teams is trying solutions out on a small scale before going into full implementation?

- What percentage of improvements is "holding the gains" six months after completion of the effort? One year after completion?

- What percentage of teams is having attendance problems at meetings?

- What is the team membership turnover rate?

The responsibilities of the sponsor or guidance team are not finished until the changes are introduced, the improvements accomplished, or the new methods systematized and the project officially completed. This may take anywhere from several weeks to a year.

Summary

The success of a project depends largely on getting everything set up correctly: establishing the goals, defining the project, selecting appropriate team members, and doing the necessary groundwork so a team will know what the project is all about. Knowing how to conduct effective meetings and establish review processes is also vital.

Once the team leader and team members are chosen, they have their work cut out for them. Their responsibilities for starting the project are described in the next chapter.

Chapter 4

Doing Work in Teams

"Toto, I've a feeling we're not in Kansas anymore!"

—Dorothy

During your team's first few meetings, it is not at all unusual to feel as though you have been transported to the Land of Oz, a place completely different from what you are used to. Many team members may be participating in an activity unlike any they've done before, perhaps working with people they've never worked with before, and using methods they may never have used before.

Being less than elegant in these circumstances is understandable. If you and your teammates feel self-conscious, awkward, or overwhelmed after your first meetings, congratulate yourselves on being normal.

Rest assured that these early feelings of inadequacy have no relationship to your team's ultimate success. Some of the most successful teams start out looking less like quality leaders and more like the Keystone Kops.

The techniques your team will be using really do work. You are not guinea pigs testing unproven approaches. There may be a lot for you to learn, and neither you nor your teammates can expect to be experts in *all* the knowledge and skills you will need. But each of you has something important to contribute: your experience and expertise. Whatever else you need to know, you can learn together.

The initial team meetings are critical for setting a proper tone: there is serious work at hand, but everyone can have fun and contribute to the organization by working together. This requires a balance between studying the problem or process and learning about each other. The following guidelines will help you develop effective meeting skills and lead you through the first few meetings.

What You Will Find Here

In this chapter we explore:

Section A: Team Techniques

Section B: Putting It All Together

Here is detailed advice on using techniques to plan and conduct team meetings.

🔦 Guidelines for Good Meetings

- Use agendas
- Fill key meeting roles
- Improve the meeting process

The "100-Mile Rule"

Once a meeting begins, everyone is expected to give it their full attention. No one should be called from the meeting unless it is so important that the disruption would occur even if the meeting was 100 miles away from the workplace.

The "100-mile rule" will need to be communicated to those who take phone messages or who would interrupt the team's work for other reasons.

Section A: Team Techniques

This section describes techniques that help teams coordinate their efforts to stay focused and develop a common understanding of issues.

I. Guidelines for Good Meetings

Although individual team members carry out assignments between team meetings, some of the team's work gets done when all team members are together—during meetings. Many people dislike meetings, but meetings don't have to be disliked. As in other processes, they can be studied and constantly improved. Productive meetings enhance the chance of having a successful project.

It is difficult to have productive meetings because few people know the rules and skills needed. In fact, the goal of having constantly improved meetings may be as hard for the team to reach as the improvement goals set for the project.

A given is that people are expected to be on time for meetings. Otherwise the time of many people is wasted. A meeting should start within a few minutes of the scheduled time, whether all of the players are present or not. If latecomers miss something, or have to be brought up-to-date, it will be an incentive for them to be on time at the next meeting.

Once most of the players are present, it's time to start. The best way to have effective meetings is to follow the guidelines given on the following pages.

Date: April 11, 1996 Time: 12:30–1:30 Place: Conference Room		Purpose: Review team progress		
TIME	TOPIC	WHO	HOW	OUTCOME
12:30	1. Check-in	All	Round-robin	
12:35	2. Review purpose & agenda	Pat	Review	Agree on agenda items
12:40	3. Recap of where we were at last review	Carl	Report	Establish where we were
12:45	4. Progress Report (Attachment A)	Team	Report	Understand current status
1:05	5. Questions of clarification	Guidance Team	Round-robin	Understand Team's work

Agendas...

Provide a structure that guides the meeting.

Use Agendas

Each meeting should have an agenda, preferably one developed prior to the meeting. It should be sent to participants in advance, if possible. If an agenda has not been developed before a meeting, spend the first five minutes of the meeting writing one on a flipchart.

Agendas should include the following information:
- **Purpose** of the meeting.
- **Topics** (including, perhaps, a sentence or two that defines each item and why it is being discussed).
- The **lead person** for each topic (usually the person who will introduce the topic).
- **Time estimates.**

Agendas for complex meetings might also include:
- **Methods** for segments of the meeting. (e.g., "First we will have a general discussion; then we will circle the group for ideas about next steps; then....")
- **Desired outcomes** for each topic. (Will this topic end with a decision, a plan, a list of options, shared understanding, etc.?)

Agendas usually include the following meeting activities:
- **Warm-up**. Short (five-minute) activities used to free people's minds from the outside world and get them focused on the meeting. (➡See Warm-Ups, p. 4-43 and C-2 to C-9.)
- **Agenda review**. Go over the agenda, adding or deleting items. Modify time estimates if necessary.
- **Meeting evaluation**. (➡See Evaluating Meetings, pp. 4-9 to 4-10.)

(➡Sample agendas also appear on pp. 4-45 and 4-47.)

For Ongoing Teams

If you are an ongoing team, such as an intact work group, the usefulness of this chapter will depend upon where your team is in its lifecycle.

An ongoing team that is starting up is just like a project team in many ways. For example, team members may have little experience being on a team and may find this chapter's step-by-step advice for their first few meetings very helpful.

On the other hand, an established ongoing team looking for ideas to improve their teamwork may prefer to read just the information on running effective meetings, facilitating discussions, and making decisions.

Chapter 4

Meeting Roles

Effective meetings include the roles of facilitator, notetaker, scribe, and time-keeper.

ROLES...

- Notetaker
- Timekeeper
- Facilitator
- Scribe

Fill Key Meeting Roles

Each meeting should have the following roles filled in order to ensure that the meeting works well:

- **Meeting leader or facilitator**

  The meeting leader or facilitator is responsible for keeping the meeting focused and moving smoothly. Often the team leader fills this role. However, your team may rotate the responsibility among its members.

  Key responsibilities are to:
  – Open the meeting
  – Review the agenda
  – Make sure someone is taking notes and someone is keeping track of time
  – Move through the agenda one item at a time
  – Keep the team focused on the agenda
  – Establish an appropriate pace
  – Facilitate discussions
  – Manage participation
  – Help the team use appropriate decision methods
  – Help the team evaluate the meeting
  – Gather ideas for the next meeting's agenda
  – Close the meeting

  (➡For more information on these responsibilities, see pp. 4-11 to 4-25.)

- **Timekeeper**

  The timekeeper helps the group keep track of time during the meeting. This keeps the team from spending all its meeting time on the first few agenda items, and thus not completing its work. Sometimes the meeting leader is also the timekeeper.

Key responsibilities are to:

- Keep track of time during meetings
- Alert the team when the time allocated for an item is almost up so the team can decide whether to continue the discussion or cut it short. Do NOT simply police the agenda. (e.g., "Time's up. Move on.")

• **Notetaker**

The notetaker records key topics, main points raised during discussions, decisions made, action items (who will do what by when), and items to be discussed at a future meeting. Notes can be written on standard forms or captured electronically during the meeting. (➡See a sample notetaking form on pp. 4-7 to 4-8.)

Key responsibilities are to:
- Capture key points for each agenda item
- Highlight decisions and action items
- Collect future agenda items
- See that the minutes are distributed or posted

• **Scribe**

The scribe posts ideas on a flipchart or whiteboard as the discussion unfolds so that everyone can see them. Posting ideas helps the team stay focused on the discussion and prevents the "team memory" from changing as the dialogue or discussion unfolds. It also shows members that their ideas have been captured for consideration, encouraging participation.

Key responsibilities are to:
- Write large enough so all can see
- Write legibly
- Check with team for accuracy
- Don't worry about spelling

Chapter 4

➤ Tip
Create an Action List

Compile action items from a meeting into a separate list. Send the list to members before the next meeting to remind them of assignments. The list includes what is to be done, by whom, by when. Start the next meeting by checking progress on the action list.

Team meeting minutes

The meeting minutes remind team members about points of discussion, tasks to be performed between meetings, and decisions made. They also help managers, and others who receive copies, to understand the issues and challenges facing the team.

Using a standard form for meeting notes that provides space for key items can help ensure that the notes capture the most useful information, and that key items, such as decisions or action items, are easy to spot in the document.

To create such a form, decide what categories of information should be part of the form. Adjust the spacing to fit your team's needs. Make the form easy to use by including ways of checking off information (such as attendance) whenever possible.

Team Meeting Record, Part 1

Instructions: Use this page and the next as a blueprint for creating a meeting record tailored to your team.

Meeting Number _____   Date _____   Location _____

1. Project charter: _____

2. ✔ To indicate "present"

       Member _____

       Member _____

       Member _____

       Member _____

       Member _____

       Team leader_____

       Others attending:

3. Agenda: Enter key words indicating the agenda topics. Check off an item when it is completed. Items you do not complete should be carried over to the next meeting.

      ( ) 1. Check-in

      ( ) 2. Agenda review

      ( ) 3.

      ( ) 4.

      ( ) 5.

      ( ) 6. Set agenda for next meeting

      ( ) 7. Meeting evaluation

4. Futures file: Items for future consideration but not for the next meeting.

5. Meeting Evaluation
      "**+**"   "**—**"

Next meeting:

Date_____ Time _____ Location _____

Notetaker:_____

Team Meeting Record, Part 2

Instructions: Take notes during the meeting on a page like this. Focus on capturing the main ideas associated with topics discussed. Summarize the discussion whenever possible.

Agenda Item	Key Discussion Points	Outcomes
Topic 1	Main points	Decisions, Action items
Topic 2	Main points	Decisions, Action items
Topic 3	Main points	Decisions, Action items
Topic 4	Main points	Decisions, Action items

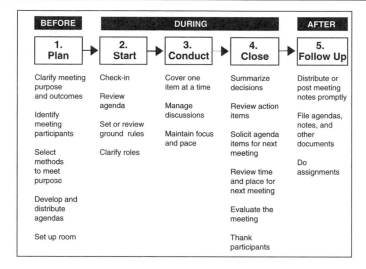

Meeting Process

Meetings are processes and can be studied and improved like other processes.

Improve the Meeting Process

Meetings are processes and can be studied and improved like any other process. The flowchart above provides a picture of the meeting process. As you can see, you plan the meeting, then conduct (do) the meeting, and then, at the end of the meeting, you evaluate, or check, the meeting to identify ways to improve it the next time. Evaluating every meeting is key to having effective meetings.

Evaluating meetings

The evaluation should include what worked well and what will be done to improve the next meeting. Some questions commonly asked are:

- How did this meeting go?
- How was the pace, flow, and tone of the meeting?
- Did we handle items in a reasonable sequence? Did we get stuck?
- How well did we stay on the topic?
- How well did we discuss the information? How clearly? How accurately?
- How well did we respond to each other's questions? How satisfied are we with answers to our questions?
- What might we do differently? What should we do that we didn't do? Do more of? Do less of? Not do at all?
- What was just right and should continue as is?
- Any other comments, observations, recommendations?

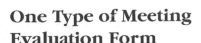

One Type of Meeting Evaluation Form

To use this format, the team leader or other facilitator asks team members to rate the meeting on criteria important to the team. Often team members work individually first, then share and discuss answers with their teammates. Other evaluation forms are less structured.

> **Example: Written evaluation form**
>
> **Our meeting today was:**
> Focused 1 2 3 4 Rambling
>
> **The pace was:**
> Too fast   Just right   Too slow
>
> **Everyone got a chance to participate:**
> Yes   Somewhat   No
>
> **Our purpose was:**
> Clear 1 2 3 4 Confused
>
> **We made good progress on our plan:**
> Yes   Somewhat   No
>
> **We followed our ground rules:**
> Yes   Somewhat   No

After a series of meeting evaluations and improvements, team members develop a common understanding of what a "good meeting" is. The evaluations provide valuable opportunities for members to identify and address problems before they become serious.

There are several ways to evaluate meetings:

- **Round-robin comments**: Go around the team and let everyone share their comments in turn

- **Written evaluations**: Forms are filled out, summarized, and discussed by the team

- **Open discussion**: Anyone speaks in any order

- **Thumbs up, sideways, down**: Everyone signals their overall evaluation (good, neutral, negative), then each in turn explains why

One useful approach to improving meetings is to monitor weak spots. For example, one team noticed that meetings were frequently sluggish at the beginning. So for the next several meetings they evaluated themselves on how quickly they got started. They also discussed reasons for slow starts, and steps they could take to prevent slow starts. For evaluations to be useful, they have to be used to improve future meetings.

(For information on teaching meeting skills, see *Running Effective Meetings*, listed on p. D-2.)

II. Guidelines for Effective Discussions

Effective discussions are necessary for effective meetings, which in turn are necessary for effective teams. Clearly the team leader should use skills for effective discussion. However, the team will be even more successful if every team member learns and practices these skills. The following techniques are presented in the framework of team meetings, but they are useful whenever an effective discussion is important.

How to Facilitate an Effective Discussion

Open the discussion

Knowing what they are talking about and why helps team members participate constructively in the discussion. It also helps the team leader plan how to handle the discussion and enables the team to check whether the desired outcome of the discussion was achieved.

Listen

Actively explore one another's ideas. Give others your undivided attention. Concentrate on understanding the speaker. Check your understanding by restating the key points in your own words.

Ask for clarification

If you are unclear about the topic being discussed, ask someone to define the purpose, focus, or limits of the discussion. If you're unclear about the logic in another person's arguments, ask someone to restate the ideas in a different way. Ask for examples, pictures, diagrams, data, etc.

 Effective Discussion Skills

- Open the discussion
- Listen
- Ask for clarification
- Manage participation
- Summarize
- Manage time
- Contain digressions
- Test for agreement
- Close the discussion

➤ **Tip**
How to Open a Discussion

- State the topic
- Give background information
- Explain intended outcome
- Suggest methods for discussion (when appropriate)

Chapter 4

Manage participation

Encourage more-or-less equal participation among team members by using techniques such as circling the group to give everyone a chance to comment. Make openings for less assertive members by asking for their opinions. (➡For more ideas on handling talkers, see p. 7-16.)

Summarize

Occasionally summarize what's been said. Check with the team to see whether your summary accurately captured the key points.

Manage time

If portions of the agenda take longer than expected, remind the team of deadlines and time allotments so work can either be accelerated or postponed, or time reallocated appropriately.

Contain digressions

Ask team members to avoid overlong examples or irrelevant discussion. If faced with a killer tangent during a meeting, suggest it be a future agenda item, or ask if the point could be finished up in the next 100 seconds. (➡For more ideas on handling tangents, see p. 7-22.)

Test for agreement

Summarize the group's position on an issue, and check whether the team agrees with the summary. (Note: This is not the same as "checking for consensus," which is described on p. 4-25.)

Close the discussion

Learn to tell when there is nothing to be gained from further discussion. Help the team close the discussion and decide the issue.

Guiding Discussion Phases

Discussions can be thought of as having two phases or stages. The first stage might be described as the exploratory phase, and the second might be called the defining phase.

The exploratory phase

During the exploratory phase, you strive to tap the team's creativity by setting up an environment in which a pool of ideas is generated for consideration. This should be a "no-holds-barred" phase of discussion in which a full range of ideas, angles, and perspectives are explored. The objective is to generate a rich set of options from which to choose. Anyone who has any experience working in teams will appreciate how difficult it is to develop creative ways to approach a task. Techniques which support openness to diverse perspectives are useful to teams in this stage of discussion. (➡See sections on brainstorming and part one of the nominal group technique, described on pp. 4-14 and 4-16.)

The defining phase

At this stage (often reached after an interval of brainstorming), a rich assortment of ideas and options has been gathered, and the challenge now is to winnow them down. Once a good list of ideas has been generated, it must be evaluated, sorted, and selected from. Options are examined, compared, and the best are chosen. Sometimes it is very difficult to select only a few items from all of the possibilities generated. Techniques that help team members prune lists and compare ideas, such as multivoting and the second stage of the nominal group technique, are useful in this stage of the group's work.

Brainstorming...

Generates a wide variety of ideas from all participants without criticism or judgment.

⚓ Discussion Techniques

Three techniques useful in managing discussion phases are:

- Brainstorming
- Multivoting
- Nominal group technique

Discussion Techniques

The following techniques can help you manage the phases of discussions.

Brainstorming

One of the easiest and most enjoyable ways to quickly generate a lot of ideas is to brainstorm. A successful brainstorm helps:

- Encourage creativity
- Involve everyone
- Generate excitement and energy
- Separate people from the ideas they suggest

Guidelines for brainstorming

- Start by reviewing the topic; make sure everyone understands the issues.
- Give people a minute or two of *silent* thinking time.
- When ideas start to flow, let them come. Freewheel—don't hold back.
- No discussion during the brainstorm. That will come later.
- No criticism of ideas—not even a groan or grimace!
- Hitchhike—build on ideas generated by others in the group.
- Write *all* ideas on a flipchart so everyone can see them.

Methods for brainstorming

Two common methods for brainstorming are:

- **Rounds**. Go around the group and have each person say one of their ideas per turn, until everyone is out of ideas.
- **Popcorn**. Anyone calls out an idea, no order, until all ideas are out.

Multivoting...

Uses voting to select the most popular items on a list with limited discussion and difficulty.

Multivoting

Multivoting is a way to conduct a straw poll to select the most important or popular items from a list with limited discussion and difficulty. This is accomplished through a series of votes, each cutting the list in half—even a list of 30 to 50 items can be reduced to a workable number in 4 or 5 votes. Multivoting often follows a brainstorming session in order to identify the few items worthy of immediate attention.

How to conduct a multivote:

1. First, generate a list of items and number each item.

2. Combine two or more similar items if the group agrees that they are the same.

3. If necessary, renumber all items.

4. Have all members choose several items they would like to discuss or address by writing down the numbers of these items on a sheet of paper. Allow each member a number of choices equal to at least one-third of the total number of items on the list (48 item list = 16 choices; 37 item list = 13 choices).

5. After all members have silently completed their selections, tally votes. You may let members vote by a show of hands as each item number is called out.

6. To reduce the list, eliminate those items with the fewest votes. Group size affects the results. A rule of thumb: If it is a small group (5 or fewer members), cross off items with only 1 or 2 votes. If it is a medium group (6 to 15 members), eliminate anything with 3 or fewer votes. If it is a large group (more than 15 members), eliminate items with 4 or fewer votes.

 Caution!

Do not confuse multivoting with data collection.

The outcome of a multivote reflects popular opinion. It is not a substitute for collecting data to identify the most important item out of a group of items.

Chapter 4

Nominal Group Technique...

Is a structured method of generating a list and then narrowing it down. The first phase is silent brainstorming. In the second phase, members vote to reduce the list.

7. Repeat steps 3 through 6 on the remaining list of choices. Continue this until only a few items are left. If no clear favorite emerges by this point, have the group discuss which item should receive top priority. Or you may take one last vote.

Nominal Group Technique

Compared to brainstorming or multivoting, the nominal group technique (NGT) is a more structured method of generating a list of options and narrowing it down. It is called "nominal" because during the session the group doesn't engage in the usual amount of interaction typical of a real team. Because of its relatively low level of interaction, the NGT is good for highly controversial issues.

NGT, Part One: A formalized brainstorm

1. **Define the task in the form of a question.** This is often done by the team leader or team facilitator before the meeting.

2. **Describe the purpose of the discussion** and the rules and procedures.

3. **Introduce and clarify the question**. The leader reads the question aloud and either writes it on paper taped to the wall or hands out sheets of paper with the question written on them. This way anyone may refer back to the question whenever he or she wants to be reminded of the session's purpose. Anyone who does not understand the question should ask for more explanation. Do not let this develop into a discussion of the issue itself.

4. **Generate ideas.** This is the most important step in the entire nominal group technique. It is important to have team members first write down their answers in silence. Experience shows this is the best way to elicit good ideas. Do not allow any distractions at this stage: no joking, no moving around, no whispering. People who finish first must sit quietly until all are finished.

5. **List ideas**. When everyone is done, go around the table and have each participant read one idea off their list; write down every answer on a flipchart. Continue the round-robin until everyone's list is complete or until time runs out (we suggest you stop at 30 minutes). No discussion, not even questions for clarification, is allowed at this point because the exercise rapidly becomes tedious and the leader must move the group through it as quickly as possible.

6. **Clarify and discuss ideas**. Display all of the flipchart pages in full view of the entire group. The leader asks if anyone has questions about any items listed. The person who contributed the idea should be the one to answer a question, but other members may join in the discussion to help define and focus the wording. The leader may choose to change the wording, but only when the person who originally proposed the idea agrees.

When there are no more questions, the leader condenses the list as much as possible. If the originators of the ideas give their approval, the leader may combine ideas. If someone suggests combining several items, but the originators think there is a difference, then leave the ideas listed separately.

Chapter 4

Results of an NGT Session

Team members first rank the items selected from the brainstorming session by filling out cards as shown (near right). The item number, taken from the brainstorming session, is placed in the upper left. Key words identifying the item are in the middle. The score, or rank, appears in the lower right. This person gave item 3 a score of 4. All votes are tallied (see flipchart, far right).

Flipchart Tally of Votes	
1. Improve Quality 8, 8, 8, 6, 7, 5, 3, 2, 6, 8	61
2. Reduce Absenteeism 1, 3, 2	6
3. Improve Planning 8, 8, 7, 6, 4, 3, 1, 1	38

NGT, Part Two: Making the selection

The second part of the NGT is much like multivoting, but again more formal. Use this to narrow the list of options and select the choice or choices preferred by the team.

1. If there are more than 50 items, use some method to reduce the list to 50 or fewer items, if possible. You could use one or two rounds of multivoting, or simply let members withdraw the less serious items they put on the list. No member is allowed to remove an item that originated with another member, unless the originator agrees.

2. Give each participant from 4 to 8 cards (three-by-five inch, or similar-sized pieces of paper). The number of cards is a rough fraction of the number of items still on the list. Hand out 4 cards apiece for up to 20 items; 6 cards for 20 to 35 items; 8 cards for 35 to 50 items.

3. Members individually make their selections from the list. They write down one item per card, one card per item (4, 6, or 8, depending on how many cards they have).

4. Have members assign a point value to each item, based on their preferences. Each person assigns the highest point value to the most important item. The value again depends on the number of items selected (4, 6, or 8). In an 8-card system, the most preferred item is numbered 8, the second most preferred item is numbered 7, and so on until the least preferred item is numbered 1. This system is the same for groups with 4 or 6 selections, except, of course, the highest point values are 4 and 6, respectively. (See sample card above.)

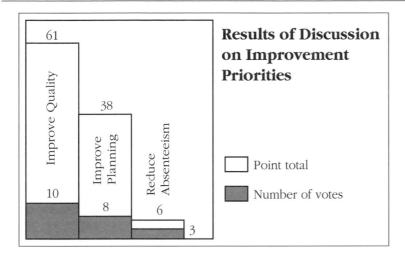

Results of Discussion on Improvement Priorities

61
Improve Quality
10
38
Improve Planning
8
Reduce Absenteeism
6
3

☐ Point total
▨ Number of votes

NGT Results

The results from an NGT session can be presented as a bar chart.

5. After each participant has given point values to the items selected, the cards are collected and the votes tallied. It is easiest to mark the flipchart page with the original list, noting the value of each vote an item received, then adding up these values. The item that ends up with the highest point total is the group's selection.

6. The group reviews the results, and discusses the reaction. If you have the time, display the results on a Pareto-like diagram so you can easily see which items received the most votes and which have the greatest point total (these are not always the same items). Were there any surprises? Any objections? Does anyone want to lobby for or against certain items and ask for another vote?

If members agree on the importance of the item that got the highest score, the NGT can end the discussion, and the team will have to decide what to do next. If members do not agree, the team could focus its efforts on investigating the two or three items that received high scores.

Chapter 4

Steps for Effective Decisions

- Understand the context of the decision
- Determine who should be involved
- Decide how to decide

III. Guidelines for Effective Decisions

Team members make decisions every day. Some of the decisions are important and affect a lot of people. Other decisions are relatively small and may only affect one member of the team. To make a good decision you need to have good information on which to base the decision. That's where being data-based comes in. When a team makes a decision, they need a good understanding of how the outcome will affect them and their particular work. However, it is important to also understand how a decision can impact:

- Other people
- Other projects
- The business as a whole
- Future decisions

Understand the Context of the Decision

When a decision is important, it is good to start by understanding the context of the decision. The following steps help you to do this:

1. Clarify the decision to be made. Make sure everyone has the same understanding.

2. Know by when the decision must be made. Understand the risks of missing the time window or not making the decision.

3. Learn how this decision affects the critical path for the team's work.

4. Gather relevant information about past decisions, pending decisions, and implicit decisions that are related to this one.

Determine Who Should Be Involved

Even when they understand the context, teams often have a lot of trouble making a decision. One reason for this difficulty is that they often aren't clear *who* should be involved in making the decision or *how* the decision should be made.

We know it's often important to involve a wide variety of people in a decision, but we often confuse that involvement with responsibility for making the actual decision. To clarify who should participate in the decision, you must decide:

- Who is ultimately responsible for the results of this decision
- Who is critically affected, both now and in the future
- Who has vital information

This will help you decide who should have input into the decision and who ultimately makes the decision. Depending on the nature of the decision, the decision-maker could be one member of the team, the whole team, the team leader, a subgroup of the team, a manager or group of managers outside of the team, or another team or group. Whoever the decision-makers are, if the decision is important, it is likely that input from others at different points in the decision-making process will make the decision more effective.

Decide How to Decide

There are many methods of making decisions. The four most common methods are: consensus, voting, assigning the decision to a subgroup (who decides by consensus), or identifying one person as the decision-maker. Each method has its strengths and weaknesses. Each is appropriate in different circumstances. The table on p. 4-22 summarizes when to use each method.

When to Use Each Method

Consensus

When decisions are important, have large ramifications, or affect a lot of people.

When groups are small (10 or fewer) you should usually consider consensus; with large groups you usually only need consensus on issues of great importance.

When you can have a rich exchange of ideas in real time, whether in person, by phone, by video conference, or with groupware.

When the group is informed and individual members feel a similar level of investment or are critical to a good decision.

When consensus can't be achieved you should have a back-up method to reach a decision.

Voting

When it is known that consensus is highly unlikely in the time allowed.

When members of the group are equally informed on the subject matter, and understand one another's viewpoints.

When it's been determined that the majority can handle the implementation without the active involvement of those who "lose" in the vote.

When you have a plan for how to handle those who "lose" to keep them from becoming defensive.

Subgroup

When a subgroup has the necessary information or expertise to make the decision.

When a subgroup is the only entity impacted by the decision and can implement it without the active involvement of the majority.

When the whole group is truly comfortable delegating their authority to representatives.

One Person

When it is an emergency.

When one person has all of the relevant information.

When one person is especially trusted to make a good decision.

When the outcome only impacts the decision maker.

What Is Consensus?

A decision by consensus is a decision in which all the group members find a common ground. Getting consensus *does not* mean that everyone must be completely satisfied with the outcome, or even that it is anyone's first choice.

Consensus *does not* mean:
- A unanimous vote
- Everyone getting everything they want
- Everyone finally coming around to the "right" opinion

Consensus *does* mean:
- Everyone understands the decision and can explain why it is best
- Everyone can live with the decision

Consensus requires:
- Time
- Active participation of all team members
- Skills in communication, listening, conflict resolution, and facilitation
- Creative thinking and open-mindedness

Consensus decision making is not just a way to reach a compromise. It is a search for the best decision through the exploration of the best of everyone's thinking. As more ideas are addressed and more potential problems discussed, a synthesis of ideas takes place and the final decision is often better than any single idea that was present at the beginning.

We often use other methods for decision making because consensus takes time. All sides of an issue have to be listened to and considered. Points of disagreement are sought out and encouraged. But getting consensus at this stage often saves time during implementation of the

 Caution!

Misunderstandings about consensus can prevent teams from obtaining its benefits.

If members confuse consensus with compromise, a creative solution is unlikely.

Also, if members think consensus means "don't rock the boat," groupthink can result. (See p. 7-3.)

➤ Tip
Handling Hot Topics

If a discussion becomes too heated, agree to disagree for now. Take time to separate and think about the issue. Come back to it in a future meeting.

decision. Either you spend time getting everyone on board at the beginning, or you may spend the time getting them on board later, when they are resentful of a decision they did not support. Sometimes the time spent getting consensus in the beginning actually saves time later.

How to do consensus

1. Discuss the issues. Take all sides into consideration. Try to find ways to address concerns.

2. Do a check. Go around the room one by one and have everyone give their current opinion. People can ask questions for clarification, but there is no criticism at this point.

3. If consensus has not been reached, repeat Steps 1 and 2.

Tips for Successful Consensus

1. **Listen carefully.** Ask for reasons and seek out the assumptions behind statements. Be open to others' reactions to your ideas and consider them carefully.

2. **Encourage all members to participate fully.** Don't assume that silence means agreement. Periodically circle the group and have each member state his or her view.

3. **Seek out differences of opinion.** Probe for alternative viewpoints. Disagreements are natural and helpful because they increase the range of information and opinions that the group can use in its decision process.

4. **Search for alternatives that meet the goals of all members.** Don't assume someone must win and someone must lose. When there's a stalemate, look for the next most acceptable alternative for all members.

5. **Avoid changing your mind ONLY to avoid conflict.**

6. **Don't just argue for your point of view.** Seek ways of combining your ideas with others' views. Try to incorporate criticism of your ideas into your proposals.

7. **Balance power.** If one or two group members have more power or authority than the others (for example, if one member supervises the group), then the member with more authority should not state his/her view until late in the discussion after all other views have been heard.

8. **Make sure there is enough time.** The "reaching consent" part of consensus takes a lot of time. Meetings should be long enough to allow for full discussion, and there should be enough meetings for a decision to emerge.

9. **Check understanding.** Check to see if everyone understands the decision and can explain why it was the best decision.

Chapter 4

For Ongoing Teams

Ongoing teams may not have discrete projects. However, it is still important to document work progress, learnings, and changes in work methods. Good records help new employees get up to speed faster and keep absent members informed. Also, regular reviews of team records help members see accomplishments and areas for improvement.

IV. Guidelines for Effective Record Keeping

Up to this point in the chapter we have been concentrating on the essentials of *conducting* effective meetings, but having effective meetings is only part of the job. With all the responsibilities team members have, it's easy to forget what transpired at meetings: what was discussed, what decisions were made, and what has to be done before the next meeting. Unless excellent records of what transpired are maintained, the team's momentum can be lost. Maintaining up-to-date files is crucial for a successful project or for documenting ongoing work. Good records are helpful for several compelling reasons:

- Projects sometimes last 6 to 12 months, so the team may lose or gain members. Good records help new members catch up and keep old members informed of developments.

- Clear, illustrated records help educate and win the support of people in the organization who may not have time to read or listen to lengthy reports.

- As the project progresses, the team may have to retrace its steps to track down problems or errors. Good records make this easier.

- Frequently, presentations about a successful project are widely circulated within the company, the industry, or local businesses. Having up-to-date records makes it easier to prepare these presentations.

For these reasons, document your team's work from the earliest stages. Talk about what kinds of records you are likely to need further down the road and plan how to maintain these records.

Communicating Project Progress

Storyboards help teams communicate the highlights of their work to others in a way that is easy to follow and graphically interesting.

We recommend keeping a central file for documents, papers, correspondence, and other pertinent records. Organize the file around the meeting agendas or a flowchart of the work plan.

The Storyboard

The storyboard is a format that has proven particularly useful in communicating the highlights of a project to others. It also helps the team track its progress. This format captures the progress of a project through a descriptive series of pictures and graphs accompanied by simple text. The format is easy to use, maintain, and read, and helps you keep track of milestones passed by the team.

A storyboard is constructed in the style of a flowchart with a sequence of boxed information. The storyboard communicates with graphs more than words. Each box represents a major step in the team's work plan or problem-solving process. Within each box are graphical data displays and the conclusions drawn from the data. The boxes lead the reader through the project's main steps. Someone completely unfamiliar with the project should be able to understand what was done and why by following the logic of the graphical data analyses and conclusions.

A team leader should begin this document before the team's first meeting, filling in the first box—labeled "Project." At the first team meeting, distribute copies of this document to help explain the team's charter or mission. As the project progresses, add boxes summarizing each stage of the team's work.

(➥A partial storyboard is shown on p. 4-28. A completed example is in Appendix B.)

Chapter 4

Storyboard Format

Description: The storyboard communicates the highlights of a team's progress through a descriptive series of pictures and graphs accompanied by simple text. There is a complete example in Appendix B.

Project

Purpose: Reduce the amount of defective product

Reason Selected: Defective product accounted for more than twice as many dollars refunded to customers over the past six months than any other single category.

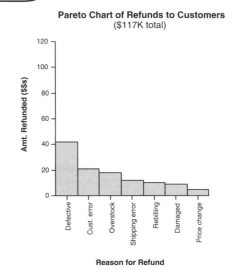

Pareto Chart of Refunds to Customers
($117K total)

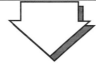

Current Situation

Further analysis showed that the Red Lake and Moonwalk A products accounted for the most defects.

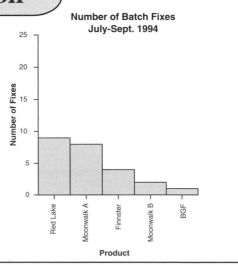

"ready, FIRE, aim!"

V. Guidelines for Planning

When undertaking a project, there is no substitute for careful planning. Unfortunately, many people have learned a "ready, fire, aim!" approach instead of "ready, aim, fire!" This encourages people to act even if it isn't the right thing to do, or the right time to do it. The essence of planning is to have teams look ahead, envision when they will do which tasks, anticipate what resources and training they might need for each, and think about what to do if they run into problems. Although planning adds time up front, it increases the chances of success and saves time in the long run.

Some advantages of planning are that it:

- Helps team members coordinate their work by providing a clear picture of what each should be doing and when. Flowcharting the steps in the plan also helps identify potential conflicts in schedules.

- Helps the team identify a series of deadlines to meet in order to complete the project on time. This allows the team to check its progress and to discuss concerns about the schedule with the sponsor well before the completion date.

- Provides a roadmap that gives the team a sense of direction and helps ensure key tasks are not missed.

- Provides the basis for improving the next project. Comparing what the team hoped would happen with what actually happened can lead to a better plan the next time.

Step #	Step and Desired Outcome	Who	Dates		Expenses	Comments
			Plan	Actual		
1	Draft the brochure	Mktg.	Start:4/1 End: 4/10	4/1 4/15		Computer breakdown on 4/8, lost some files
2	Circulate draft for comments	George	Start: 4/12 End: 4/20	4/16 4/20	$50 for FedEx	
3	Review input and create second draft	Whole team	Start: 4/23 End: 4/30	4/23 4/29		Must complete this step by 4/30 to make final deadline

Creating a Plan

There are several tools that help teams plan their work. Deployment flowcharts (◄see p. 2-18) help team members see the sequence of steps and who is involved in each step. This tool is particularly useful when the work is moving from one team member to another. For example, one member might be leading a data collection activity. Then the data she collects might be analyzed by two other team members who bring their analysis to the whole team for discussion.

A planning grid is another useful tool for short-term planning of single events or simple projects. The grid helps a team organize the tasks needed to reach a goal. It does not help you choose the goal; it only helps you reach it. The team lists the steps or tasks down the side of a page and adds other important information, such as who is involved and how much time is needed, in adjacent columns.

Here is how to set up a plan like the one pictured above:

- **Identify what you want to accomplish**
  How will you know when this project or activity is completed? Agree on what you will have accomplished and write it down.

- **Identify the final step or task**
  What is the last task that officially indicates the end of the project or activity? For example: signing a contract, giving a final report to the sponsor, or the sixth flawless run of the newly designed work process.

- **Identify the starting point or first step**
  What will be (or was) the first action that signaled the beginning of this activity or project? For example: being invited to be on the team, noticing a problem, or agreeing that a key process should improve.

- **Brainstorm a list of separate and distinct activities that should take place between the starting and ending point**

- **Organize and refine the brainstorm list**
  Clarify what is unclear. Eliminate redundancy. Break up tasks that are too large and combine those that are too small.

- **Prepare the grid**
  Feel free to add columns other than those discussed here to your grid. For example, you might include notes on limits or boundaries, reminders, or cautions. For each step, list:
  - The steps, in sequence, and the outcome of each
  - Who is responsible for each step or task
  - The planned start and end dates

  Leave room to write in when the steps actually start and end. This will help you understand how to improve next time. Also leave room to capture comments and lessons learned.

- **If necessary, revise**
  After looking over the whole plan, the team may want to rework some items.

If you are working on more complex or longer term projects, you may need to create a planning grid for each stage of the project, or use other planning tools or computer software.

Chapter 4

Planning Grid

Instructions: Use this page as a blueprint for creating a planning grid for your team.

Step #	Step and Desired Outcome	Who	Dates		Expenses	Comments
			Plan	Actual		
1						
2						
3						
4						
5						
6						

Section B:
Putting It All Together

This section offers detailed advice to team leaders on how to use many of the methods, tools, and techniques described earlier when preparing and conducting the first few team meetings.

I. The First Few Team Meetings

The previous pages describe the skills needed for effective team meetings. The trick is to apply these skills to your work. The remainder of this chapter provides detailed plans for the first few meetings of a new team. We hope these plans will help you use the skills to get your team off to a good start.

Preparing for the First Team Meeting

The team leader or manager is the driving force behind the first team meetings. He or she drafts a preliminary work plan. He or she also handles all of the logistical details, and develops meeting agendas that help the team get to know one another, understand the project, and begin to learn new skills.

It is usually a good idea for the sponsor or a member of the guidance team to attend the first team meeting to orient the team, answer questions about the charter, and explain how progress will be regularly reviewed. (◄See Chapter 3 pp. 3-25 to 3-28 for details on reviewing projects.) The team leader should review the agenda with the sponsor before the meeting and clarify who will lead which parts of the meeting. Organizations with coaches or quality advisors recommend that the team leader and the coach prepare together for the team's first few meetings.

 Preparing for the First Team Meeting

- Review the charter or mission statement and discuss the project
- Clarify roles
- Draft a plan
- Identify pertinent existing data
- Set the meeting logistics
- Draft an agenda

Chapter 4

For Ongoing Teams

The goals of an ongoing team's first meeting are similar to those of a new project team. They should clarify the purpose, function, and expectations of the team. Roles, ground rules, limits of authority, and methods of working together must be developed and agreed to. The team also needs clear connections to others in the organization.

Before the first team meeting, the team leader should:

- **Review the charter or mission statement**

  Are the goals realistic? Is the definition clear? Do you anticipate any controversial issues? Are the team's boundaries and limitations clear? What are the expectations about deadlines? How will workloads and priorities be handled? List your questions and arrange a meeting with the team's sponsor to discuss them.

- **Clarify roles**

  If you are working with a coach or quality advisor, clarify what responsibilities each of you will have. (Review Chapter 3.) How will you communicate and coordinate with each other? Schedule weekly meetings for the two of you to review the last team meeting and plan and prepare for upcoming meetings.

- **Draft a plan**

  How might this project unfold? What activities are needed to complete the project and in what sequence should they occur? (➡See Chapter 5 for help developing a plan). This plan will inevitably change as the team progresses, but preparing one before the team meets makes it less likely that you will stall in the starting gate or get stuck in unimportant details.

- **Identify pertinent existing data**

  Review previous work in this area. Has anyone worked on this problem or issue before? If you are improving a process, find out how the process came to be designed the way it is. Determine if anyone is currently collecting data on the process you intend to study.

- **Set the meeting logistics**

  The time you choose for the first meeting need not be the time members select for regular meetings. At the first meeting everyone can decide on a best time for regular meetings.

  The first team meeting may need to be longer—perhaps two hours—to cover all of the issues and answer questions. Once the effort is well under way, your team will usually meet weekly for one hour or longer. You will also meet with the sponsor and/or guidance team for 1 1/2 hours about once a month.

  There should be a regular time and place for all meetings. Holding meetings in the same room at the same time saves members from wondering, "When and where are we meeting this week?" The team leader should make certain that there are sufficient:

  - **Tables and chairs:** Have enough table space and chairs to accommodate the team and any visitors. A square or round table allows team members to see and hear each other, encouraging equal participation.

  - **Flipcharts, markers, masking tape, and other supplies**: Each meeting room should have a flipchart mounted on the wall or on an easel. Have adequate flipchart pads, markers, and tape. Tape the flipchart pages to the wall as the meeting progresses so your team can track its progress. You may also need notepaper, graph paper, pencils, and pens.

- **Draft an agenda**

  The team leader drafts the agenda prior to each of the first several meetings. As the team gains experience, agendas can be developed during the prior meeting. A sample agenda for the first meeting is described in the next section. (◄Also see p. 4-3 for more on agendas.)

Chapter 4

Goals of the First Few Meetings

Team-Building Goals
- Get to know each other
- Learn to work as a team
- Work out decision-making issues
- Set meeting ground rules

Project Goals
- Understand your assignment
- Understand your resources
- Develop a work plan
- Identify stakeholders

Educational Goals
- Learn the scientific approach and other new skills needed to be an effective team and to successfully start the project.

Goals of the First Few Meetings

The goals of your team's first meetings are built around three themes: building relationships between team members, starting to do the work, and learning about methods and ways of doing work that may be new to you. Though the temptation is to plunge right into the project, you will do better in the long run if you spend some time in the beginning on all three aspects.

The following catalogue of issues that a team should address may seem intimidating. Keep in mind you need not pack them all into one or two meetings. The time needed depends on team members' experience and the nature of the project.

Team-building goals for the first few meetings

Get to know each other

As a team, you're going to be working closely together and will need to rely on each other. Take time to learn each other's background and skills, and how each learns and works best. You will be most effective when members can compliment each other without embarrassment and disagree without fear.

Learn to work as a team

When team membership is drawn from various departments and levels within the organization, allow time for the group to become a team. Find ways to use each member's strengths. (➡See Chapter 6 and Appendix C.)

Work out decision-making issues

Too often decisions just "happen" in a team; members go along with what they think the group wants. Teams should discuss how they will make decisions. (◀See pp. 4-20 to 4-25 for more information on methods of decision making.)

Set meeting ground rules

Every team establishes ground rules, or "norms," concerning how meetings will be run, how team members will interact, and what kind of behavior is acceptable. Some are stated aloud; others are understood without discussion. Each member is expected to respect these rules, which usually prevents misunderstandings and disagreements. A few of the ground rules to establish are:

- **Attendance**: Teams should place a high priority on attending meetings. Identify legitimate reasons for missing a meeting and establish a procedure for informing the team leader if you'll miss a team meeting. Decide how to bring absent members up to speed.

- **Promptness**: Team meetings should start and end on time. This makes it easier on everyone's schedule and avoids wasting time. How strongly does your team want to enforce this rule? What can you do to encourage promptness? What does "on time" mean to your team?

- **Participation**: Everyone's viewpoint is valuable. Therefore, emphasize the importance of both speaking freely and listening attentively.

- **Interruptions**: Decide when interruptions (phone calls, for example) will be tolerated and when they won't. (◀See the 100-Mile Rule, p. 4-2.)

- **Basic conversational courtesies**: Listen attentively and respectfully to others; don't interrupt; hold one conversation at a time; and so forth.

- **Confidentiality**: Decide whether there are kinds of information which should not be discussed outside of the meetings.

- **Assignments**: Much of a team's work is done between meetings. When members are assigned responsibilities, it is important they complete their tasks on time.

- **Smoking and breaks**: Decide whether and under what circumstances smoking will be allowed, whether to take breaks, and how long breaks will be.

- **Rotation of responsibilities**: Decide who will be responsible for taking notes, setting up the meeting room, etc., and how to rotate these duties among members.

- **Meeting place and time**: Specify a regular meeting time and place, and establish a procedure for notifying members of meetings.

Understand Your Project

One of the team's first tasks is to understand the boundaries of its project.

Project goals for the first few meetings

Understand your assignment

Your sponsor, guidance team, or manager has identified what you are expected to work on. Make sure you understand the assignment and the sponsor's expectations. What boundaries or limitations does the team have? Are there deadlines? What decisions can the team make? (◀See Discussing Your Mission, p. C-27.)

Understand your resources

Discuss what resources you will have—budget, time, people, etc. What expertise or technical abilities will you need that are not represented by team members? What access will you have to that expertise or information? On a more detailed level, how will the team have access to typing or copying services? Where can you get meeting supplies?

Develop a work plan

A work plan is a road map for your team to follow, enabling you to progress steadily and keep on track. The importance of such a plan cannot be overstated. Chapter 5 presents two general plans—one for improving processes and one for solving problems. One of these approaches is likely to be useful. Each of the two approaches then links to more detailed plans or strategies to help you carry out each step of the work.

The team leader may have drafted a work plan before the first meeting. In that case, team members should discuss the plan in detail at one of the first meetings, revising it if necessary. The team will continue to review and revise the plan as more is learned about what is needed to successfully complete its project, or carry out its work.

Chapter 4

Chapter 4

Identify stakeholders

Once you are clear about your purpose and goals, it is important to identify others who might affect or be affected by your work. Some examples of stakeholders are: regulatory agencies, employees in other work areas, suppliers, etc. The better you understand and take into consideration the needs and concerns of your stakeholders, the smoother your team's work is likely to be. Knowing who your stakeholders are can help you create more buy-in to changes you might recommend down the road.

Educational goals for the first few meetings

If your team is expected to use methods new to them, then part of the team's meeting time should be spent learning these new skills. Since the ideal time to learn a skill is just when that skill is needed, it is likely that some training and education will happen throughout the team's life. Some of the topics that might need to be discussed in the first few meeting are:

- **The scientific approach**: Discuss what it is and how it may be different from the way problems have been solved in the past. Help team members understand how this approach may influence their actions and decisions. (◀To refresh your memory on the Scientific Approach, see p. 2-8.)

- **Teams and teamwork**: Talk about why it is important for a team to do this work. Also explain why each member is important on the team. You may need to spend time talking about the difference between doing individual work and doing teamwork, which is highly interdependent and collaborative.

- **Processes**: If your team will be working with processes, then it might be helpful to discuss what processes or steps are represented by members of the team, and how these relate to one another. Viewing your work as part of a process can revolutionize the way you approach making improvements.

- **Variation**: All processes show variation. Your team may need to understand what it is, how to measure it, and how it should influence your reactions to problems.

- **The Pareto Principle**: Your team may need to use the Pareto Principle to quickly focus its efforts on the "vital few" important problems. Review the definition of this principle and discuss how it will govern selection of team activities.

Of course, the work plan developed for your project will determine when each topic will be most useful. (◀See Chapter 2 for more information on the topics above, as well as for descriptions of the tools you may need to do the work.)

Chapter 4

The First Team Meeting

The main focus of the first team meeting is to understand and agree to the purpose of the team.

Conducting the First Meeting

We have found the following sequence of activities to be useful for the first team meeting. Use this as a guide for your first meeting. The outline follows the accompanying sample agenda (p. 4-45) very closely. Decide which agenda items will be led by the sponsor or guidance team member, and which by the team leader.

1. Set up the room

Arrive early. Arrange tables and chairs so everyone will be able to see one another easily. Write the following information on flipchart pages that are taped to the wall so everyone can see them:

- The meeting agenda
- Project name
- Charter or mission statement
- Improvement goals

Check to make sure all the supplies are ready.

2. Greet arrivals

Greet members by name or introduce yourself as they enter the room. Welcome each one personally.

3. Get started

Establish a precedent for a prompt start. We suggest you begin at the announced starting time, even if some members have not yet arrived. If people are talking, get their attention by meeting their eyes and saying, "It's time to get started."

Introduce yourself and explain your role.

4. Review the agenda

Explain the goals of this meeting. Add or delete items. Review the time needed for each item. Note which items must be completed today.

Also outline the goals for the first few meetings (e.g., to build the team, clarify the task, learn necessary new skills, and further develop the work plan).

5. Have members introduce themselves

Begin with a five minute warm-up activity. Some warm-ups focus people's attention on the task at hand, but at the first meeting you might want to pick one that helps team members get better acquainted. Simply go around the table and have members introduce themselves and say a few words about what they do. The quality advisor and sponsor could discuss their roles when it is their turn. (➡See Appendix C for more on warm-ups.)

6. Review the team's purpose

Review the charter or mission, and the project's goals. This is the team's purpose. Say a few words about why you are excited about this project. Indicate why the work is important to the organization and its customers. If appropriate, discuss how each team member and all the employees who are part of this work process will benefit. As part of this orientation, you might place this project in the context of the organization's business strategies. (⬅See Chapter 1 for more on the importance of *alignment*.)

7. Define roles

Discuss how the team will operate. If appropriate, describe the roles of team leader, sponsor, and coach or quality advisor in more depth. Discuss the responsibilities of team members to contribute to understanding the problem or process, and to carry out some of the

Warm-Ups

Warm-ups are quick activities to use at the beginning of meetings. They signal the start of the meeting, preparing the group to work together. There are many different warm-ups described in Appendix C. Here is one that is almost always appropriate:

The "Check-In"

Going around the room, have each member say a few words about how they are and what concerns or distractions they are "checking at the door." This helps each member put aside personal concerns in order to focus on the meeting, and also lets the team know what may be influencing their participation.

Some examples of check-in comments: "The baby was up all night with an ear infection and I'm exhausted"; "We're trying to get a rush job out and everyone in my unit is giving me grief for coming to this meeting, so I'm kind of distracted"; "I'm fine today"; "Glad to be here; it's a zoo down there today!"

Team-Building Exercises

Certain activities are designed to help members learn to work better as a team. Several of these team-building activities are described in Appendix C.

Here is one that is especially useful for a team working to improve a cross-functional process:

Touring Each Other's Workplace

Each team member can use part of a team meeting (or a session between regular meetings) to guide other members through their work area. That way team members get a firsthand look at how different parts of the company operate.

Each tour typically takes about 30 minutes.

The host member:

- Explains the main processes involved, perhaps providing a flow-chart
- Describes the part of the process that is related to the team's project
- Introduces the team to other people working in this area
- Allows time for questions from the team members

data collection and analysis. Discuss how the team will draw conclusions from the data, develop proposed improvements, and make links to other employees in related parts of the company. Briefly describe the guidance team, who is on it, and its purpose. (◀See Chapter 3 for more on these roles.)

8. Set ground rules

Have team members discuss ground rules for what the team will expect in terms of general courtesy (such as not interrupting conversations) and team members' responsibility for their behavior (such as promptness and carrying out assignments). Review the list on pp. 4-37 and 4-38 for more detail.

9. Introduce basic concepts or skills

This is an opportunity to introduce the team to a few key skills or concepts (such as the scientific approach or the Pareto Principle), which will help them do the work expected of them.

10. Review assignments

Go over any readings or project work to be done before the next meeting. Help members understand that much of the team's work will occur in between meetings.

11. Meeting evaluation

Choose a method of evaluating the meeting. Make sure you gather suggestions for improving the next meeting. (◀See pp. 4-9 to 4-10 for more information about meeting evaluations.)

Sample Agenda for a Team's First Meeting

Instructions: Use this agenda as a model for your first meeting. We have included time estimates for each item. Keep track of the actual times so you get better at predicting how much you can accomplish in each meeting. If you think you will not have enough time to finish all the items, indicate which are "musts" for this meeting.

Project _____ Meeting Date _____

Team charter and goals:

> Note: Have your charter and goals listed on the agenda. They can be typed onto the master form before it is copied.

1. **Review this agenda (5 mins.)**

   Explain the goals of this meeting. Add or delete items. Review the time needed for each item. Note which items must be completed today.

2. **Brief self-introductions by team members (10 mins.)**

3. **Review the charter or mission statement (15 mins.)**

4. **Discuss the roles of team leader, coach or quality advisor, and team members (15 mins.)**

5. **Set ground rules (15 mins.)**

6. **Introduce basic concepts or skills needed for the work (15 mins.)**

7. **Discuss assignments for the next meeting: date, time (10 mins.)**

   Discuss possible readings or activities that team members can undertake before the next meeting.

8. **Meeting evaluation (10 mins.)**

The Meeting Cycle

After the initial flurry of activity dies down, a team's meetings will settle into an effective, comfortable routine in which agendas, set ahead of time, incorporate work that members will do between meetings.

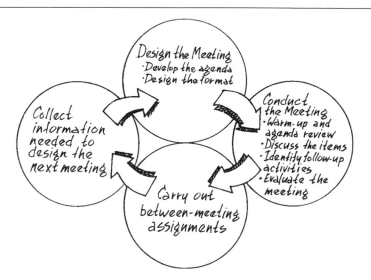

II. Regular Team Meetings

Once past the hurdle of the first meeting or two, team members will become more comfortable with the meeting process and the project or work. Discussing all the issues described previously in "Goals of the First Few Meetings" will probably take you at least two or three meetings—and some of the items will carry through the entire effort. Filling agendas for these meetings will therefore pose little difficulty.

By the end of that time you should have a work plan and be able to structure agendas around the team's activities. Your work should settle into a routine of planning, carrying out meetings, and completing between-meeting activities.

Each agenda should include the items we've already pointed out: warm-ups, evaluations, agenda items, persons responsible, and time estimates. Keep track of the type of activities you usually have at your meetings, and make space for them on your standard meeting agenda. (See the sample agenda formats on the next page.)

Overall, the flow of your meetings—and the project or work itself—will be determined largely by the work plan you develop. (➡See Chapter 5 for help developing a work plan.)

Sample Agenda for a Team's Regular Meetings

Instructions: Below is a list of topics commonly covered in regular team meetings. Use this list as a basis for developing a standard agenda for your team. Note: When creating an agenda, be sure to indicate who is responsible for each item and how much time you will allot. See p. 4-3 for more details.

Project_____ Meeting Date _____

Team charter and goals:

1. **Warm-up or check-in.**

2. **Agenda review.**

3. **Status reports on action items and assignments from last meeting.**

4. **Issues to be discussed or decided. Work that needs to be done with everyone present.**

5. **Review progress relative to work plan and schedule.**

6. **Assignments for work to be done in between meetings (who will do what by when).**

7. **Reminders of upcoming special meetings or events.**

8. **Review action items from this meeting.**

9. **Draft agenda for next meeting.**

10. **Meeting evaluation.**

Chapter 4

III. Work Reviews

Taking time periodically throughout the project to stop and ask, "How are we doing?" can be one of the most important and difficult activities a team can undertake. Self-critique can help a team identify problems early, before they become crises.

Structure any evaluation around two points:

- **Effectiveness:** Are we doing the right things?—Asking the right questions? Tackling the right problems? Working on issues related to the project?

- **Efficiency**: Are we doing things right?—Are we taking unnecessary steps? Repeating ourselves? Spinning our wheels?

We recommend that teams pause to review their work at the end of each major step in their work plan.

Reviews by Management

One of the ways sponsors, guidance teams, or other managers may keep in touch with projects is to review them regularly. These review meetings are an opportunity for the team to summarize their work thus far, and share both their successes and their problems with managers who are committed to the work.

One of the main functions of these joint meetings is to keep the sponsor or guidance team informed of the unfolding of the work. For example, the team's early investigative work can lead to redefining the project. The review meetings also give both the team and sponsor or guidance team a chance to clarify ambiguous issues. (◄See Chapter 3, pp. 3-25 to 3-28, for more information about review meetings.)

The team usually gives a brief presentation on its progress as part of the joint review meeting. A very effective way to communicate the key messages about the team's work is to use a storyboard format. (◀See p. 4-27 for more information about storyboards.)

IV. Project Closure

Eventually every project or initiative reaches an end point, yet it can be surprisingly difficult for some teams to recognize when it's time to end. Here are some ways to tell when it is time to say good-bye:

- When the purpose of the project has been fulfilled
- When the work plan has been completed
- When the data, or other indicators of improvement, show some progress and it is clear that further progress would require a new breakthrough effort
- When there is agreement that this is the wrong team to continue the work (e.g., investigation has revealed the real problem to be different from the team's charter)

It is important to have a formal closure to a project. This can be a time to recognize the considerable time and effort that went into the initiative. It is also an opportunity to capture the learnings from the initiative and to share them with the sponsor or guidance team. The point of closure can signal that responsibility for standardization and monitoring the changes now shifts over to the appropriate ongoing work teams and supervisors.

Chapter 4

The following elements should be part of a good closure:

- **Evaluate the team's work**

  Although this effort or project is ending, it is likely that team members will be involved with other efforts in the future. Taking time to do a final evaluation of the current effort reinforces key learnings and provides a sense of closure for the team. This evaluation often includes:
  - A list of key learnings
  - A review of the team's strengths and achievements
  - A discussion of the team's weaknesses, and major roadblocks that stood in the way
  - Ideas for how the next project could be improved

- **Complete your documentation**

  The team's documentation serves as the organization's memory of the team's work; therefore, it is important to finish writing up the results and what was learned.

- **Share your results**

  There are many ways your team can share its results with the rest of the organization. One way is to give a presentation on the highlights of your team's work. A sample outline of such a presentation is on p. 4-52.

  Another way to share results is to write up an article for your organization's newsletter, or to post the storyboard of the highlights of the team's work in an area where others can read it.

• **Celebrate**

Finally, be sure to celebrate everyone's efforts! Have a pizza lunch, or give out token gifts such as T-shirts to recognize everyone's efforts. Be sure to include people who supported the team's efforts by covering for them while they were in meetings, or who helped collect or analyze data, or who will be implementing the changes in their jobs. In short, include everyone in the celebration.

For Ongoing Teams

Ongoing teams need to celebrate too. Notice when a challenging task is completed or when a phase of work is done and celebrate!

Another celebration idea is to occasionally have an "accomplishment lunch" or special coffee break. While people eat lunch or cookies, have everyone identify one accomplishment from the past week and write it on a self-stick note. Go around the room; share the accomplishments and stick them to a flipchart or wall.

Chapter 4

Team Presentations

Your team may be asked to make a presentation to mark key milestones in its project. Some examples are when the team has documented the causes of a problem, when a remedy has been tested and proven successful, or at the conclusion of a project.

These presentations usually take about 20-30 minutes. They should be self-contained, covering the context, purpose, key activities, and results of the work in a way that is understandable to anyone unfamiliar with the project. Try to involve every team member in the presentation.

Potential audiences for these presentations include: the guidance team, other employees, suppliers, customers, other local businesses, and professional organizations.

Here's one recommended outline for these presentations:

1. Introduction

1.1 Purpose of the project or work.

1.2 Reason it was selected (why it is important to customers, the organization, or employees in the work area).

2. Highlights of activities and investigations

2.1 Main conditions found at outset of the work.

2.2 Major investigations done. Emphasize why avenues were pursued rather than give detailed descriptions of each step.

2.3 Outcomes of investigations. Show results and charts. Describe impact and implications of outcomes/problems.

2.4 Achievements or major findings. Show savings, potential savings, or potential improvements. If costs or savings in approximate dollars are available, show them. If not, give examples of costs that cannot be quantified.

3. Conclusions

3.1 Impact of findings on system being studied.

3.2 Suggestions for future work.

3.3 Other recommendations.

3.4 Acknowledgments.

Closure Checklist

Instructions: Teams often have problems bringing their projects or work to an end. This checklist will help you determine when you have accomplished your tasks, and help you plan activities that will signal the end of the project. Sometime before the end of the project you can also use this list to spur discussion among team members regarding the topic, "How will we know when we're finished?" Add any items the team agrees to that are not already on this list.

____ **Evaluate the Team's Process.**

- Nostalgia—what was it like working with this team early on?
- What have you learned from this experience?
- Organizational learnings from this experience—what advice would you give to other teams?
- How well did you work with your sponsor or guidance team?

____ **Evaluate the Team's Product.**

- Did you accomplish your charter or mission? What helped your team? What hindered it?
- What were your technical accomplishments?
- Have the improvements been standardized and error-proofed? How will the improvements be maintained? How were these improvements communicated among and between work groups?
- What other discoveries did you make? How were they communicated among and between work groups?
- What suggestions for future improvements can you make?

____ **Document the Team's Improvement.**

- Is your storyboard up-to-date? Does it contain your final results and conclusions?
- Is your document file completed?
- Did you make a final report to the management team?

____ **Communicating the Ending.**

Note: This is a joint task for the team and its sponsor or guidance team.

- How will the team's improvements be communicated to the rest of the organization?
- How can the end of this project or work sow the seeds for future initiatives?
- How will this team's learnings be communicated to management?
- What recommendations will the team make for follow-up after the work is completed?

____ **The Celebration!**

- What is the appropriate way to celebrate this closure? (Lunch/dinner/dessert?)
- How will you say good-bye?

Model of Progress

This is a top-down flowchart showing one possible progression of events for project teams. In the early part of an improvement project, team members clarify what it means to be on the team: what process they will work on and what kinds of improvements are expected. From these goals and expectations they draft an improvement plan. The first few meetings may be devoted largely to team building and education. After team members have been exposed to scientific principles, they are ready to begin work in earnest on the process or problem. Usually, they study the process or problem to learn more about it. Theories are checked by collecting data, and appropriate actions determined after analysis. The loop of problem analysis and data collection continues until the team is satisfied that it has identified and addressed the root causes of problems.

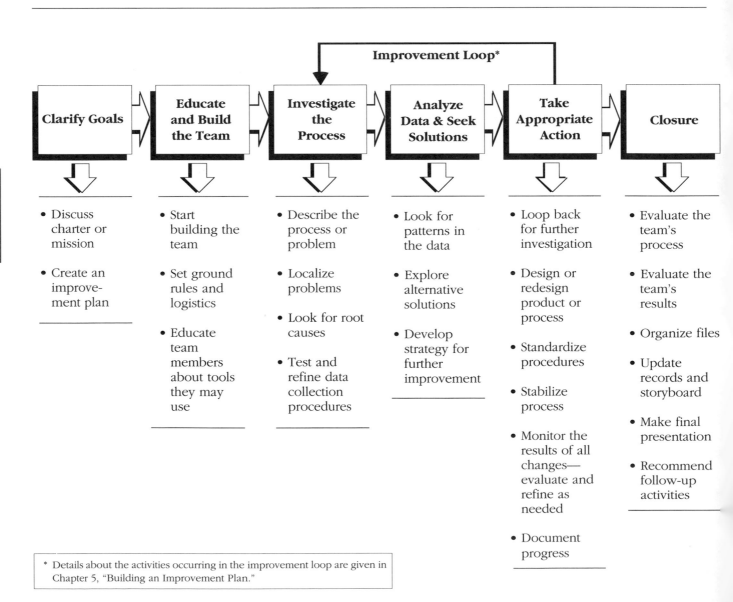

Improvement Loop*

Clarify Goals	Educate and Build the Team	Investigate the Process	Analyze Data & Seek Solutions	Take Appropriate Action	Closure
• Discuss charter or mission	• Start building the team	• Describe the process or problem	• Look for patterns in the data	• Loop back for further investigation	• Evaluate the team's process
• Create an improvement plan	• Set ground rules and logistics	• Localize problems	• Explore alternative solutions	• Design or redesign product or process	• Evaluate the team's results
	• Educate team members about tools they may use	• Look for root causes	• Develop strategy for further improvement	• Standardize procedures	• Organize files
		• Test and refine data collection procedures		• Stabilize process	• Update records and storyboard
				• Monitor the results of all changes—evaluate and refine as needed	• Make final presentation
				• Document progress	• Recommend follow-up activities

* Details about the activities occurring in the improvement loop are given in Chapter 5, "Building an Improvement Plan."

Chapter 4

Progress Checklist

Instructions: Refer to this list occasionally to monitor the team's progress. Some of these items may not pertain to your team—or you may be able to identify other milestones not listed here that you want to add.

Charter or mission statement

__ Clarify; modify if necessary

__ Get management approval for revisions

__ Define goals and objectives related to mission

Planning

__ Develop logistical system for team meetings

__ Create an improvement plan

__ Review and revise plan as needed

Education/Team-building activities

__ Introduce team members

__ Explain roles and expectations

__ Orient to group's process

__ Introduce new skills or methods team may need

__ Provide training in scientific tools as needed

__ Develop ownership in project

Study the process or problem

__ Construct flowchart of process

__ Interview customers to identify needs

__ Design data gathering procedures

__ Gather data on process or problem

__ Analyze data to see if process is stable

__ Identify problems with process

Localize problems

__ Identify possible causes of problems

__ Select likely causes

__ Gather data to establish root causes

__ Analyze data

__ Rank causes

__ Develop appropriate solutions that address causes

Make changes/Document improvement

__ Develop a plan to test changes

__ Implement test

__ Gather data on new process

__ Analyze data, critique changes in light of data

__ Redesign improvements in process and repeat this step if necessary

__ Implement further changes, or refer matter to appropriate person or group

__ Monitor results of changes

__ Establish a system to monitor in the future

Closure

__ Prepare presentation on project

__ Deliver presentation

__ Evaluate team's progress

__ Evaluate team's product

__ Document

Chapter 4

Summary

Meetings are an essential tool for team success. Effective meetings are those which pay attention to the meeting process as well as to the work underway. Good meetings are invaluable in helping a team focus on the problem or process that it needs to address.

Whether a team has been up and running for some time, or is just getting started, the meeting process can sometimes be a frustrating and difficult one. Nevertheless, without effective meetings, it is difficult for a team to make meaningful progress. Effective meetings require well-designed agendas, the careful assignment and practice of meeting roles, guidelines for effective discussions, decision making, and good record keeping. Early meetings must establish clearly defined goals, focus the efforts of the team, and make clear to team members what is expected of them. Regular meetings are needed to monitor, direct, and review ongoing efforts, as well as to evaluate results.

In the next chapter, we will concentrate on the components of a work or improvement plan, which the team will need to achieve its goals.

Chapter 5

Building an Improvement Plan

Teams that proceed with improvements without thinking ahead are probably headed for disaster. Without a road map, teams often collect the wrong kind of data, invest in unnecessary gadgets or machines, or ignore customer or other key stakeholder needs. As a result, their solutions may not be solutions at all. They end up with a process no better than at the start, an expensive investment that has done little good, or a product or service the customers don't want. Perhaps worst of all, these winless projects create a crowd of once-hopeful managers and employees who now conclude "improvement just doesn't work here."

Lasting improvements come most often from careful forethought and planning. Teams must envision how projects are likely to unfold, anticipate data collection and resource needs through different stages, and plan how to deal with these needs. They must pay close attention to the sequence in which actions will occur. And they must attend to people issues: how to involve people affected by the effort; what to do if they run into people opposed to their work; how to open communication lines throughout the organization.

In time, knowing how to cope with these issues will become second nature. Starting out, however, it's easy to get confused, and some direction is helpful. This chapter outlines two approaches, or road maps, for making improvements. Each approach is made up of a series of steps, and each step has one or more strategies that can be used to help accomplish that step. If you already know which approach most likely fits your situation, you can turn to it now. If not, make a quick scan of the whole chapter, then dig deeper in those areas that seem most useful.

What You Will Find Here

In this chapter we explore:

I. The 5 Step Plan for Process Improvement (pp. 5-7 to 5-14)

   This approach helps you manage and improve daily work.

II. The Joiner 7 Step Method™ for Problem Solving (pp. 5-15 to 5-24)

   This approach helps you solve specific problems.

III. The 15 Improvement Strategies (pp. 5-26 to 5-59)

   These strategies can be used in different combinations to accomplish both process improvement and problem solving.

IV. Seven Key Ingredients for Successful Improvement Efforts (pp. 5-60 to 5-64)

   No matter which approach you use, there are seven key ingredients that need to be part of every effort.

Chapter 5

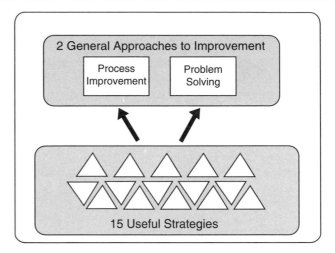

Two General Approaches to Improvement

There are two general approaches that cover most improvement situations: process improvement and problem solving.

5 Step Plan for Process Improvement—Managing and Improving Daily Work

The process improvement approach should be used when the team will seek to establish and document the current best-known process or when the team will be involved in the ongoing management and improvement of its own daily work. Examples of charters or missions are:

- Identify and document today's best-known process for designing new products
- Continuously improve how we sell our products and services
- Assume responsibility for the management and improvement of the work area

The Joiner 7 Step Method™ for Problem Solving

This general approach is useful when you have a specific problem to solve. Examples of problems needing solutions might be:

- A new coating material results in too many imperfections
- It takes too long to process expense reimbursements
- Some stores wind up with too much stock, others with too little

Problem Solving or Process Improvement

Generally, it doesn't matter whether you start off trying to improve a process or solve a problem—each approach can lead to the other.

How to Know Which Approach to Use

In some cases it will be quite clear which general approach fits best. In other cases you may find yourself a ways down one of these roads before you discover you'd be better off on the other. In most cases, that won't be a big deal because much of the work you've done will still be useful. In fact, in many cases when solving a problem, you will need to engage in process improvement as you go. And vice versa. Often in process improvement you will need to solve problems. Here are two questions we find helpful to get started:

- Do you want ongoing improvement?
  - If so, use the 5 Step Plan for Process Improvement.

- Is there a specific problem you need to fix?
  - If so, use the Joiner 7 Step Method™ for Problem Solving.

For Ongoing Teams

Ongoing teams trying to improve daily work processes should use the 5 Step Plan for Process Improvement.

Chapter 5

The 15 Improvement Strategies

There are 15 basic strategies which can be used in different combinations to accomplish the two general approaches to improvement. In Sections I and II these strategies are referenced within each of the two approaches where they can be used. Section III maps out the details for each strategy and shows how they fit with the two different approaches. (The chart on p. 5-5 provides a cross-reference of the strategies and improvement approaches, and how they fit together.)

The first time through this material, you may find it easier to read all the way through Sections I and II and then look up the relevant strategies, rather than trying to flip back and forth as you go. This will give you a better understanding of the "big picture" before you focus on the details. Charts on pages 5-9 and 5-18 show how the strategies fit within each of the improvement approaches. In addition to their use within these two approaches, the various strategies can also be used in other contexts not covered in this book.

How the Improvement Strategies and General Approaches Fit Together

This chart shows the relationship between the 15 improvement strategies and the two different approaches to improvement: process improvement and problem solving.

Process Improvement
The 5 Step Plan

Step 1. Understand the Process
Strategies: 8, 5, 9, 3

Step 2. Eliminate Errors
Strategies: 10, 15, 14

Step 3. Remove Slack
Strategies: 11, 14

Step 4. Reduce Variation
Strategies: 12, 13, 1, 3

Step 5. Plan for Continuous Improvement
Strategies: 4

Problem Solving
The Joiner 7 Step Method™

Step 1. Project
Strategies: 1, 5, 7, 6, 8

Step 2. Current Situation
Strategies: 1, 7, 8, 6, 5, 13, 15, 14

Step 3. Cause Analysis
Strategies: 2, 1

Step 4. Solutions
Strategies: 3, 4, 9

Step 5. Results
Strategies: 1, 13

Step 6. Standardization
Strategies: 9, 1, 10, 11, 12, 13, 14

Step 7. Future Plans
Strategies: 1, 3, 4, 6

Chapter 5

15 Improvement Strategies

1. Collect Meaningful Data	6. Study the Use of Time	11. Streamline a Process
2. Identify Root Causes of Problems	7. Localize Recurring Problems	12. Reduce Sources of Variation
3. Develop Appropriate Solutions	8. Describe a Process	13. Bring a Process Under Statistical Control
4. Plan and Make Changes	9. Develop a Standard Process	14. Eliminate Waste
5. Identify Customer Needs	10. Error-Proof a Process	15. Clean Up and Organize the Workplace

Examples of People Making Improvements

Monitoring a Process

A company needed to make sure the parts they manufactured met customer specifications, and they were worried about the reliability of their measurements. So they used control charts to make sure the instruments remained in statistical control.

Getting a Focused Problem

The collection department of a company had a large number of late payments. Before they could take effective action, they needed more specific information about which customers posed the biggest problems and what caused the delays. They examined the issue by localizing recurring problems and then searching for root causes. Once they found out when and why some problems were occurring, they realized many were beyond their control. For example, they could do little about incorrect orders caused by customers changing their minds.

What they could control was the variation in their work methods. They decided to develop a standard process that all would follow. As the new standard process was further refined, the employees in this division set and held onto the best collection record in the entire company—despite the fact that they were limited by problems inherited from other departments.

Patients Monitoring Their Status

A healthcare clinic teaches diabetic patients to monitor and manage their blood sugar levels using time plots and control charts. Patients adjust diet, exercise and/or insulin based on whether special causes, or only common causes, are present.

Listening to the Customer

An equipment maintenance department in a government agency realized that to cut the number of complaints they received, they'd have to find out what their customers wanted and start addressing those needs.

A group of mechanics and supervisors talked to representatives of each department they served to identify customer needs. They found two key concerns. First, the customers had different priorities than the maintenance department—despite severe budget cutbacks, the customers were still more concerned about safety than repair costs. Second, the customers felt the repair process took too long.

The maintenance team then split into two groups. One found ways to resolve conflicting priorities by developing appropriate solutions. The second studied the repair process, localizing problems, looking for causes, and developing solutions.

Conflicts in priorities are now settled between a maintenance supervisor and a designated contact person in each department. The repair process has been streamlined with unnecessary steps cut out entirely. Other delays in repairs have been eliminated by revising purchasing policies so equipment is more standardized, and by keeping better records on failures so they can stock the right spare parts.

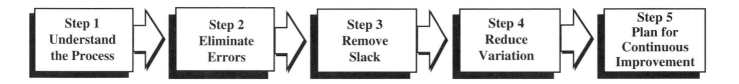

I. The 5 Step Plan for Process Improvement

It is natural for inexperienced teams to have difficulty planning their first efforts. Typically, they are faced with many problems clamoring for their attention. Our 5 Step Plan is a general improvement framework useful for all kinds of processes. It has teams tackling common problems in an order that increases the likelihood of success—peeling off layers of problems as you would peel layers from an onion. While processes differ widely from one company to the next, there is a general approach that applies in almost all situations. We have divided this approach into five stages, each composed of one or more strategies.

The sequence of stages is based on recognizing that most process problems arise from six sources:

1. Inadequate knowledge of how a process works

2. Inadequate knowledge of how a process *should* work

3. Errors and mistakes in executing the procedures

4. Current practices that fail to recognize the need for preventive measures such as maintenance of machines or files

5. Attitudes that encourage unnecessary steps, inventory buffers, and other wasteful measures

6. Variation in inputs and outputs

Chapter 5

Most likely, a process will have problems arising from each source. Each type demands a different approach to finding solutions. A team can increase its effectiveness by focusing on one type of problem at a time, an idea we have incorporated in the 5 step improvement plan described here. This plan attacks the problems in the order listed above, allowing a team to gradually expose problems and tailor solutions to each situation. Each step is made up of one or more *strategies*, described in Section III, that indicate the kinds of questions teams will have to answer during that step of the plan. (See the chart on the next page.)

The following improvement plan works equally well on manufacturing and non-manufacturing processes, though the strategies on variation may be used less often in non-manufacturing situations. Sometimes you will follow the sequence straight through; other times you will loop through some steps several times as you learn from your data.

The first step in process improvement projects is to understand the process—how it currently operates, what it is supposed to accomplish, who its customers are and what they expect. When teams know what the process should be doing, they can often find simple ways to standardize procedures, which usually makes a process run more smoothly.

With one layer of problems stripped away, others will be exposed, and teams will have a clearer picture of what further changes are appropriate. As they continue to work on the process, it will gradually show less waste and complexity. At that point, the team will be able to see where they can cut down on unnecessary buffers. Then comes the difficult task of removing and controlling variation.

Finally, teams must foster ongoing improvement. They must put in place systems for continuous improvement.

Strategies to Use in the 5 Step Plan for Process Improvement

The table below shows how various strategies fit into each of the five steps in the 5 Step Plan for Process Improvement. The following pages describe each step in more depth and explain the purpose of those strategies listed below as "Usually Needed."

	Step 1 Understand the Process	Step 2 Eliminate Errors	Step 3 Remove Slack	Step 4 Reduce Variation	Step 5 Plan for Continuous Improvement
Strategies Usually Needed	8. Describe a Process (p. 5-45) 5. Identify Customer Needs (p. 5-39) 9. Develop a Standard Process (p. 5-47)	10. Error-Proof a Process (p. 5-49)	11. Streamline a Process (p. 5-50)	12. Reduce Sources of Variation (p. 5-52) 13. Bring a Process Under Statistical Control (p. 5-54)	4. Plan and Make Changes (p. 5-37)
Strategies Sometimes Useful	3. Develop Appropriate Solutions (p. 5-34)	15. Clean Up and Organize the Workplace (p. 5-58) 14. Eliminate Waste (p. 5-56)	14. Eliminate Waste (p. 5-56)	1. Collect Meaningful Data (p. 5-29) 3. Develop Appropriate Solutions (p. 5-34)	

Chapter 5

Chapter 5

Benefits of Studying a Process

- Arriving at a common understanding
- Eliminating inconsistencies
- Highlighting obvious problems

Step 1: Understand the Process

Before a process can be improved, it must be understood. To really know what is right and what is wrong with a process, you must answer three questions: How does the process currently work? What is it supposed to accomplish (that is, how does the output relate to customer needs)? What is the current best-known way to carry out the process?

Investigating these questions is the best way for your team to gather information that will let you set goals and objectives for the rest of the improvement effort.

Benefits of studying a process include:

Arriving at a common understanding

When team members work through the recommended strategies, they gain a common understanding of the process. They will start using the same terminology, and won't waste time pulling in different directions or gathering irrelevant information.

Eliminating inconsistencies

These strategies lead you systematically through a process and have you compare how various people associated with the process carry out their work. You are bound to find inconsistencies, many of which can be traced to a lack of documentation and inadequate training about the best way to run the process. Quality and productivity often increase dramatically once employees who do the same job start sharing and using a "best-known way" to do their work.

Highlighting obvious problems

Looking closely at a process almost always highlights glaring problems that have gone unnoticed but can be fixed easily. This is particularly true of paperwork processes.

Our recommended strategies for understanding a process:

Describe a Process (Strategy 8, p. 5-45)

This strategy leads your team through the process step-by-step. By the end, you will know which of your fellow employees work on the process, what materials or information go in and come out, and what happens in between.

Identify Customer Needs (Strategy 5, p. 5-39)

This strategy focuses your team on the purpose of its work: doing something to benefit the customer. Skip this step temporarily if you have found glaring problems that can readily be fixed with benefit, or at least no harm, to the customer.

Develop a Standard Process (Strategy 9, p. 5-47)

Armed with the knowledge of how the process currently works and what it is supposed to do, your team will almost always be able to devise better approaches. Get everyone who works with the process to use and contribute to best-known methods. You will be amazed by the dramatic gains in product or service quality, productivity, and job satisfaction brought about by a standard approach.

Chapter 5

Why Streamline?

Having large inventories or doing work in large batches is like driving down the road with a dirty windshield. As long as you can't see the road ahead, you might think you're in good shape. Streamlining a process—removing slack, getting rid of buffers—lets you clean off that windshield and avoid potential disaster.

Step 2: Eliminate Errors

Everyone makes mistakes. Yet we fail to realize that many mistakes can be prevented by making simple changes to a process. For instance, if people forget to fill in a certain blank on a form or to get certain key information before calling on a customer, it's often easy to make changes that dramatically reduce the error rate (such as highlighting the step that is missed). (➡See Strategy 10: Error-Proof a Process, p. 5-49).

Step 3: Remove Slack

Increasing numbers of organizations are realizing that traditional practices of keeping large inventories and doing work in batches are more harmful than helpful. These practices mask problems instead of solving them. In addition, all processes tend to grow over the years, many steps losing whatever value they once had.

To get out of this trap, move towards just-in-time flow and examine each step to see if it is necessary and adds value to the product or service. The result of this critical examination is often dramatically reduced time required to complete a process. The resulting improvements usually increase quality, too.

Strategy 11: Streamline a Process (p. 5-50) lets team members trim the fat from a process. This strategy is in Step 3 because few people can recognize slack and unnecessary work until the most glaring problems are eliminated. The process should already be in relatively good shape by the time your team gets to this step.

Step 4: Reduce Variation

As discussed in Chapter 2, the sources of variation come in two flavors: common causes and special causes. The trick is to tell them apart. Common causes typically come from numerous, ever-present sources of slight variation. Special causes, in contrast, are not always present, and usually cause greater fluctuations in the process. Eliminating common causes requires changes within the process; special causes usually require changes outside the process.

Getting rid of variation usually happens in two stages: taking it out of measurement processes, then out of the work process. Reducing measurement variation must come first because it obscures the performance of a work process and masks the effects of changes.

Example: One company knew that a 1% increase in yield would be worth $1 million a year. But they discovered their yield measurements could be off by as much as 16%—so even if the yield appeared to increase, they would have no way of knowing whether it was because the measurement was off or the solution worked. It was no use trying to get rid of process variation before they had fine-tuned their measurement systems to the point where they could detect real 1% increases in yield.

The techniques for reducing measurement variation are almost identical to those for reducing work process variation. Thus the following recommended sequence has some repetition.

To reduce variation:

Use Strategy 12: Reduce Sources of Variation (p. 5-52) on measurement processes.

> If you can't measure precisely, you will miss important improvement opportunities, or worse yet, waste your time chasing ghosts.

Chapter 5

Then use Strategy 13: Bring a Process Under Statistical Control (p. 5-54) on measurement processes.

Repeatedly measuring one item will help you identify and eliminate special causes of variation in your measurement processes. Omitting this step is, in our experience, a false saving—whatever time or money you save by skipping this step you will lose later in rework.

After the measurement process is in control, return to Strategy 12: Reduce Sources of Variation (p. 5-52), but this time use it on the targeted work process.

With measurements that are in control, you will be in a much better position to detect real changes in your work process.

Finally, use Strategy 13: Bring a Process Under Statistical Control (p. 5-54) on the targeted work process.

Here, every person working on the process is a detective tracking down special causes. Keep monitoring the work process and removing special causes until they are all gone.

Step 5: Plan for Continuous Improvement

By this stage, the most obvious sources of problems will have been eliminated from a process. Now your team must look for ways to make improvement a constant, never-ending part of your jobs. Use Strategy 4: Plan and Make Changes (p. 5-37) to monitor the effectiveness of changes you made in the process. Ongoing training and education in areas related to the process, as well as instruction in the skills associated with statistical tools, are critical. Active experimentation programs can be helpful. Before closing, discuss ways to keep the improvement philosophy alive. Keep records about the process and procedures up-to-date; make sure they are used.

| Step 1 Project | Step 2 Current Situation | Step 3 Cause Analysis | Step 4 Solutions | Step 5 Results | Step 6 Standard- ization | Step 7 Future Plans |

II. The Joiner 7 Step Method™ for Problem Solving

If you have a "simple" problem, chances are you know, or think you know, what to do about it. In that case use Strategy 4: Plan and Make Changes (p. 5-37).

But with a complex problem, chances are you don't know what to do, at least not with the resources at your disposal. In many cases, effective use of data will allow the detective work needed to come up with a focused, cost-effective solution pinpointed right at the heart of the problem. The Joiner 7 Step Method can be used on any problem, but it is vital for more complex problems.

It helps to define a problem carefully. For our purpose *a problem is the unsatisfactory result of a job.* Many common "problem" statements do *not* meet this narrow definition. Instead, they are often theories about solutions. But, if you ask, "So what? What's the impact on the customers?" you can usually get to a problem as we have defined it.

Because many teams bog down when they tackle inappropriate problems, it is a good idea to first define the problem as the undesirable result of a job, and then work to discover an effective solution.

For example, the team might ask, "What is the impact of inadequate staffing on customers?" Perhaps the problem turns out to be errors in medications. If so, start with medication errors, not inadequate staffing.

The Joiner 7 Step Method is a framework that increases the odds of asking the right questions, making the right links, and finding the deep causes of problems. The table on pp. 5-16 and 5-17 provides an overview of the Joiner 7 Step Method. Each of the seven steps has a clearly defined aim and a set of questions that helps us achieve that aim.

Examples of Good Problem Definitions

- Meals served cold
- Wrong invoices
- Customers lost due to mistakes made
- Slow responses
- Misplaced equipment

Examples of Poor Problem Definitions

- Lack of planning
- Inadequate staffing
- Lack of computerization

Chapter 5

Joiner 7 Step Method Overview

Step	1. Project	2. Current Situation	3. Cause Analysis
Goal	Define the project's purpose and scope.	Focus the improvement effort by gathering information on the current situation.	Identify deep causes and confirm them with data.
Output	A clear statement of the intended improvement and how it is to be measured.	A more focused problem statement.	A theory that has been tested and confirmed.
Issues	What is the project's purpose? What problem or "gap" are you addressing? What impact will closing this gap have on customers? What other reasons exist for addressing this gap? How will you know if things are better? What is the history? What is your plan for this project?	Can the problem or situation be shown in a sketch or flowchart? What are the symptoms? What happens when the problem appears? Where do symptoms appear? Where don't they appear? When do symptoms appear? When don't they? Who is involved? Who isn't?	What are the possible causes of the symptoms described in Step 2? What are possible deeper causes of these confirmed causes? Based on the causes you have confirmed, who should be working on this project?

4. Solutions	5. Results	6. Standardization	7. Future Plans
Develop, try out, and implement solutions that address deep causes.	Use data to evaluate both the solutions and the plans used to carry them out.	Maintain the gains by implementing the new work methods or processes consistently.	Anticipate future improvements and preserve the lessons from this effort.
Planned, tested actions which should eliminate or reduce the impact of the causes identified in Step 3.	Data which shows how well the goals were met and the plan was followed.	Documentation of the new method. Training in the new method. A system for monitoring its consistent use and for checking the results.	Completed documentation and communication of results, learnings, and recommendations.
What solutions could address the deep causes confirmed in Step 3? How can you compare possible solutions? What are the pros and cons of each solution? Which solutions seem to best address the original problem? How will you try them out on a small scale? Which trial solutions turned out to be most effective? What are the plans for implementing them on a full scale?	How well do the results meet the targets set for this project? How well was the plan executed?	What is the new standard method or process? How will all of the employees who do this work be trained? What's in place to assure that gains are maintained? How will the methods, procedures, and results be monitored? What means are in place to encourage ongoing improvement?	What are the tangible results? What are the intangible results? What remaining needs were not addressed by this project? What are your recommendations for investigating these remaining needs? What did you learn from this project? How will the documentation of this project be completed? How will this project be brought to a close?

Chapter 5

Strategies to Use in the Joiner 7 Step Method™

	Step 1 Project	Step 2 Current Situation	Step 3 Cause Analysis	Step 4 Solutions	Step 5 Results	Step 6 Standard-ization	Step 7 Future Plans
Strategies Usually Needed	1. Collect Meaningful Data (p. 5-29) 5. Identify Customer Needs (p. 5-39) 7. Localize Recurring Problems (p. 5-43)	1. Collect Meaningful Data (p. 5-29) 7. Localize Recurring Problems (p. 5-43)	2. Identify Root Causes of Problems (p. 5-32) 1. Collect Meaningful Data (p. 5-29)	3. Develop Appropriate Solutions (p. 5-34) 4. Plan and Make Changes (p. 5-37)	1. Collect Meaningful Data (p. 5-29)	9. Develop a Standard Process (p. 5-47)	1. Collect Meaningful Data (p. 5-29) 3. Develop Appropriate Solutions (p. 5-34) 4. Plan and Make Changes (p. 5-37)
Strategies Sometimes Useful	6. Study the Use of Time (p. 5-41) 8. Describe a Process (p. 5-45)	8. Describe a Process (p. 5-45) 6. Study the Use of Time (p. 5-41) 5. Identify Customer Needs (p. 5-39) 13. Bring a Process Under Statistical Control (p. 5-54) 15. Clean Up and Organize the Workplace (p. 5-58) 14. Eliminate Waste (p. 5-56)		9. Develop a Standard Process (p. 5-47)	13. Bring a Process Under Statistical Control (p. 5-54)	1. Collect Meaningful Data (p. 5-29) 10. Error-Proof a Process (p. 5-49) 11. Streamline a Process (p. 5-50) 12. Reduce Sources of Variation (p. 5-52) 13. Bring a Process Under Statistical Control (p. 5-54) 14. Eliminate Waste (p. 5-56)	6. Study the Use of Time (p. 5-41)

Step 1: Project

The first step of the Joiner 7 Step Method is to define the project's purpose and scope—what problem or opportunity is being addressed, why it is important, and how much progress or improvement is expected. A team often defines the problem it is going to attack, while ignoring why the problem is important and how much improvement is necessary. This can cause the team to focus on irrelevant aspects of the problem, or spend long hours trying to make a process perfect when efforts could be better spent elsewhere.

Defining the problem means looking at how the current level of performance differs from the level of performance the organization needs and the customers want. Learning what's important includes looking at the effects a change will have on customers. And knowing how much progress is expected requires that the team know how it will measure improvements and what the targets are.

Next, it is important to learn the history of the problem. When did the problem first appear? What else was happening? Have other fixes been tried in the past? What happened? By understanding what has happened the team can learn from the past and avoid repeating unsuccessful efforts.

Finally, the team needs to plan for the project. They need to know who will be involved, what the budget and schedule are, and what the boundaries are. It is also important to decide how to document the work. Although these decisions may have to be revised as the team gets deeper into the project, it is vital to have a place to start and to set some parameters for the work. Without these decisions in the beginning, it is easy for a project to get out of control.

Chapter 5

For help in understanding the gap between the current situation and the desired outcome, see Strategy 1: Collect Meaningful Data (p. 5-29). To learn what is important, see Strategy 5: Identify Customer Needs (p. 5-39); to have some idea of where to focus your efforts, see Strategy 7: Localize Recurring Problems (p. 5-43).

Step 2: Current Situation

The most important aspect of Step 2 is to further focus, refine, or narrow the improvement effort by examining specifics of the current situation. What is happening? When is it happening? Where is it happening? Who is involved? This refined focus will help the team come up with a well-targeted solution.

In this step, the process is often sketched out or flowcharted. The team can then try to focus on a specific part of the process where the problem occurs. By collecting data on when and where the problem occurs you can also look for patterns that will help narrow your focus. The outcome of this step should be a focused aspect that appears to be a major contributor to the problem. The sharper the focus, the better the chances for making real improvements.

To learn more about the symptoms of problems, see Strategy 1: Collect Meaningful Data (p. 5-29). To help you continually narrow your focus, see Strategy 7: Localize Recurring Problems (p. 5-43).

Step 3: Cause Analysis

Once the team has a focused problem, it needs to look for the root cause of that problem. The first part of Step 3 is to identify *potential* causes of the problem; the second part is to verify which of the potential causes are *actual* causes.

If the problem still lacks focus at this stage in the process it is difficult to find a verifiable cause. When the problem is global, the causes tend to be global as well. If the problem is defined as "projects take too long to complete," you will end up with a lengthy list of possible causes that are related at many levels. Trying to collect meaningful data to confirm any one of them would be impossible. However, if you define the problem as "the alpha test phase in computer software development takes three times as long as is usually scheduled," you can start identifying and testing possible causes.

Recognizing that potential causes are only that—*potential*—until they have been tested and confirmed with data is critical at this stage. Too often teams come up with theories that sound good and jump to the conclusion that they must be true. So to save time, they skip the data collection and confirmation. Later, when the solution fails to make a significant difference, they wonder where they went wrong.

For help identifying possible causes and verifying them with data, see Strategy 2: Identify Root Causes of Problems (p. 5-32).

Chapter 5

Step 4: Solutions

In this step it is finally time to try out a solution to the problem. You will probably come up with several possible solutions to the cause identified in Step 3. To select the best one, consider whether each solution is aimed at a quick fix or if it is a lasting remedy; whether it has any side effects, either negative or positive; and how well it really addresses the original focused problem.

Next try out the selected solution *on a small scale.* Too often a team will think it has the answer and will implement it immediately without testing it, only to discover that some critical aspect was overlooked. Making changes is usually difficult for people. Making one change only to have it followed by another change is particularly frustrating and likely to create ill will for both this change and any future changes you propose. So start small, but plan how you will conduct a full-scale implementation based on what you learn in the small-scale test.

For help selecting the best solution, see Strategy 3: Develop Appropriate Solutions (p. 5-34). For help implementing that solution, see Strategy 4: Plan and Make Changes (p. 5-37).

Step 5: Results

Step 5 evaluates both the small-scale test and the full-scale implementation from Step 4. Were the goals met? In Step 1 you decided what your targets were for improvement and how you would measure those improvements. Now you can use those measures to see how well your solution met your target. Without having a target or measures, it is difficult to evaluate a solution.

Sometimes, even if you have done all of the previous steps, you get to Step 5 and discover that your proposed solution didn't give you the results you expected. Although this can be disheartening, it often provides a lot of valuable data that can be used to repeat Steps 2 through 4.

The team also needs to evaluate the implementation of the solution. Did the plan work? In some cases the solution may have been right, but the team did such a poor job of implementing it that people were upset or alienated. If this was a small-scale test, there is now the opportunity to improve the implementation plan before full-scale implementation.

To learn how successful the solution really is, use Strategy 1: Collect Meaningful Data (p. 5-29).

Step 6: Standardization

All too often, when a team discovers that the solution works, it figures the work is done. "We've solved the problem, so let's get on with something else—or just go back to our real work." This approach usually means that someone else, down the road, will have the opportunity to solve the same problem again, and again.

In order to maintain the gains it is necessary to implement new work methods or processes. New methods need to be documented. People need to be trained in the new ways of doing things. The team needs to make sure the new methods are being used and that they continue to work as expected. Otherwise, being human, we all tend to backslide and go back to doing things the way we always have in the past—even though we know those ways didn't work as well.

Chapter 5

To document, monitor, and maintain the changes you have made, use Strategy 9: Develop a Standard Process (p. 5-47).

Step 7: Future Plans

This step is the end of the 7 Step Method, but it may also be the beginning of new projects and plans. In an environment of continuous improvement and ongoing change, it is always important to look to the future.

One way to look ahead is to preserve what was learned so that teams working on future improvement efforts won't have to start from scratch. Regardless of the type of improvement effort, there are always new learnings to document and pass along.

The second way to look ahead is to see how this effort can become the starting point for additional improvement projects.

To see what worked and what didn't, use Strategy 1: Collect Meaningful Data (p. 5-29). To develop better methods for the future, use Strategy 3: Develop Appropriate Solutions (p.5-34). And to put those solutions in place, use Strategy 4: Plan and Make Changes (p. 5-37).

What to Do If You Get Stuck: The PDCA Cycle

Even experienced teams sometimes have difficulty knowing what to do next. If you get stuck, we suggest you use a P-D-C-A (Plan-Do-Check-Act) approach:

Plan:

Refer to your improvement plan; have team members discuss their readiness to begin the next stage or step. What have you learned so far? What should you do next? What understanding or skills will your team need in the next stage? How will you learn what you need to know? If the team is reluctant to move to the next step, read through the discussion of "Floundering" (p. 7-13). If you have no improvement plan, create one.

Do:

Make some early attempts at the next steps in the strategy or plan you are following. Allow yourselves to make mistakes.

Check:

Reflect on your trial efforts and identify ways to improve them. What worked or went well? What didn't work well? What resources, training, or knowledge do you need to do a better job? Can your sponsor(s) help you fulfill these needs?

Act:

Have the team discuss how to capture and use the lessons learned from your PDCA cycles, and plan for the next cycle.

P-D-C-A or P-D-S-A?

Dr. Deming attributed the basis for the Plan-Do-Check-Act (P-D-C-A) cycle to Dr. Walter Shewhart. He recommended the Shewhart cycle, as he called it, be written as "Plan-Do-*Study*-Act." Here's how Dr. Deming drew it for us:

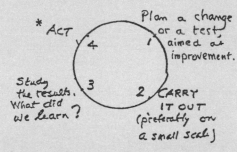

Although it may be more properly called P-D-S-A, we chose to stick with the terminology of P-D-C-A because it is so firmly rooted in improvement language.

Still another version of this cycle is known as S-D-C-A, or "*Standardize*-Do-Check-Act." This reference is used particularly when people are improving the methods used on a process. The goal is to have all employees involved with a process share common best-known methods. In this case, the S-D-C-A Cycle is used to check how well the work is going. It also indicates that the work of improving how we do things is never done.

Chapter 5

Chapter 5

III. The 15 Improvement Strategies

There are 15 strategies all told. Each is key to a specific aspect of problem solving or process improvement. As shown in both the 5 Step Plan for Process Improvement and the Joiner 7 Step Method for Problem Solving, these strategies can be used in various sequences to accomplish different goals. They simplify the planning process by providing a framework around which teams can create improvement plans.

These strategies can be divided into three categories according to their use:

- Those forming the basis of the scientific approach
- Those for identifying improvement needs (selecting an improvement project)
- Those for improving processes

On the next two pages you will find answers to some commonly asked questions and a list of the 15 strategies. Detailed instructions for each strategy start on page 5-29.

Common Questions About Using the Strategies

1. Do we have to do every step?

For beginning teams, the answer is "yes, for the most part." Most of us rebel a little at being told we must follow a particular set of rules. After all, we have experience and "gut knowledge" that has gotten us to where we are today. But when we are learning a new approach it is good to follow the steps until we have a good feel for the process and understand what we may miss if we leave out a step.

When you first learn to cook you follow the recipes exactly, but as you become more skilled you know how to make adjustments and substitutions. Even then, though, if you are having an important dinner party you may want to follow recipes because the risk of making a mistake is greater than if you are just cooking for yourself. The same is true for these strategies.

Each strategy has a logic. To skip any step is to risk missing something that you may need later on down the road. The truth is that you may find some of the steps won't help very much. But there is no way for inexperienced people to know ahead of time which ones will ultimately be useful and which won't. As you become more experienced you will be able to skip steps, or combine them, or make some modifications. However, even then, if you are working on a project where there is a lot of risk involved, you may decide to follow the steps precisely.

We ask a series of questions with each step. These questions are there to spur your own thinking. You may not need to answer absolutely every question listed, and you may come up with other questions pertinent to your work that we have not included.

2. Do we have to follow these steps in order?

We have carefully chosen a sequence that will help you proceed with the least amount of rework. So we recommend following this sequence, especially in the beginning.

However, few processes are ever strictly linear. Sometimes it makes sense to skip ahead; often it is necessary to go back to a previous step to get more details or reconsider a decision in light of new understandings.

3. Should we be able to answer each question at the meetings?

Each strategy will be a mixture of questions you can resolve right at the meeting and goals that you must work on outside the meeting (such as collecting data). Even for the activities you will pursue outside of the team meeting, you must discuss them first in the meeting.

For instance, if there are assignments to be done outside the meeting, be clear about what is expected of any team member involved—when the person or people will be expected to report back to the team, what it is they will have to report (conclusions, recommendations, charts or graphs of data, items for further discussion, and so forth), what resources they have access to, and their limits of authority or responsibility.

4. Are there any time limits set on when we should finish?

In a sense, the answer is yes. Projects that last several months often run out of steam. Work at a comfortable pace and don't try to do everything at once, but keep things moving. Typically, at first you will spend too much time on some steps and not enough on others. With experience, you will learn how much time is needed for each step.

5. Can we use tools other than those mentioned here?

Yes. Feel free to use whatever tools are appropriate for your project. We have just listed tools used commonly in the steps we outline. You may find that you need others.

Chapter 5

The 15 Improvement Strategies

Strategies of the Scientific Approach

1. Collect Meaningful Data
Used to point out common sources of inaccurate data and indicate how they can be combatted.

2. Identify Root Causes of Problems
Used to identify and verify actual causes of a problem.

3. Develop Appropriate Solutions
Used to identify changes that attack the root causes of problems.

4. Plan and Make Changes
Used to implement changes smoothly and effectively.

Strategies for Identifying Improvement Needs

5. Identify Customer Needs
Used to describe useful ways to get information from customers.

6. Study the Use of Time
Used to identify which activities consume people's time and to highlight opportunities for improvement.

7. Localize Recurring Problems
Used to identify where and when problems occur and don't occur.

Strategies for Improving a Process

8. Describe a Process
Used to identify obvious improvements or to begin a more detailed study.

9. Develop a Standard Process
Used to increase the uniformity of a product or service by developing standard procedures that everyone follows.

10. Error-Proof a Process
Used to eliminate and prevent the most common mistakes made in the execution of a process.

11. Streamline a Process
Used to eliminate slack from a process: reduce inventory sizes, shorten cycle times, etc.

12. Reduce Sources of Variation
Used to eliminate the most obvious causes of variation.

13. Bring a Process Under Statistical Control
Used to make a process more predictable by bringing variation under control.

14. Eliminate Waste
Used to increase awareness of the many types of waste and systematically eliminate them.

15. Clean Up and Organize the Workplace
Used to create a clean, well-organized workplace.

Strategy 1: Collect Meaningful Data

Purpose:

The goal of this strategy is to collect meaningful data. This is one of the most important things to do well no matter where you work. There are just too many ways in which data can be in error: it may be the wrong kind of data for what you need; it's easy to combine data that should not be mixed; data collectors often use different procedures unless they are specifically taught what to do; there may be some bias in the process you don't know about. The possibilities for error are almost endless. Thus it always pays to be suspicious of data and data collection procedures until they are proven reliable.

1. Clarify Data Collection Goals

It is easy to become swamped with useless data, especially when data collection is done without a clear purpose.

• Why are you collecting data?

• Is the data you need already available? If not, what data do you need to collect?

• How will the data help you to meet customer needs? To improve operations?

• Imagine you have the data in hand: What could this data tell you? What will you do with the data? What will you do after that? Would another kind of data be more helpful?

• How much data do you need? Over what time period do you need to collect data?

2. Develop Operational Definitions and Procedures

Most people approach data collection with a concept they would like to understand—for example, measuring "on-time delivery," "smoothness," "strength," or "length." An operational definition translates the concept into procedures that everyone can follow when measuring or discussing it.

• What is the concept you are trying to evaluate?

Examples: length, volume, hardness, ease of use, uniformity, completeness.

• What data will allow you to attach a value to this concept? By what standards or measures will you judge it? How far off from perfect does the measurement have to be to count as a defect or problem?

Examples: Does "on-time" mean within five minutes? two hours? three days? What size of bump makes something "unsmooth"? Do you have samples of the defects to show people, or samples that are "defect-free"? Would typos, blank spaces, and wrong information all count as errors on a form? Think of different ways to define this concept and see which comes closest to what you mean.

continued...

Chapter 5

- What is your plan for collecting the data? What procedures will be used? Will the data collectors have to take samples? How often? How many? Can you get the measurement immediately or will there be a delay?

  Write down clear descriptions of how to measure the characteristic. Be specific. Compare possible procedures with an eye towards places where the data collectors could easily make mistakes. Look for procedures that are less error-prone. Procedures that give faster results are generally a better choice, even if they are a little less precise than other alternatives. Note: When collecting a physical sample, specify a precise method of drawing the sample. For example, the temperature of a bath might be defined as the average of two readings taken from the center of the vat, one from two inches above the bottom, the other from two inches below the surface.

- How will the data be recorded?

  Practice using whatever form and procedures you devise. Modify them as needed.

- Do your customers or suppliers collect the same kind of data? What procedures or instruments do they use? Are your definitions, standards, and procedures comparable to those used by customers and suppliers?

  If you and your customers or suppliers use different methods, the data will probably not be comparable. Many disputes with customers revolve around measurement issues.

3. Plan for Data Consistency and Stability

Meaningful data must be both consistent and stable. Data is consistent if any two people who measure the same things arrive at essentially the same answer. Data is stable when the results do not show signs of special causes of variation over time. Ignoring these issues usually leads to wasted effort.

- What are some factors that might cause measurements of the same item to vary?

  Each situation is unique, with a unique set of factors that are important. Brainstorming a list of factors and arranging them on a cause-and-effect diagram is a good way to identify possible sources of variability in your measurement process. For example, if everyone does not follow the exact procedure, how might that affect results?

- How can you reduce the impact of these factors?

  For example, work to eliminate the differences in measurements taken by you and a customer or supplier. You can reduce variability among employees by having them all use the same methods for measuring or categorizing items. Calibrate instruments and replace materials frequently to combat problems of decay or wear. Get all employees to walk through the processes and reach consensus on procedures.

continued...

Strategy 1: Collect Meaningful Data

4. Begin Data Collection

Explain the procedures to all data collectors, especially if there are some who are not on the team. Have all data collectors follow the procedures you developed. Have someone who knows what to do watch and instruct beginning data collectors.

5. Continue Improving Measurement Consistency and Stability

Continuing to check data consistency and stability often exposes problems that, if left uncorrected, could lead to incorrect conclusions.

- Are measurements stable?

  If practical, evaluate measurement stability by repeatedly measuring the same item periodically. Plot the results on a control chart; take action if measurements are out of control. More elaborate procedures may be needed if you have destructive tests or standards that degrade over time.

- Are measurements consistent?

  Periodically check consistency by having data collectors measure an identical item. (If the tests are destructive, have a pool of items from which to randomly draw samples.) How much variability is there? Can you reduce the variability?

- Do dot plots of the data show any strange features?

  Many strange patterns can appear in plots. For example, does the data stop abruptly at a barrier? If so, data collectors may be reluctant to record points above or below a certain level (often at specification limits). At first, have a statistician, quality advisor, or someone with equivalent experience evaluate your plots.

When gathering data over time or from different units, make sure the data is standardized so you can compare data collected at different points. For example, accident figures should be adjusted for number of employees or number of working hours; monthly production figures should be adjusted to account for different numbers of working days per month.

Chapter 5

Strategy 2: Identify Root Causes of Problems

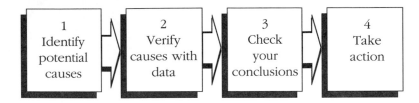

Purpose:

Jumping to conclusions without understanding the root causes of problems often leads to wasted time and resources. Usually it's best to have localized the occurrence of a problem before attempting to identify its root causes. Before starting, be sure everyone agrees on the definition of the problem. You may also need to resolve issues concerning methods of measurement.

1. Identify Potential Causes

- What are possible causes of the problem you are studying?

  Consider inviting people not on the team to a meeting to discuss these issues. The more areas of the process and different types of people that are represented, the more likely you are to identify new potential causes.

  Use brainstorming and cause-and-effect diagrams to bring out ideas. Write down all possibilities at first; later you can discuss and eliminate some. One way to get at root causes is to think of what might be the cause of each possible cause you list. Example: Suppose you find that a leading cause of delays is supplies running out. Ask next, "Why do supplies run out?" Continue exploring the "causes of the causes" until you run into a question you can't answer with facts.

2. Verify Causes With Data

- How could you detect the influence of these potential causes? What patterns would you expect to see in data?

- Do you have any existing data that could help you decide which are the actual causes of problems? Are you sure the existing data is relevant to the problem being studied?

- Does the problem always appear when any of the possible causes you identified are active?

- What additional information or data do you need? How can you get it?

  This is often the heart of the project in complex situations—observing the process, trying changes, counting, measuring, plotting data, and so forth. Review Strategy 1: Collect Meaningful Data (p. 5-29) to help you get the data you need.

- Who will collect the data? By when?

- How will it be analyzed? By when?

  Use graphs, charts, and other visual summaries whenever possible.

continued...

Strategy 2: Identify Root Causes of Problems

3. Check Your Conclusions About Causes

After you collect the data and draw conclusions, show your summaries to people knowledgeable about the process.

- Do people with knowledge of the process agree with your conclusions? If not, what additional data could you get that might support or contradict your conclusions?

4. Take Action

- Are there any obvious changes that would eliminate some causes of problems?

  Fix obvious problems immediately; monitor your solutions to make sure they work.

- In most cases, the obvious changes won't fix everything. What steps should be taken next?

  You may next want to use Strategy 3: Develop Appropriate Solutions (p. 5-34).

Strategy 3: Develop Appropriate Solutions

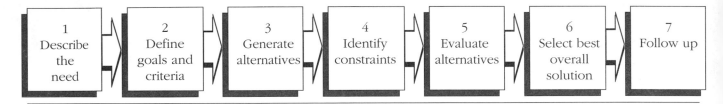

| 1 Describe the need | 2 Define goals and criteria | 3 Generate alternatives | 4 Identify constraints | 5 Evaluate alternatives | 6 Select best overall solution | 7 Follow up |

Purpose:

The crux of improvement is to develop changes that really *make things better*. You should always be on the lookout for obvious changes that are easy to implement and have few, if any, potential negative side effects. Use this strategy to come up with those changes that aren't so obvious, at least not at the beginning.

1. Describe the Need

- Precisely what problem, need, or opportunity are you addressing?

- What people or departments are involved?

- What problems are customers having because of this situation?

  Think of both your organization's customers as well as others in your organization who use your products or services.

- What operational definition best fits this problem, need, or opportunity?

  Example: What is an "excessively long waiting period"?

2. Define Goals and Criteria

- Given the need, problem, or opportunity, what are the goals of your solution? What are your desired outcomes?

  Develop a statement that describes these outcomes or goals.

- What are the criteria or characteristics of an "ideal" solution?

  Examples: Be inexpensive, easy to implement, and substantially increase yield. Refer to "Developing Criteria for Solutions" (p. 5-36) for more details.

- Which criteria MUST a solution meet to be seriously considered?

  Proposed solutions that fail to meet MUST criteria are automatically rejected.

- Which criteria are only WANTS?

  WANTS are criteria that are desirable, but not necessary. You might give weights to the WANTS to reflect their importance, for example, 3 points if very important, 2 points if moderately important, 1 point if less important.

3. Generate Alternatives

Use brainstorming techniques to stimulate people's imaginations.

- What are minor (not very disruptive) solutions that you could put in place right away?

- What are the most conventional solutions?

- What are some workable solutions that would be a substantial change to the present system?

- What are some unconventional solutions?

  Listen to and build on team members' wild ideas. Even if they seem totally impractical at first, you might find later that you can use pieces of them.

continued...

Strategy 3: Develop Appropriate Solutions

4. Identify Constraints

Constraints are unchangeable factors that will limit the options you can realistically consider. Do not be overly pessimistic or overly optimistic. Before accepting the factor as unchangeable, do some trial tests. "Unchangeable" factors are commonly more flexible than people think, but paying attention to real constraints will help you avoid naive solutions and wasted time.

- How much money will you realistically be able to use?

- What written or unwritten rules—sacred cows or taboos—might make a solution easier or more difficult to carry out?

- What limits are there on the present technical ability of team members and other involved parties? How might these limits change in the foreseeable future?

- Are there factions, rivalries, or ongoing issues between individuals or groups to be considered?

5. Evaluate Alternatives

Develop a list of the final candidates. Keep it varied. Look for ways to combine the ideas generated in Step 3. Allow for at least two or three basic approaches, each with some slight variations. Often, the options include features borrowed from the wild or unconventional ideas proposed in the brainstorm.

- Do any solutions deal directly with known root causes of problems?

- Which solutions are easiest to introduce, implement, and maintain?

- Could major changes be phased in?

- Which solutions increase work in the system the least? The most?

- What are possible disadvantages, negative consequences, or other weaknesses of each alternative? What would make each alternative misunderstood, unwelcome, unsupported, or unsuccessful? How likely are these to happen? How might you revise the proposed solution to avoid or minimize these factors?

This evaluation is important because it can open your eyes to ways of turning a mediocre solution into a highly desirable one.

- How does each candidate measure up to the goals, criteria, and constraints you identified?

Eliminate solutions that do not satisfy the goal and the MUST criteria, or see if they can be changed to conform. Rank others according to how many WANTS they meet in addition to the MUSTS.

- Can the best solutions be blended or used simultaneously?

If possible, develop a workable network of solutions.

continued...

Chapter 5

Developing Criteria for Solutions

To guide any major decision, you must have the right goals in mind and know what criteria an appropriate action needs to meet. There are four categories of criteria to assess and weigh carefully:

- **Organizational/Cultural**

  – Do you have systems in place to support changes?
  – Will the environment and culture of your organization support such changes?
  – Are there champions for the changes? Is there leadership support for the changes?

- **Safety/Health/Environmental**

  – What factors in the decision are likely to affect the safety and health of employees?
  – Are there environmental regulations or concerns in the community that you need to respect? Do you know enough about these regulations or concerns to make sound judgments?

- **Developmental/Educational**

  – What skills, training, and education do involved personnel have? Will this limit your options in any way?
  – Do you have capable advisors with additional skills and training?
  – Do you have the resources to provide training or education if necessary?

- **System/Operational**

  – Into what process does the solution have to fit?
  – How will changes affect the current process? Will you be able to change your procedures, equipment, or setup if you need to?
  – What processes for supplying raw materials and information will be affected?
  – What processes for handling and delivering finished goods or services are involved?
  – What aspects of these processes are unchangeable? Are you sure?

6. Select the Best Overall Solution

Compare the proposed solution and choose several of the most likely alternatives. Get feedback from anyone involved in or affected by the proposed changes. The changes should be as simple as possible to make and maintain. Where practical, aim for changes that address the root causes of problems. Try to avoid changes that increase the amount of work or complexity in the process.

7. Follow Up

- What changes should be implemented right away?

  Document how you make your choice. If your team is authorized to take action, proceed immediately to Strategy 4: Plan and Make Changes (p. 5-37). This strategy will lead you through careful planning and execution of the solution(s) you decide to try. Success will depend on how well you anticipate the resources needed to carry off the change, how much training and preparation everyone receives, whether key leaders lend their support, and so forth. If your team is not authorized to take immediate action, write up your recommendations for how the change should be made and give it to your sponsor or other appropriate people.

- What possible solutions need further revision or development?

  Ideally, you are looking for lasting, upstream changes that prevent a problem from recurring. However, it may be necessary to use temporary or downstream "band-aids" while longer-term approaches are being developed.

- What other groups or people need to be involved in further action?

Strategy 4: Plan and Make Changes

(Plan-Do-Check-Act)

| 1 Assure awareness among stakeholders | 2 PLAN the change | 3 DO the change | 4 CHECK the change | 5 ACT to refine and standardize |

Purpose:

The goal is to implement changes smoothly and learn how to make future changes go even more smoothly. Smaller changes need less planning and involvement. Larger changes need more. A planning tool that can help you keep on track is the planning grid, described on p. 4-32.

1. Assure Awareness Among Stakeholders

Very little will happen with your solutions unless key stakeholders support them. These include the formal and informal leaders of those who may be affected by the changes. Involve them as you go.

- Who should be alerted to the existence of the problem or opportunity? How should it be brought to their attention?

- Which leaders are likely to support efforts to solve the problem or address the opportunity? What must be done to develop a group of leaders who will stand behind the effort and give it support and guidance?

2. Plan the Change

- Precisely what change is to be made?

- How do you know the planned change is appropriate? Have other alternatives been explored?

  If no other alternatives have been explored, you may want to first work through Strategy 3: Develop Appropriate Solutions (p. 5-34).

- What sequence of major steps is needed for this change? What are the major substeps of each step?

Map out the change sequence on a planning grid (p. 4-32) or on a flowchart. (◀See pp. 2-16 to 2-19.)

- Who will be directly involved in carrying out each step and substep? Who will need to be consulted?

- Whom will the change affect? Who will need to change the way they do their jobs? How will they be trained? How will you get qualified trainers? How will the effects of the training be checked?

  Do not surprise people with the change. Get information to everyone before they hear rumors. Seek input from people who will be affected by the change. Explain the change and explain how it will affect them and how they will be kept informed. Ask them what they need to know to be comfortable with the change. Incorporate their helpful suggestions into the plan.

- How long will the change take? How long will each step and substep take?

- How will you know when each step is completed? What milestones of progress will there be? What will be the product of each step or substep? How will you acknowledge and celebrate milestones?

continued...

Chapter 5

Strategy 4: Plan and Make Changes

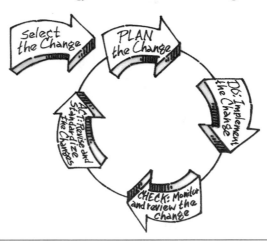

- How will you monitor the change's effectiveness? What might go wrong in implementing the plan? What side effects might there be? How can you check or avoid these side effects?

  Imagine that it is a year from now and the change has not been fully successful. What were the most likely causes of problems? Pay particular attention to the people involved, their understanding, their buy-in, their training, and how their time was allocated. Imagine what a successful change would look like one year from now. What made it successful? What constitutes a reasonable amount of success after one year?

- What will you do about unexpected problems? Who will have the authority to take action?

- Taking all these factors into account, what can be done to increase the likelihood of success?

- How will you monitor and check the progress of the change? The effectiveness of the change? How will you measure the benefits of the change? What are the key points to monitor to determine if the change is proceeding as expected?

- How will you collect, review, and act on this information?

3. Do the Change

It is often best to carry out a small-scale study of the change before making it widespread. *Personally supervise the trial.* Train those whose jobs will

change. After reviewing lessons from the trial, refine your plan. Then carry it out. *Personally supervise execution of the change.*

4. Check the Change

Monitor the progress and effectiveness of the change according to your plan. Gather data from key points. Watch for side effects and backsliding.

5. Refine and Standardize the Change

- What did the information you collected tell you about the effectiveness of the change?

- What can be done to error-proof the process?

  (See Strategy 10: Error-Proof a Process, p. 5-49, for hints.)

- How can the change be refined?
  Do another Plan-Do-Check-Act cycle if refinements are substantial.

- What do you need to do to complete the documentation of the change?

  Standardize the new procedures. Transfer responsibility for ongoing monitoring and improvement to those who do the work regularly.

- What lessons learned here about the new procedure and about implementing changes apply elsewhere? How can these lessons be communicated?

Strategy 5: Identify Customer Needs

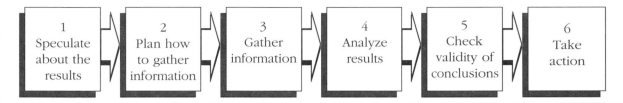

| 1 Speculate about the results | 2 Plan how to gather information | 3 Gather information | 4 Analyze results | 5 Check validity of conclusions | 6 Take action |

Purpose:

The goal should be to exceed customer expectations, not merely meet them. Your customers should boast about how much they benefit from what you do for them. To attain this goal, you must *absorb their needs* and understand where they are trying to go. This strategy can be used to identify potential improvements or to clarify the goals of a particular improvement.

1. Speculate About the Results

Checking your initial guesses against what you learn is a good way to keep track of how well you know your customers.

- What do you think you will learn about your customers' needs and directions?

- What do you think they will say about your current products and services?

Write down your answers, seal them in an envelope, then open them again in Step 5.

2. Plan How to Gather Information

- From which customers will you seek information? From which potential customers?

- How will you find out where customers are headed? What they are trying to achieve?

  Review published or on-line information. Look at when customers get excited; when they get frustrated. Arrange conversations with those in the best position to know. Personal discussions with customers, singly and in groups, are best. Questionnaires with fixed categories of response are seldom as useful.

- How do customers use your product or service? What problems do they have even when your product is working well? What problems do they have that are in any way associated with your products or services?

  Watching customers use your product or service is a quick way to discover areas ripe for improvement and to see how they can get more out of your product. Absorb their needs.

- How will the above information be collected? By whom? How will the information be analyzed? By whom?

  Review suggestions given under Strategy 1: Collect Meaningful Data (p. 5-29). Be open to hearing customers' suggestions. Be open to learning what they like about competitors and why they like it. Record comments in the customer's language. Once you translate to your own language you've lost the chance for new thinking.

3. Gather Information

A pilot study is often useful. Gather information from a few customers, then review your plan before gathering more information.

continued...

4. Analyze the Results

- What are different groups of customers trying to achieve?

- What problems did customers have that are in any way connected with your products and services? How many customers had each kind of problem?

- What problems did you notice when watching the customers use your product or service?

- If appropriate, develop graphs and other summaries to aid communication.

5. Check the Validity of Your Conclusions

- Do the customers and other people in your organization agree with your summaries?

- Open the envelope you sealed in Step 1. What did you learn about customers? About yourself?

6. Take Action

Make obvious changes immediately. Plan ways to address deeper issues. Tell customers what you have heard and what you plan to do. Plan for regular contact with customers so you can keep in touch with their problems and ideas. Follow up.

Which Customers?

Almost everyone has multiple customers. The soup company sells to the wholesaler, who sells to the retailer, who sells to the consumer. All three—the wholesaler, the retailer, and the consumer—are customers, often with very different needs. In addition, most employees do work that goes to other employees rather than directly to any external customer. Obviously, the more you know about all of these different types of customers, the more you'll be able to make changes that are really valuable. But you can't learn it all at once. We suggest you focus first on the most important group with whom you can establish regular contact.

"Internal Customers"?

Perhaps your work goes to other people in your organization rather than directly to your company's customers. If so, should you call them your "internal customers"? Some organizations stopped using this term because it created strife: "I'm your customer, therefore you will do as I say." Needless to say, such attitudes are not helpful. In these cases it may be better to speak of "partners" or "internal customer partners." The term "partner" better describes the desired relationship.

Strategy 6: Study the Use of Time

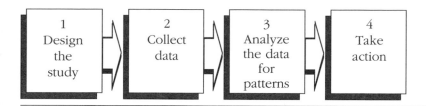

Purpose:

Use this strategy to find out which activities consume people's time and which of these add little value to your products or services. This strategy is used to identify and further refine improvement needs. It is particularly effective for administrative and service processes, although it also has applications in manufacturing. Note: The more that people fear the results will be used against them, the less your chances of getting accurate data. Work hard to eliminate fear. Focus on improving processes and systems and eliminating unnecessary work and hassles—not on judging people! Work only with groups that are receptive: don't force the study on any group that remains unconvinced of its purpose. Success and improvement with receptive groups will go a long way towards convincing cautious groups to give it a try.

1. Design the Study

- What do you hope to accomplish? How will the data be used to help you accomplish your purpose?

  Explain this to the people involved in the study. Have them participate in planning the study.

- How many people will be involved?

- How will the data be collected?

  There are several kinds of data that reflect how people spend their time. Often, people program a watch to beep regularly, and mark down what they are doing when it goes off. For example, the watch beeps every 47 minutes and people record what they are doing. Have someone with statistical training help you look at several possible data collection schemes and decide which suits your purpose best.

- What data collection forms will be used?

  Open-ended forms (ones without fixed categories) are best at the beginning. Later on, forms with fixed categories—such as "tracking down an error" or "searching for equipment"—can be used.

- Who will need to be trained to do the study? How will they be trained?

- What do you think will turn out to be the biggest time-consumers?

2. Collect Data

Review suggestions given under Strategy 1: Collect Meaningful Data (p. 5-29). Reminder: a pilot study is almost always useful.

- What problems do people have when collecting data?

- Do people understand the procedures? The forms?

  Make refinements as needed.

- Are the results giving you the information you want? If not, what changes are needed?

- Collect the data you will need.

continued...

Chapter 5

3. Analyze the Data for Patterns

- How many observations are there in each category? Where is the most time spent?

  Order the categories from most frequent to least frequent; display them with a Pareto chart (p. 2-20).

- Which time-consuming tasks would be unnecessary if the process worked flawlessly?

- Are there problems that arise from other operations in your area? What can you do about them?

- Are there problems in your area that are inherited from other areas? How can these be addressed?

- Are people spending time on the right things? Have they been told what activities they *should* be spending time on?

- What necessary activities take the bulk of the time? What can be done to reduce this time?

4. Take Action

- What changes can you make right away?

- Which problems need further study? What is your plan for them?

- What other recommendations can you make?

Strategy 7: Localize Recurring Problems

Purpose:

To clearly define recurring problems you must learn precisely when and where they occur. This knowledge is essential in finding causes underlying these problems. This strategy is used both to identify a general improvement need and to further pinpoint a problem within a general area.

1. Define Recurring Problems

Often people will have an idea of what problems they want to eliminate. However, in complex situations, precise operational definitions are needed (p. 2-10). For example, what is an "unclear instruction" or a "late invoice"?

2. Assess the Impact of Each Problem

- How often does this problem occur?

- How severe is it when it occurs?

- Do you already have any data on its occurrences? On its impact?

- Do you need additional data to determine its total impact? How can you get it?

3. Localize Each Major Problem

- What data do you need in order to know:

  - When the problem tends to occur and when it doesn't occur

  - Where it tends to occur; where not

  - Where first observed

  - Which products or equipment tend to have the problem; which not

  - Which customers; which not

    Which employees; which not

  Note: Be careful to avoid finger-pointing. Look for problems in processes, not individuals to blame!

- Do you have appropriate data now? If not, how can you get what you need?

  Use the suggestions under Strategy 1: Collect Meaningful Data (see p. 5-29).

- What does the data tell you about the occurrence of this problem?

  Prepare graphs and other summaries to aid communication. Pareto charts (p. 2-20) are often used here.

continued...

Chapter 5

Strategy 7: Localize Recurring Problems

4. Discuss Conclusions With Key Players

- Do the results of your data collection seem logical to the people involved?

- Do they agree with the conclusions you reached about the occurrence of this problem? If not, what other data do you need?

5. Take Action

Determine what actions to take next. Typically, this means moving on to another strategy, which is often Strategy 2: Identify Root Causes of Problems (p. 5-32).

- Are there obvious changes that would eliminate the problem? Are there obvious ways to prevent similar problems in the future?

  Fix the obvious problems immediately; monitor your solutions to make sure they work.

- What steps should be taken next?

Strategy 8: Describe a Process

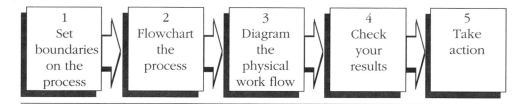

Purpose:

The goal is to develop a useful description of your process as it currently works. This often leads to discoveries of obvious improvements. It also becomes a solid basis for more detailed study of the process. This strategy is part of a general process improvement approach.

1. Set Boundaries on the Process

- Precisely where does the process you are going to study start and stop?

  Example: In studying the order entry process, does it start when the order form arrives in the mail room? On a clerk's desk?

- What inputs and suppliers feed this process?

- What are its outputs (products or services)?

- Who are the customers of this output?

- Who will "acquire" the product or service? Who will use the product or service? (These are not always the same people.)

2. Flowchart the Process

- Who does the work of this process? Are they involved in drawing the chart? They should be!

- What kind of flowchart is most helpful in this situation?

  There are several kinds of flowcharts. (◀See Chapter 2 for examples of different flowcharts—pp. 2-16 to 2-19.) In many cases, it works best to first draw the process as it *would* work if everything in the process went perfectly. Then, if necessary,

add in steps where adjustments, rework, inspection, and delays occur.

- How much detail in the chart will be useful at this point?

  Start with just the 5 to 15 major steps, then add further details later if necessary.

- Who does what? When? Where? Why? How?

- What steps does everyone agree are a part of this process?

- Who should be consulted after drawing the chart?

3. Diagram the Physical Work Flow

Having pictures of how the products and people actually move in the process helps to highlight wasted motion, unnecessary handoffs, unnecessary delays, complexity, and other inefficiencies. Trace the movement of people or materials on a diagram of the floor plan (◀see the work-flow diagram on p. 2-15). Create a deployment flowchart to understand handoffs. Living Flowcharts may also be useful here, too (▶see Appendix C, p. C-31).

continued...

Chapter 5

4. Check Your Results

Get the reactions of others to the flowchart and work-flow diagrams. Improve the diagrams, as appropriate.

5. Take Action

- Are there obvious changes that would improve the process?

  Fix obvious problems immediately. Monitor your solutions to make sure they work. Watch for side effects.

- What steps should be taken next? Consider the following:

  - Strategy 10: Error-Proof a Process (p. 5-49)

  - Strategy 11: Streamline a Process (p. 5-50)

  - Strategy 12: Reduce Sources of Variation (p. 5-52)

  - Strategy 13: Bring a Process Under Statistical Control (p. 5-54)

Strategy 9: Develop a Standard Process

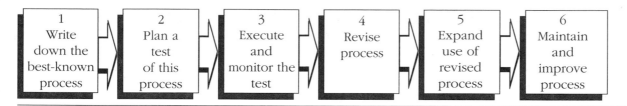

| 1
Write down the best-known process | 2
Plan a test of this process | 3
Execute and monitor the test | 4
Revise process | 5
Expand use of revised process | 6
Maintain and improve process |

Purpose:

The goal is to strengthen the organization's ability to provide value. The basic approach is to start from today's best-known process, and build a way to share, document, and use lessons learned.

1. Write Down the Current Best-Known Process

The current best-known process describes how you do the job today when you're at your best. It's not how you might do it in the future. Sometimes it may be best to have one person write it out; at other times, it might be more effective to involve the whole work group. Employees might, for instance, discuss how they do each step, then choose a best method. Alternatively, they might start by observing the employee who everyone agrees is the best at this job. Use flowcharts, pictures, and drawings when describing the process. For tips see Strategy 8: Describe a Process (p. 5-45).

2. Plan a Test of This Process

Get a small group of people to try out the best-known process.

- How many people will be involved in the test?

  If there are only a few people who work with the process, consider involving all of them in the test. If there are many people, select a few to test this current best-known process.

- How will the participants be trained? Who will train them? How will the trainers be trained?

- How will participants keep track of their progress? How will you know what works and what doesn't work?

- How will the process and any changes be documented? How will documentation be kept up-to-date?

3. Execute and Monitor the Test

Actively collect information and gather ideas for improvement from the group trying to use the best-known process.

- Are any of the instructions unclear? Unnecessary?

- What problems occur?

- What things come up that aren't covered in the description of the best-known process?

- Has waste been reduced? Can it be reduced even more? See Strategy 14: Eliminate Waste (p. 5-56).

- Have results improved? Has undesired variation in the process been reduced? Could it be reduced any further? See Strategy 12: Reduce Sources of Variation (p. 5-52).

continued...

Chapter 5

4. Revise the Process

Use the information you gathered to improve the process. Work hard to simplify the documentation. Keep it as simple and graphical as possible. Find ways to error proof and make visible key aspects of the process. For tips see:

– Strategy 14: Eliminate Waste (p. 5-56)

– Strategy 10: Error-Proof a Process (p. 5-49)

– Strategy 11: Streamline a Process (p. 5-50)

– Strategy 12: Reduce Sources of Variation (p. 5-52)

– Strategy 13: Bring a Process Under Statistical Control (p. 5-54)

5. Expand Use of the Revised Process

If only a few employees were involved in the test, expand use of the revised process to others. Use Strategy 4: Plan and Make Changes (p. 5-37) to help carry off this expansion.

6. Maintain and Improve Process

Have everyone use the newest, most improved process; challenge them to develop further refinements. Develop ways to capture, try out, and implement people's ideas. Develop methods to systematically review and improve the process at least once every six months. Keep documents up-to-date and make sure they are used, particularly to train new employees and to retrain and cross-train current employees.

Managing and Improving Daily Work

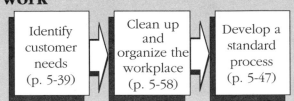

Some teams have the opportunity to help manage and improve how daily work gets done in their area. Linking three strategies provides a useful roadmap.

1. Identify Customer Needs

To be able to manage and improve any work, we must know the current needs and future directions of our customers. Helpful tips can be found in Strategy 5: Identify Customer Needs (p. 5-39).

2. Clean Up and Organize the Workplace

It's hard to stay organized and productive when there's a lot of clutter in the workplace and people have to continually look for working equipment, price lists, forms, etc.

A good first step in managing and improving daily work is to clean up and organize the work area. For tips on how to do this see Strategy 15: Clean Up and Organize the Workplace (p. 5-58).

3. Develop a Standard Process

Knowing customer needs and having a clean workplace lays the foundation, but now you must prepare to execute quickly and flawlessly. If you continually forget lessons learned, or have problems whenever someone new is involved, your work will be an embarrassment to you and everyone else. Developing and using a standard process is the third component of managing and improving daily work (Strategy 9, p. 5-47).

Strategy 10: Error-Proof a Process

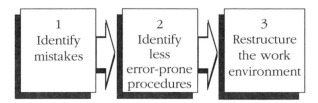

Purpose:

Many errors in processes can be prevented through simple measures once employees know what to look for and how to combat common oversights.

1. Identify Mistakes

- What errors or mistakes occur at each process step?

  Use the process flowchart as a guide to think through each step. Picture each step and think of what goes wrong in its execution. Begin to collect data on errors.

2. Identify Less Error-Prone Procedures

- Would changing the order of steps prevent mistakes?

  If a step is often forgotten, consider revising the sequence to make it more prominent.

- Would changing a form prevent mistakes?

  Use shading, different type sizes and looks, a different layout, or an altered sequence of information to make forms easier to read, understand, and follow.

- Would using a checklist prevent mistakes?

  Checklists are a simple way to make sure everything that is supposed to happen does happen, and in the proper sequence. Use them in almost any situation.

- Would clear directions, graphically illustrated and prominently displayed, prevent mistakes?

  The less frequently a procedure is used, the more likely it is that employees will need easy-to-understand instructions to remind them how to perform the task. Even frequent procedures need instructions displayed for the benefit of newcomers and temporary replacements.

- Can you think of entirely new procedures that are less error-prone?

  Be creative. Pretend you were designing this process from the ground up. What could you do to prevent the kinds of errors that appear in the current process? Should you adopt the new approach or incorporate key ideas into your current procedures?

3. Restructure the Work Environment

With enough ingenuity you can prevent most errors.

- Would changing the work layout prevent any of the mistakes you found? What would an ideal layout look like?

- Would a gadget that checks the completion of an action be useful?

  Simple, inexpensive gadgets that stop a process or sound an alarm can eliminate many costly mistakes, especially in assembly operations. Computers can catch many data entry errors.

- A useful trick is to immediately stop the work flow when an error is discovered. This is a dramatic way to highlight problems and foster solutions.

Chapter 5

Strategy 11: Streamline a Process

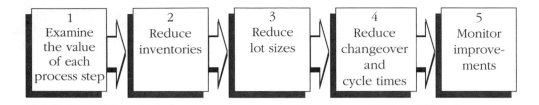

| 1 Examine the value of each process step | 2 Reduce inventories | 3 Reduce lot sizes | 4 Reduce changeover and cycle times | 5 Monitor improvements |

Purpose:

Many process problems and inefficiencies lie buried beneath blankets of inventory and work-in-process buffers. Streamlining processes is critical to meeting the demand of customers for quicker and quicker response at lower and lower cost. In addition, a well-honed process increases joy in work.

1. Examine the Value of Each Process Step

- Which steps merely undo or patch problems caused upstream? Can upstream problems be solved?

- Are some steps a result of excessive caution or mistrust? Can something be done to remove the mistrust?

  For example, forms should require no more than one signature to be approved. Getting multiple signatures is a waste of time and indicates that people do not trust one another's judgment. Perhaps creating consensus around operational definitions of "completed" or "acceptable" forms would reduce this mistrust.

- Do all steps add value to the product or service, or can you eliminate some?

2. Reduce Inventories

- What are the current "inventory" sizes of each step in the process? How much do they vary?

  In administrative processes, backlogs of work or "in-boxes" represent inventory.

- How much can inventories be reduced without changing the process?

- How could you change the process to allow extremely low inventories?

  The goal is always zero inventory.

3. Reduce Lot Sizes

- What are current lot sizes at each step? For administrative processes, do a certain number of forms or orders accumulate before they are handled?

- How can lot sizes be sharply reduced? How much efficiency would be lost with a much smaller lot size?

  Work towards lot sizes of one.

continued...

Strategy 11: Streamline a Process

4. Reduce Changeover and Cycle Times

- When there are multiple products or services, how much time does it take to change from one to another at each step in the process?

- How can you reduce changeover times?

The goal is single-motion, nearly instant changes. Jigs, fixtures, and spare parts and equipment ease this process in manufacturing. Changing the work area layout may help in administrative processes.

- What is the current total cycle time? How long does it take for a product or form to get through the entire process? From customer request until customer receipt?

Identify the steps in the process and estimate how long each step would take if there were no waiting time. Gather data on how long each step actually takes. Usually there is a huge difference between this theoretical minimum time and the actual total cycle time. This difference represents a huge opportunity to reduce total cycle time.

5. Monitor Improvements

As changes are made, continue to gather data on their effect on total cycle time. Constantly look for ways to improve any of these process characteristics.

> ### Reducing Total Cycle Time
> Total cycle time is the time from the start of the process until the end of the process. In many cases this is time from customer request until customer receipt of product or service. In most cases the actual time spent working on the product or service is only a small percentage of the total elapsed time. Working to reduce substantially this total cycle time has many benefits:
>
> - Improves customer service
> - Reduces work-in-process inventories in manufacturing
> - Forces the organization to work as a team across boundaries
> - Surfaces the sources of errors and delays

Chapter 5

Strategy 12: Reduce Sources of Variation

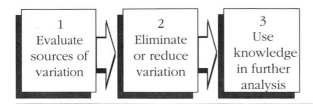

Purpose:

This strategy provides a way to eliminate the most obvious sources of variability in a product, service, or measurement process. To evaluate a measurement process, measure the same item repeatedly, if possible. If the measurement is destructive, get a set of items as close to identical as possible, and select from this pool randomly. This strategy is part of a general approach to process improvement.

1. Evaluate Sources of Variation

Look for places in your process where different conditions or procedures lead to differences in results. Stratification analysis is a useful tool here (see p. 2-12). Prepare graphs and other summaries to aid communication and encourage action.

For example, after coding points on time plots or dot plots, do you see differences between:

- Different people (such as new employees versus experienced employees)?

- Different machines? Different heads on the same machine? Different tools?

- Different measurement instruments? Different inspectors?

- Different sources of materials? Materials of varying ages?

- Different operating conditions (temperatures, humidity, etc.)?

- Different times of the day, different days of the week? The beginning or end of the month? Different shifts?

2. Eliminate or Reduce Variation

- Which of the sources you identified above can be eliminated?

  For example, training and documentation might eliminate differences among employees.

- Can the impact of other sources be reduced?

  Example: Sometimes products, equipment, or facilities can be redesigned to be less sensitive to variation in inputs. Working with a single supplier could reduce variability in raw materials.

- Which sources cannot be eliminated or reduced? Are you sure? Could you do trial experiments to make sure?

continued...

3. Use Knowledge (of Variation) in Further Analysis

Avoid mixing data that may not have been collected with comparable methods and under comparable conditions. Mixing data from different sources can be dangerous. Guard against the possibility of combining data that should be kept separate.

- Is there any way the data can be standardized to eliminate consistent differences that you know about and find necessary or appropriate?

  Example: If some months have more working days than others, consider reviewing sales per day or production per day. If product A has twice as many components as product B, try measuring the assembly time per component rather than total time.

- Can you tell whether the variation arises from special or common causes? How would that affect your future actions?

  For example, in Strategy 13: Bring a Process Under Statistical Control (p. 5-54), separate charts may be needed for products from different machines.

Strategy 13: Bring a Process Under Statistical Control

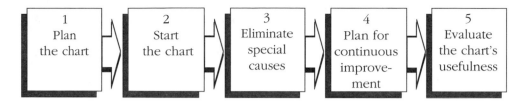

| 1 Plan the chart | 2 Start the chart | 3 Eliminate special causes | 4 Plan for continuous improvement | 5 Evaluate the chart's usefulness |

Purpose:

You can get rid of many obvious sources of variation through the use of stratification analysis, as described in Strategy 12: Reduce Sources of Variation (p. 5-52). However, you need more sophisticated tools for tracking down less obvious sources of variation in order to bring the process under statistical control. When a process is under statistical control, its performance is more predictable and you have a good starting point for making more fundamental improvements. Control charts are the best way to bring a process under statistical control. Processes can speak to us through these charts, telling us when to track down and eliminate special causes of variation. When this is done, the performance of the system will be predictable within certain limits. Everyone involved in the charting or analysis should have some training on the nature and use of control charts. Such training is critical for managers, superintendents, foremen, and supervisors. It is also important to have the guidance of someone with statistical knowledge. That person needs to understand how to construct the various types of control charts and know when each is appropriate.

1. Plan the Chart

Involve a control chart expert in the planning stage and throughout the effort; this guidance is necessary each time you use control charts during the first year or two of the quality effort.

- What should you measure and plot? For products, what key quality characteristics are related to what your customers want? For measurement processes, what items should you measure?

- How, when, and where will the data be collected? How will accuracy be checked? How will you select samples?

- What kinds of charts and scales are appropriate?

- Who will collect the data? Who will plot the data?

Typically, operators collect the data and plot the chart. They then work on identifying and removing special causes of variation. It is extremely useful to have places on the chart where operators can make notations about process conditions.

- What will happen when there is a signal of a special cause? Who will have the authority to take action?

Managers need to actively support corrective actions, but many times the operators themselves are in the best position to know what actions are most appropriate.

2. Start the Chart

Begin taking data and charting. Develop appropriate control limits when sufficient data has been collected. On the charts, note process conditions, describe special causes that you find, and mark down any other useful information.

- Are sampling procedures appropriate?

- Is the chart revealing the kind of information you need in order to track down special causes? If not, should it be modified or discontinued?

continued...

Chapter 5

Strategy 13: Bring a Process Under Statistical Control

3. Eliminate Special Causes

Seek out special causes of variation in response to signals from the chart. Evaluate process capability.

- Is action being taken when there are signals of special causes? Are root causes of problems being identified and removed? Can you reduce the impact of known sources of variation?

Example: Product variability may be related to incoming raw materials. Working collaboratively with a sole supplier is an upstream answer to this problem.

4. Plan for Continuous Improvement

As you get nearer to statistical control, you can start making fundamental improvements to the process. Once variation starts to disappear, other problems may surface. Plan ways to deal with the problems and to make obvious improvements.

- How will changes you recommend be implemented? Who will be responsible for monitoring these changes?

5. Evaluate the Chart's Usefulness

Review the chart periodically. If special causes are still occurring or if the variable being charted is critically important, continue to use the chart. If no special causes have occurred for some time, you should examine the relative importance of the chart. Ask yourself if the effort spent maintaining this chart is more important than other opportunities in the work area.

Chapter 5

Strategy 14: Eliminate Waste

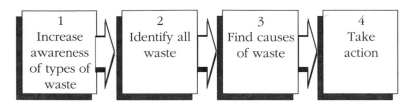

Purpose:

The goal is to increase awareness of the many different types of waste and to institute methods to continually remove waste from work processes.

1. Increase Awareness of Types of Waste

- Waste is all around us. It is any action that does not add value to a product or service in the eyes of a customer. It is non-value-added time and effort.

  You have probably had times during your work day in which you have not been able to find a pen, paper clips, book, customer record, price list, or tool. You spend time looking for the item. This is waste.

- Close examination of any workplace will find large amounts of non-value-added work and much smaller amounts of value-added work.

  Keep in mind that the process of eliminating waste is continuous improvement. Any work done to improve a workplace process and reduce waste is value-added work.

- Waste takes many forms. In the manufacturing process, we find eight major types of waste:

  ### – Waste Due to Defect/Rework

  Waste due to defect/rework is the largest type of waste because work should have been done right the first time. Correction of defects adds cost to the product or service because of extra labor, material, transportation, inventory, motion, and energy expenses.

  ### – Waste of Material (overproduction)

  Waste of material is producing more product than is necessary, or producing at a rate faster than required. Waste of material is a violation of just-in-time principles, that is, producing what is needed when it is needed. Any product produced before it is needed, sold, or ordered by a customer is waste.

  Costs due to overproduction can be incurred in damage (waste of rework), handling (waste of transportation), labor (waste of motion), and paperwork (waste of processing).

  ### – Waste of Processing

  Waste of processing is unnecessary work that does not add value to the product. Example: Additional paperwork that does not improve the product or the timely delivery of the product.

  ### – Waste of Transportation

  Waste of transportation is any transportation of material not needed for just-in-time production, the supply of information, or the delivery of tools and parts.

continued...

Strategy 14: Eliminate Waste

– **Waste of Inventory**

Material builds up at the work site, between processes, or as an end product that could be delivered to a customer. Inventory is usually used as a buffer or as insurance against shortages.

Excess inventory in the system is a violation of just-in-time principles and is a major source of waste.

– **Waste of Motion**

Waste of motion is any motion of people or machinery that does not contribute value to the end product.

Examples: A tool is misplaced or lost and a team member has to take time to look for the tool. The work site is poorly arranged and too many steps have to be taken between processes.

– **Waste of Waiting**

Waste of waiting occurs when you have to wait for another process to finish before you can do your work.

Examples: Waiting in line to use the copy machine; waiting to use the crane; or waiting for a machine to finish an automatic process.

– **Waste of the Human Mind**

Waste of the human mind—not involving the person doing the job (the real expert)—results in poor quality, lost productivity, and higher costs.

Waste of the human mind is a direct cause of the other seven wastes.

2. Identify All Waste

- Systematically go through the workplace making a log of all the waste you can identify. Don't worry now if you can't figure out how to eliminate all of it. Fix the obvious as you go.

- Make a visible record, in priority order, of all the waste you have identified. Continue to add to this list. Continue to fix the obvious.

- Keep a log and create a visible chart that shows how many actions you have taken to make things better.

3. Find Causes of Waste

- Unless you can find the deeper causes of waste, it will continually reappear. Use Strategy 2: Identify Root Causes of Problems (p. 5-32).

4. Take Action

Take action to eliminate the waste and to keep it from coming back. Use Strategy 3: Develop Appropriate Solutions (p. 5-34), Strategy 4: Plan and Make Changes (p. 5-37), Strategy 9: Develop a Standard Process (p. 5-47), Strategy 10: Error-Proof a Process (p. 5-49), and Strategy 15: Clean Up and Organize the Workplace (p. 5-58).

Chapter 5

Strategy 15: Clean Up and Organize the Workplace

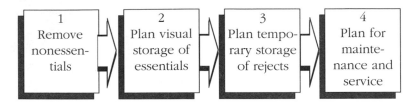

Purpose:

Creating a well-organized workplace is fundamental to improving the quality and productivity of daily work. Having a place for everything helps make the work go more smoothly and quickly surfaces problems when they arise.

1. Remove Nonessentials

- Remove from the workplace everything that is not essential to the ongoing work.

  Identify all defective spares, tools, equipment, supplies, and products. Make the decision to fix, scrap, or surplus and take immediate action.

  Identify all "junk" and sell or eliminate.

  Fix or eliminate everything that is broken or needs repair. List by location on a layout plan and prioritize, find, and remove or repair.

2. Plan Visual Storage of Essentials

- Classify essential items in the workplace by frequency of their use. Store accordingly.

- Plan for installation of visual storage with places for all essential items.

  Items in constant use:
  - At desk or work station: store visibly; use label-, color- or icon-coded storage rack
  - On person: use compartmentalized tool belt or pouch
  - Items special to a machine or operation: store visibly at the machine or operation site

  Items used occasionally should be stored visibly near where they are used.

Need	Description	Action
Low	• Items not used for 1 year	• Determine if it is needed for emergency. If yes, store in central stores; if no, sell, surplus, or scrap.
	• Items used in the last 6-12 months	• Store in central stores.
Medium	• Items used once or twice a month	• Store in a central location in the workplace.
High	• Items used frequently: – Once per week	• Store near the work site.
	– Once per day – Once per hour	• Store at the area where used.
	– 2 or more times per hour	• Carry on person.

Create a storage rack, board, or shelf that clearly shows: where each item or group of items is to be placed (stored); when an item is missing; when supply items should be reordered, as well as the order quantity.

continued...

Strategy 15: Clean Up and Organize the Workplace

3. Plan Temporary Storage of Rejects

- In manufacturing and some service jobs, a defective product may sometimes occur. If so, in each work area identify a specific location where defective products will be temporarily stored. The location should be highly visible to all and be clearly marked and separated from quality output. The area should be purposely small to "force" decision on disposition.

4. Plan for Maintenance and Service

- Develop a system for regular maintenance, service, and sanitation of all areas, including service areas (rest rooms, locker rooms, lunch rooms, meeting rooms, and offices).

- Audit the mechanical and aesthetic condition of all areas at present.

- Plan and fund upgrading as appropriate.

- Audit (or establish) standard service and sanitation methods; develop service checksheets for use by the service/sanitation staff.

- Review service checksheets to develop methods to assist in maintaining cleanliness and sanitation.

- Audit service areas according to service checksheets. Use these checksheets to evaluate conditions between scheduled service and sanitation visits.

- Revise service and sanitation frequency and develop other improvements based on this data.

Foundations of the Visual Workplace

Organization—Sort through and sort out. Distinguish between needed and unneeded items. Eliminate unnecessary parts, adjustments, documents, etc.

Orderliness—Organize the necessary items close to where they are needed and in such a way that any waste or abnormality is apparent. Set limits to the amounts stored. Make the location self-explanatory so that everyone clearly perceives what goes where.

Cleanliness—Cleaning is a form of inspection. Ensure that equipment, tools, and the entire workplace shines. Eliminate dirt, dust, oil, trash, and scrap.

Neatness—When organization, orderliness, and cleanliness are practiced for awhile, a new state of efficiency is achieved. This becomes permanent by sharing information and following standards so that abnormalities are quickly recognized and eliminated.

Discipline—Scrupulously stick to the rules, including wearing safety equipment. Make maintaining correct procedures a steady habit.

Chapter 5

Seven Key Ingredients for Successful Improvement Efforts

- Maintain communications
- Link to organizational priorities
- Bite off what you can chew
- Fix obvious problems
- Look upstream
- Document progress and problems
- Monitor changes; publicize and celebrate successes

IV. Seven Key Ingredients for Successful Improvement Efforts

No matter which approach you use for improvement, we have found seven ingredients that must be incorporated into every step of every project. Teams that forget to use them will run into barriers, such as opposition from people who feel ignored or misused. Teams who follow these suggestions will travel a much smoother road to longer-lasting improvements.

1. Maintain Communications

A project's success depends on how well team members communicate what they are doing, not only among themselves, but also to their sponsor and to anyone else likely to be affected by or interested in their activities. For example, if a team was about to collect data from a work area, team members should notify all supervisors and employees in advance and tell them exactly why, how, and when the data will be collected. Similarly, a team studying how employees in an office use their time should explain that the goal is to identify inefficient systems not lazy people.

This kind of communication is simply being considerate of fellow employees. It encourages cooperation from coworkers and often leads to suggestions for improvement.

Later, when you have ideas for changes, someone, often several people, will need to change what they do. You will need their enthusiastic cooperation, and the time to start building it is now. Involve them as you go!

The strategies in this chapter generally do not mention "notify supervisors and employees" or "explain to the people working with the process what you are about to do" as specific steps. But you should include these activities throughout your project. It's one thing to come up with wonderful ideas—it's a whole different thing to get them implemented.

2. Link to Organizational Priorities

You will have a far greater chance of success if you make it clear to everyone how what you are doing links to organizational priorities. Close cooperation with your team's sponsor can help to make this clear.

3. Bite Off What You Can Chew

Focus first on changes you can make cheaply in your own work area. Do this even if you have support and encouragement for changes in other areas. Making changes in your own area will build credibility and will enhance your ability to design other changes that work.

Also focus on changes you can make quickly. Those that look like they will take more than three months should probably be broken into stages.

 Caution!

When making changes in your area, stay in touch with others in the organization to ensure that you don't inadvertently suboptimize the larger system.

Chapter 5

4. Fix Obvious Problems

The better you get at studying processes, the more problems you will find that need fixing. Generally we recommend exploring problems in depth and collecting data to make sure you have developed appropriate solutions. But there are also times when a problem is easily fixed, and in those cases we urge you to go ahead and make the change. Do not wait until the end of a project to fix obvious problems.

Before making any change, however, ask yourselves these questions: "What's the worst that could happen if this solution doesn't work? How easy will it be to undo the change? Will this delay other actions? How expensive will this change be in terms of money, time, and the disruption and inconvenience to coworkers?" If it looks like the solution you propose could have substantial negative effects if it doesn't work, take the time to explore other options. If it is simple to put into place and is easily done, go ahead and try it out.

5. Look Upstream

Most problems we see are only symptoms of other problems buried upstream in the process. For example, variation in a product may be the result of variation in materials; mistakes in a customer's bill may be the result of mistakes in the original order or any steps in between. In such cases, after you have fixed what you can in your own area, begin to move upstream. To make long-lasting improvements, someone must eventually seek out these causes and find ways to prevent them. Whenever your team is faced with a problem, mentally walk through the entire process and see if you can identify upstream conditions that may be the cause. Fix what you can locally, then seek upstream cooperation. You'll get much more respect when you have data and have already done your part.

6. Document Progress and Problems

In every organization, there are problems that get "solved" over and over—problems you hear about year after year. You try something once, it doesn't do much good, so somebody else tries something different the next time (with little idea of what has gone before). If you're lucky, the problem will decrease or disappear for awhile, but it always returns because the solutions tried are aimed at symptoms rather than causes of the problem.

For example, one company was plagued with a recurring defect that resulted in 35% of the product being scrapped. Three technicians set out to eliminate the problems, experimenting with various adjustments in the control of the machinery. Sure enough, the defects disappeared. But the technicians weren't sure what they had done that finally got rid of the problem. Three months later, the problem reappeared, defects were right back to 35%, and the technicians couldn't figure out why. Now the company thinks that the process is capable of working better than its current level, and projections of production are based on the higher figure obtained during the three-month period when the defect disappeared. But since they have no record of what adjustments eliminated the problem, the company has never been able to duplicate their brief success, and production has never met the higher predictions.

The simple way to get out of this trap is to keep and use good records of everything tried on the process. Records provide valuable data for future efforts. (◀See the discussion in Chapter 4, p. 4-26, about team records and documentation.)

Chapter 5

7. *Monitor Changes; Publicize and Celebrate Successes*

Rarely does something turn out exactly the way you planned. Changes made to a process or system are no exception. Though careful planning reduces the chances of unanticipated problems, there is no guarantee that everything will work perfectly. The only sensible plan of action, therefore, is to personally monitor changes so you can quickly catch problems and prevent them from becoming bigger ones.

Then, as you have successes, publicize them and celebrate. The road to improvement is constantly under construction. Without celebrations of milestones, the journey can begin to feel overwhelming!

Summary

Understanding the two general approaches to improvement described in this chapter and being able to call on the 15 strategies as needed can take a team a long way. A little time spent early in a team's life getting a top-level view of these two approaches and a sampling of the 15 strategies gives them a bird's-eye view of the territory ahead. The team is then much more capable of continuing to make progress even when the going gets tough.

Chapter 6

Learning to Work Together

The ordinary team is a complicated creature. Members must work out personal differences, find strengths on which to build, and balance commitments to the project against the demands of their everyday jobs.

Dealing with internal group needs that arise from these pressures is as important as the group's task of solving problems, improving processes, or completing daily work. Teams often underestimate the need for team development. When a team works together well, members can concentrate on their primary goal of solving problems or improving processes. In contrast, a team that fails to build relationships among its members will waste time on struggles for control and endless discussions that lead nowhere.

The more you know about what to expect as your team progresses, the better equipped you will be to handle challenges as they emerge. With a strong foundation in place, you will be better able to recognize and avoid many disruptions, and better able as a group to work through those that cannot be avoided. In Chapter 7 we will be looking at what to do when the team runs into trouble, but it is far better to prevent problems than have to manage them later. (An ounce of prevention is worth a pound of cure!) In this chapter we will explore how to help prevent problems before they happen.

I. Undercurrents in Team Dynamics

If all teams had to do was have meetings, gather data, plan improvements, make changes, write reports, and so on, progress would be very swift. But when people form into teams, something always seems to get in the way of efficient progress.

What You Will Find Here

In this chapter we explore:

Chapter 6

For Ongoing Teams

Ongoing teams face the same emotional issues, experience the same stages of growth, and ride the same roller coaster of highs and lows as project teams.

The problem is that there are hidden concerns that, like undercurrents, pull team members away from their obvious tasks. When they walk through the door into a meeting, team members are beset by conflicting emotions: excitement and anxiety about being on the team, loyalty to their divisions or departments, nervous anticipation about the project's success.

If left unattended these undercurrents can inhibit a group's chance of becoming an effective team. Every group must therefore spend time on activities not directly related to a task, activities that build understanding and support in the group. You need to resolve issues that fall into what one author, William Schutz, calls the "interpersonal underworld."

These are issues not often spoken about, but common to us all, and they fall into three categories.

1. Personal identity in the team

It is natural for team members to wonder how they will fit into the team. The most common worries are those associated with:

- **Membership, Inclusion:** "Do I feel like an insider or outsider? Do I belong? Do I want to belong? What can I do to fit in?"

- **Influence, Control, Mutual Trust:** "Who's calling the shots here? Who will have the most influence? Will I have influence? Will I be listened to? Will I be able to contribute? Will I be allowed to contribute?"

- **Getting Along, Mutual Loyalty:** "How will I get along with other team members? Will we be able to develop any cooperative spirit?"

2. Relationships among team members

With few exceptions, team members want the team to succeed, to make improvements, and to work cooperatively. They extend personal concerns to the team: "What kind of relationships will characterize this team? Will members make and keep commitments? How will members of different ranks interact? Will we be friendly and informal or will it be strictly business? Will we be open or guarded in what we say? Will we be able to work together, or will we argue and disagree all the time? Will people like or dislike me? Will I like or dislike them?"

3. Identity with the organization

Team members usually identify strongly with their departments or divisions, and they will need to know how membership in the team will affect those roles and responsibilities: "Will my loyalty to the team conflict with loyalty to my coworkers? Will my responsibilities as a team member conflict with my everyday duties?" Usually it is the team's work that suffers if the two compete.

Just as team members must reach outside the group to maintain ties with their departments, so must the team as a whole build relationships throughout the organization. Political astuteness is crucial. Finding influential people to champion the team and its project can make a big difference in the support your team receives from the organization. A team's relationship with its manager or sponsor is one avenue for creating such support within the organization.

Chapter 6

Chapter 6

Forming

When a team first forms, team members are like hesitant swimmers standing by the side of the pool and dabbling their toes in the water.

➤ Tip
Leading a Team Through Forming

As teams move through stages of growth, team leaders should adapt their behavior to the team's shifting needs.

To build trust and confidence during the forming stage, the leader should:

- Help members get to know each other
- Provide clear direction and purpose
- Involve members in developing plans, clarifying roles, and establishing ways of working together
- Provide the information the team needs to get started

II. Stages of Team Growth

As the team matures, members gradually learn to cope with the emotional and group pressures they face. As a result, the team goes through fairly predictable stages.

Stage 1: Forming

When a team is forming, members cautiously explore the boundaries of acceptable group behavior. Like hesitant swimmers, they stand by the pool, dabbling their toes in the water. This is a stage of transition from individual to member status, and of testing the leader's guidance both formally and informally.

Forming includes these feelings...
- Excitement, anticipation, and optimism
- Pride in being chosen for the team
- Initial, tentative attachment to the team
- Suspicion, fear, and anxiety about the job ahead

...and these behaviors.
- Attempts to define the task and decide how it will be accomplished
- Attempts to determine acceptable team behavior and how to deal with team problems
- Decisions on what information is needed
- Lofty, abstract discussions of concepts and issues; or, for some members, impatience with these discussions
- Discussion of symptoms or problems not relevant to the task; difficulty in identifying relevant problems
- Complaints about the organization and barriers to the task

6-4   © 1996 Joiner Associates Inc. All Rights Reserved.

Storming

As team members start to realize the amount of work that lies ahead, it is normal for them to almost panic. Now they are like swimmers who have jumped into the water, think they are about to drown, and start thrashing about.

Because there is so much going on to distract members' attention in the beginning, progress on work or team goals is slow. This is perfectly normal.

Stage 2: Storming

Storming is probably the most difficult stage for the team. It is as if team members jump in the water, and, thinking they are about to drown, start thrashing about. They begin to realize that the task is different and more difficult than they imagined, and become testy, anxious, or overzealous.

Impatient about the lack of progress, but still too inexperienced to know much about decision making or the scientific approach, members argue about just what actions the team should take. They try to rely solely on their personal and professional experience, resisting any need for collaborating with other team members.

Storming includes these feelings...
- Resistance to tasks and methods of work different from what each individual member is comfortable using
- Sharp fluctuations in attitude about the team's chance of success

...and these behaviors.
- Arguing among members even when they agree on the real issue
- Defensiveness and competition; factions and "choosing sides"
- Questioning the wisdom of those who selected this project and appointed the other members of the team
- Establishing unrealistic goals; concern about excessive work
- Creation of a perceived "pecking order"; creating disunity, increased tension, and jealousy

➤ **Tip**
Leading a Team Through Storming

At the storming stage, to build self-direction the leader should:

- Resolve issues of power and authority. For example, don't allow one person's power to squash others' contributions.
- Develop and implement agreements about how decisions are made and who makes them.
- Adapt the leadership role to allow the team to become more independent. Encourage members to take on more responsibilities.

Chapter 6

Norming

As team members get used to working together, their initial resistance fades away. They start helping each other stay afloat rather than competing with one another.

➤ Tip
Leading a Team Through Norming

In the norming stage, to build cooperation the leader should:

- Fully utilize team members' skills, knowledge, and experience
- Encourage and acknowledge members' respect for each other
- Encourage members to "roll up their sleeves" and work collaboratively

Again, these many pressures mean team members have little energy to spend on progressing towards the team's goal. But they are beginning to understand one another.

Stage 3: Norming

During this stage, members reconcile competing loyalties and responsibilities. They accept the team, team ground rules (or "norms"), their roles in the team, and the individuality of fellow members. Emotional conflict is reduced as previously competitive relationships become more cooperative. In other words, as team members realize they are not going to drown, they stop thrashing about and start helping each other stay afloat.

Norming includes these feelings...

- A sense of team cohesion, a common spirit and goals
- Acceptance of membership in the team
- Relief that it seems everything is going to work out

...and these behaviors.

- An attempt to achieve harmony by avoiding conflict
- More friendliness, confiding in each other, and sharing of personal problems; discussing the team's dynamics
- A new ability to express criticism constructively
- Establishing and maintaining team ground rules and boundaries (the "norms")

As team members begin to work out their differences, they now have more time and energy to spend on their work. Thus they are able to start making significant progress.

Performing

As team members become more comfortable with each other, and as they better understand the work and what is expected of them, they become a more effective unit with everyone working in concert.

Stage 4: Performing

By this stage, the team has settled its relationships and expectations. They can begin performing—diagnosing and solving problems, and choosing and implementing changes. At last, team members have discovered and accepted each other's strengths and weaknesses, and learned what their roles are. Now they can swim in concert.

Performing includes these feelings...
- Members having insights into personal and group processes, and better understanding of each other's strengths and weaknesses
- Satisfaction at the team's progress
- Close attachment to the team

...and these behaviors.
- Constructive self-change
- Ability to prevent or work through group problems

The team is now an effective, cohesive unit. You can tell when your team has reached this stage because you start getting a lot of work done.

The duration and intensity of these stages vary from team to team. Sometimes Stage 4, *performing,* is achieved in a meeting or two; other times it may take months. Use the descriptions here to compare your team with the normal pattern for maturing groups. Understanding these stages of growth will keep you from overreacting to normal problems and setting unrealistic expectations that only add to frustration. Don't panic. With patience and effort this assembly of independent individuals *will* grow into a team.

➤ Tip
Leading a Team Through Performing

In the performing stage, to build openness to change the leader should:

- Update the team's methods and procedures to support cooperation
- Help the team understand how to manage change
- Represent, and advocate for, the team with other groups and individuals
- Monitor work progress and celebrate achievements

Chapter 6

Roller Coaster of Highs and Lows

Every team goes through cycles of good times and bad times. The duration of these highs and lows will vary for each team, depending on how quickly they progress, work through obstacles or problems, and so forth. Team members should know that such cycles are normal and do not signal a team's ultimate success or failure.

- Excited, Proud
- Satisfied, Pleased
- Optimistic
- So-So, Bored
- Impatient, Discouraged
- Frustrated

First 3-4 wks. "The Honeymoon"   Early Planning & Training

III. Roller Coaster of Highs and Lows

Knowing about the typical stages a team passes through—forming, storming, norming, and performing—should relieve much of the fear team members have about the project's success. It is also helpful to be aware of the roller coaster of highs and lows every team experiences.

A team's mood usually reflects its fortune: with every step forward, the future looks bright and team members are optimistic. But no matter how well a team works together, progress is never smooth. As progress swings from forward to stalled, and then from stalled to backward, the team mood will swing, too. These swings are only partly linked to the stages of growth, and they are usually unpredictable.

As shown above, the team begins with hopefulness and optimism. These positive feelings may last awhile, but usually change to boredom and impatience as the project gets underway. Members begin to feel overwhelmed when they realize just how much they have to learn about making improvements. Somewhere in here the storming starts.

When they finally begin collecting data, team members again feel encouraged—at last they are making progress! Rarely does this elation last: since few people are experts in scientific methods the first time out, team members almost always uncover mistakes in data collection procedures, and realize they must go back and do it again. The mood swings down. Recovery comes as the team learns from experience, makes another attempt, and gathers good, reliable data.

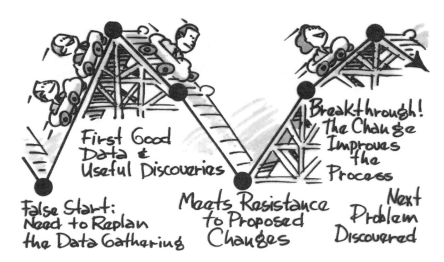

First Good Data & Useful Discoveries

Breakthrough! The Change Improves the Process

False Start: Need to Replan the Data Gathering

Meets Resistance to Proposed Changes

Next Problem Discovered

The pattern is different for each team. Team members' attitudes depend on both the speed of progress and the resistance or encouragement they receive from their manager or sponsor and their departments.

The best way to deal with this cycle is to understand and accept it with a "this too shall pass" attitude. Changes in attitude, just like growth stages, are normal. The team must cultivate patience. Eventually, everyone will better understand how the work unfolds and will be able to set a more realistic pace.

Teams can also take a more active approach to dealing with the stages and cycles they experience by learning when and how to avoid or work through group problems. The rest of this chapter describes approaches for improving the group's ability to solve and prevent problems.

For Ongoing Teams

Ongoing teams also experience highs and lows about the progress of their work. Initial excitement about defining how work will be done can shift into frustration or defensiveness as work methods are examined and changed. Recovery comes as the team learns to work together and as improved work methods remove daily hassles. Then new deadlines, adding or losing members, or other changes can cause the team to slip back into discouragement. Take time to review what's going on and give the team time to readjust.

Chapter 6

🗼 Ten Ingredients for a Successful Team

1. Clarity in team goals
2. An improvement plan
3. Clearly defined roles
4. Clear communication
5. Beneficial team behaviors
6. Well-defined decision procedures
7. Balanced participation
8. Established ground rules
9. Awareness of the group process
10. Use of the scientific approach

IV. Recipe for a Successful Team

No team exists without problems. But some teams—particularly those who have learned to counter the negative team dynamics—seem to be especially good at preventing many typical group problems. How close a team comes to this ideal depends on the following ten essential ingredients.

1. Clarity in Team Goals

A team works best when everyone understands its purpose and goals. If there is confusion or disagreement, they work to resolve the issues.

Ideally, the team:
- Agrees on its charter or mission, or works together to resolve disagreement
- Sees the charter as workable or, if necessary, narrows the charter to a workable size
- Has a clear vision and can progress steadily towards its goals
- Is clear about the larger project goals and about the purpose of individual steps, meetings, discussion, and decisions

Indicators of potential trouble
- Frequent switches in directions
- Frequent arguments about what the team should do next
- Feelings that the project is too big or inappropriate
- Frustration at lack of progress
- Excessive questioning of each decision or action
- Floundering

Recommendations

If team members feel they don't understand the charter or mission, try working through the exercise "Discussing Your Mission" (p. C-27). Emphasize the right of each team member to ask questions about a decision or event until satisfied with the answers. If you find the mission is too broad, work with the sponsor or manager to find something workable.

2. An Improvement Plan

Work plans help the team determine what advice, assistance, training, materials, and other resources it may need. They guide the team in determining schedules and identifying mileposts. The plans described in Chapter 5 are built from strategies that incorporate the scientific approach, which can be difficult for early teams.

Ideally, the team:

- Has created a work plan, revising it as needed
- Has a flowchart or similar document describing the steps of the work
- Refers to these documents when discussing what directions to take next
- Knows what resources and training are needed throughout the work, and plans accordingly

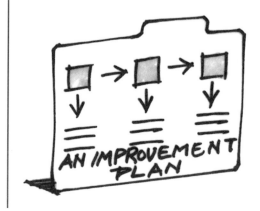

Indicators of potential trouble

- Uncertainty about the team's direction (the team muddles through each step without a clear idea of how to get the information it needs)

- Being "lost in the woods" (when one step is completed there is little or no idea of what to do next)

- "Fishing expeditions" (the team plunges ahead, hoping to stumble across improvement ideas)

- "Filling the sky with lead" (launching many activities without thinking about what each is supposed to do, hoping at least one will hit the target)

Recommendations

Seek assistance from a competent technical advisor. Work through the improvement plans in Chapter 5; ask yourselves what you need in order to fulfill your mission. Ask your guidance team to review or, if necessary, help formulate your plan.

3. Clearly Defined Roles

Teams operate most efficiently when they tap everyone's talents, and when all members understand their duties and know who is responsible for what issues and tasks.

Ideally, the team:

- Has formally designated roles (all members know what is expected of everyone, especially the leader, facilitator, technical expert, and coach)

- Understands which roles belong to one person and which are shared, and how the shared roles are switched (for instance, using an agreed-upon procedure to rotate the job of meeting facilitator)
- Uses each member's talents, and involves everyone in team activities so no one feels left out or taken advantage of

Indicators of potential trouble
- Roles and duty assignments that result from a pecking order
- Confusion over who is responsible for what
- People getting stuck with the same tedious chores

Recommendations
The team must decide on how roles will be assigned and changed. Review the role descriptions in Chapter 3 (pp. 3-14 to 3-22). Have the team leader discuss the responsibilities and roles of all involved with the team. The team leader might facilitate discussions on what duties must be assigned, how they will be assigned, and how they can be changed. Reach consensus about roles within the team.

4. Clear Communication

Good discussions depend on how well information is passed between team members.

Ideally, team members should:
- Speak with clarity and directness
- Be succinct; avoid long anecdotes and examples
- Listen actively; explore rather than debate each speaker's ideas
- Avoid interrupting and talking when others are speaking

Chapter 6

- Share information on many levels by offering:
  - **Sensing statements** ("I don't hear any disagreements with John's point. Do we all agree?")
  - **Thinking statements** ("There seems to be a correlation between the number of errors and the volume of work.")
  - **Feeling statements** ("I'm disappointed that no one has taken care of this yet.")
  - **Statements of intention** ("My question was not a criticism. I simply wanted more information.")
  - **Statements of action** ("Let's run a test on the machine using materials of different thickness.")

Indicators of potential trouble

- Poor speaking skills (mumbling, rambling, speaking too softly, little eye contact)
- Members are unable to say what they really feel; cautiousness; lots of tentative, conditional statements ("Do you think, maybe, that sometimes it might be that...")
- Everyone senses there is more going on than meets the eye; people's words do not match their tone of voice or mannerisms
- Opinions expressed as facts or phrased as questions
- "Plops": statements that receive no acknowledgment or response
- Bullying statements ("What you don't understand is...")
- Discounts ("That's not important. What's worse is...")

Recommendations

Develop communication skills, and learn to recognize problems that result from poor communication. Use the meeting evaluation to discuss

how well team members communicate. Have observers (team members or outsiders) watch the group and give honest feedback on communication dynamics (➡see Observing Group Process, p. C-19).

5. Beneficial Team Behaviors

Teams should encourage all members to use the skills and practices that make discussions and meetings more effective (⬅see pp. 4-2 to 4-25).

Ideally, team members should:
- Initiate discussions
- Seek information and opinions
- Suggest procedures for reaching a goal
- Clarify or elaborate on ideas
- Summarize
- Test for agreement
- Act as gatekeepers: direct conversational traffic, avoid simultaneous conversations, manage participation, make room for reserved talkers
- Keep the discussion from digressing
- Be creative in resolving differences
- Try to ease tension in the group and work through difficult matters
- Express the group's feeling and ask others to check that impression
- Get the group to agree on standards ("Do we all agree to discuss this for 15 minutes and no more?")
- Refer to documentation and data
- Praise and correct others with equal fairness; accept both praise and complaints

Chapter 6

Indicators of potential trouble

- Failure to use discussion skills
- Reliance on one person (the leader) to manage the discussion; no shared responsibility
- People repeating points, unsure whether anyone heard them the first time
- Discussions that are stuck; wheel-spinning; inability to let go of one topic and move onto the next
- Discussions in the hallway after the meeting that are more free and more candid than those during the meeting

Recommendations

Refer to Constructive Feedback, p. 6-23; Ten Common Problems and What to do About Them, p. 7-13; and the Meeting Skills Checklist, p. C-13. The team leader can also create an exercise out of effective discussion skills. For example, team members could pick two or three skills for the whole team to practice at a meeting, reviewing their performance during the meeting evaluation.

6. Well-defined Decision Procedures

You can tell a lot about how well a team is working by watching its decision-making process. A team should always be aware of the different ways it reaches decisions.

Ideally, the team should:

- Discuss how decisions will be made, such as when to take a poll or when to decide by consensus (are there times when a decision by only a few people is acceptable?)

- Explore important issues by polling (each member is asked to vote or state an opinion verbally or in writing)

- Test for agreement ("This seems to be our agreement. Is there anyone who feels unsure about the choice?")

- Use data as the basis of decisions

Indicators of potential trouble

- Conceding to opinions that are presented as facts with no supporting data

- Decisions by one or two people in the group, without team members agreeing to defer to their expertise

- Too-frequent recourse to "majority rules" or other easy approaches that bypass strong disagreement

- Decision by default; people do not respond to a statement (the "plop"); silence interpreted as consent

Chapter 6

Recommendations

Have the team leader (or, if appropriate, the coach) lead a discussion on decision making in the team. Occasionally designate a member or outsider to watch and give feedback on how decisions are made so the group can talk about necessary changes it needs to make (➧see Observing Group Process, p. C-19).

7. Balanced Participation

Since every team member has a stake in the group's achievements, everyone should participate in discussions and decisions, share commitment to the project's success, and contribute their talents.

Ideally, the team should:

- Have reasonably balanced participation, with all members contributing to most discussions
- Build on members' natural styles of participation

Indicators of potential trouble

- Some team members have too much influence; others, too little
- Participation depends on the subject being discussed (for example, only those who know the most about a subject are actively involved; others do not even ask questions)
- Members too often contribute only at certain times in a conversation or meeting
- Some members speak only about a certain topic ("hot buttons"—participation only when the subject touches, for example, money or training)

Recommendations

Use brainstorming (p. 4-14) and the nominal group technique (p. 4-16) to elicit input from all team members during discussions. If problems persist, adapt the Disruptive Group Behavior exercise (p. C-16) to your group.

8. Established Ground Rules

Teams invariably establish ground rules (or "norms") for what will and will not be tolerated in the team. A complete list of typical issues included in ground rules is given in Chapter 4 (pp. 4-37 to 4-38).

Ideally, the team should:

- Have open discussions regarding ground rules, where the group discusses what behaviors are acceptable and unacceptable

- Openly state or acknowledge norms ("We all agreed to decide the issue this way")

Indicators of potential trouble

- Certain important topics are avoided; too many subjects are taboo; conversations recur that are irrelevant to the task and harmful to the group

- No one acknowledges the norms; everyone acts as they *think* the group wants them to act; no one is able to say exactly what ground rules the team follows (for example, no one cracks jokes even though it was never stated that jokes would be out of place)

Chapter 6

- Recurring differences about what is or is not acceptable behavior
- Behavior that signifies irritation; for example, repeated disregard for starting and ending times
- Conflict over assumed norms or conflicting expectations

Recommendations

Right from the start, teams must take time to discuss and agree on obvious ground rules. From time to time, review the ground rules, adding, deleting, or revising them as needed. Particularly pay attention to current and possible ground rules during times of conflict and antagonism.

9. Awareness of the Group Process

Ideally, all team members will be aware of the group process—how the team works together—as well as pay attention to the context of the meeting.

Ideally, team members should:

- Be sensitive to nonverbal communication; for example, be aware that silence may indicate disagreement, or know that physical signs of agitation might indicate someone is uncomfortable with a discussion
- See, hear, and feel the team dynamics
- Comment and intervene to correct a group process problem
- Contribute equally to group process and meeting content
- Choose to work on group process issues and occasionally designate a team member or outsider to officially observe and report on group interactions at a meeting

Indicators of potential trouble

- Avoidance of undercurrent issues particularly when the group is having difficulty

- Pushing ahead on the task when there are nonverbal signs of resistance, confusion, or disappointment

- Inattention to obvious nonverbal clues and shifts in the team's mood

- Members attributing motives to nonverbal behavior ("You've been quiet during the last 30 minutes. You must not be interested in what's being said.")

- Remarks that discount someone's behavior or contribution ("Let's get on with the task and stop talking about that stuff.")

Recommendations

Use the series of observation formats described in "Observing Group Process" (starting on p. C-19) to work through pertinent team issues before they become a problem. Use the coach as an observer to evaluate how well the team handles problems, confusion, discussions, and so forth. Encourage the team to have several "process checks," times when members can say how they think the meeting is going, or express thoughts for which there are no appropriate times in the meeting. Routinely include group process issues in meeting evaluations.

Chapter 6

10. Use of the Scientific Approach

Teams that use a scientific approach have a much easier time arriving at permanent solutions to problems. Failure to use a scientific approach can lessen the team's chance for success. The scientific approach helps avoid many team problems and disagreements. Many arguments are between individuals with strong opinions. The scientific approach insists that opinions be supported by, or at least defer to, data.

Ideally, the team should:

- Ask to see data before making decisions and question anyone who tries to act on hunches alone

- Use basic statistical tools to investigate problems and to gather and analyze data

- Dig for root causes of problems

- Seek permanent solutions rather than rely on quick fixes

Indicators of potential trouble

- Team members insist they don't need data because their intelligence and experience are enough to tell them what the problems and solutions are

- Wild stabs at supposed solutions: jumping to conclusions, too many inferences and assumptions, shooting from the hip

- Hasty action, a "ready, *fire*, aim!" approach

Recommendations

Make sure the team has access to an expert for training and guidance (usually this is the coach or quality advisor). Every team should talk about the importance of using a scientific approach, especially when decisions or actions are needed.

V. Constructive Feedback

A fundamental message of this handbook is that no matter what pressures a team encounters, it can work hard at its task *and* support members' needs. The single most important skill to have in working through any problem is the ability to give constructive feedback.

Why? Because most often problems are expressed as criticism of someone's action. When you are criticized by someone, it is difficult to know what to do. A common reaction is to feel critical of them. "What right do they have to criticize *me?*" Suppose it is you reacting negatively to behavior that truly disrupts the team's progress. Do you sit on your negative feelings for the sake of group harmony? Is there a way to express dissatisfaction without provoking a confrontation that might disrupt the team even more?

There are proven methods for giving and receiving criticism, methods that work equally well for giving and receiving praise. The goals are to give constructive feedback, whether positive or negative, and to make sure that any feedback you receive is constructive. While there is no guarantee, following the guidelines below will minimize the possibility of provoking a bad scene. Use them to help you decide when to give feedback, how to tell a person or team what you think, and how to listen to feedback given to you.

Chapter 6

Guidelines for Constructive Feedback

- Acknowledge the need for feedback
- Give both positive and negative feedback
- Understand the context
- Know when to give feedback
- Know how to give feedback
    - Be descriptive
    - Don't use labels
    - Don't exaggerate
    - Don't be judgmental
    - Speak for yourself
    - Talk first about yourself, not about the other person
    - Phrase the issue as a statement, not a question
    - Restrict your feedback to things you know for certain
    - Help people hear and accept your compliments when giving positive feedback
- Know how to receive feedback
    - Breathe
    - Listen carefully
    - Ask questions for clarity
    - Acknowledge the feedback
    - Acknowledge valid points
    - Take time to sort out what you heard

Guidelines for Constructive Feedback

Useful feedback comes in several forms. *Statistical data* provides feedback from a process, measurements that tell you how well a process is running, whether changes you tried were effective, and so forth. *Market research* provides feedback from customers, telling you how well your organization is doing and whether your product or service meets customers' needs. The most common form of feedback (and our focus here) is simply *one person talking to another.*

Many people know that to get good data or useful market information you must plan carefully and follow established rules and guidelines. Few people know that the same ideas apply to person-to-person feedback. Thinking ahead of time about what you are going to say and how you are going to say it, and following the guidelines given below, will increase the value of what you say to another person.

To make personal feedback constructive, you must:

Acknowledge the need for feedback

The first thing to recognize is the value of giving feedback, both positive and negative. Feedback is vital to any organization committed to improving itself, for it is the only way to know what needs to be improved. Giving and receiving feedback should be more than just a part of a team member's behavior; it should be part of the whole organization's culture.

You will need good feedback skills to improve your team meetings, and, more generally, interactions between team members. These skills will also help you communicate more effectively with customers and suppliers (both internal and external). In fact, you will find many opportunities to apply these skills in your work. First, however, your team should agree that giving and receiving feedback is an acceptable part of how you will improve the way you work together. This agreement is necessary so that no one is surprised when he or she receives feedback.

Give both positive and negative feedback

Many people take good work for granted and give feedback only when there are problems. This is a bad policy. People will more likely pay attention to your complaints if they have also received your compliments. It is important to remember to tell people when they have done something well.

Understand the context

The most important characteristic of feedback is that it always has a context: where it happened, why it happened, what led up to the event. You never simply walk up to a person, deliver a feedback statement, and then leave. Before you give feedback, review the actions and decisions that led up to the moment.

Know when to give feedback

Before giving feedback, determine whether the moment is right. You must consider more than your own need to give feedback. Constructive feedback can happen only within a context of listening to and caring about the person.

Do not give feedback when:

– You don't know much about the circumstances of the behavior.

Chapter 6

– You don't care about the person or will not be around long enough to follow up on the aftermath of your feedback. Hit-and-run feedback is not fair.

– The feedback is about something the person has no power to change.

– The other person seems low in self-esteem.

– You are low in self-esteem.

– Your purpose is not really improvement, but to put someone on the spot ("gotcha!"), or demonstrate how smart or how much more responsible you are.

– The time, place, or circumstances are inappropriate (for example, in the presence of outsiders).

– Your emotions or theirs are still running high.

Know how to give feedback

If the circumstances are appropriate for giving feedback, use the following guidelines for compliments as well as complaints. Use the "Easy-to-Remember Guide for Giving Constructive Feedback" (facing page) the first few times—though it may feel awkward, you will soon get more comfortable and be able to give constructive feedback without having to refer to the guide.

– **Be descriptive**

Relate, as objectively as possible, what you saw the other person do or what you heard the other person say. Give specific examples, the more recent, the better. Examples from the distant past are more likely to lead to disagreement over "facts."

An Easy-to-Remember Guide for Giving Constructive Feedback

Sequence	Explanation
1. "When you..."	Start with a "When you..." statement that describes the behavior without judgment, exaggeration, labeling, attribution, or motives. Just state the facts as specifically as possible.
2. "I feel..."	Tell how the behavior affects you. If you need more than a word or two to describe the feeling, it's probably just some variation of joy, sorrow, anger, or fear.
3. "Because I..."	Now say why you are affected that way. Describe the connection between the facts you observed and the feelings they provoke in you.
(4. Pause for discussion)	Let the other person respond.
5. "I would like..."	Describe the change you want the other person to consider...
6. "Because..."	...and why you think the change will alleviate the problem.
7. "What do you think?"	Listen to the other person's response. Be prepared to discuss options and compromise on a solution.

How the feedback will work:

When you [do this], I feel [this way], because [of such and such]. (Pause.) What I would like you to consider is [doing X], because I think it will accomplish [Y]. What do you think?

Example:

"When you are late for meetings, I get angry because I think it is wasting the time of all the other team members and we are never able to get through our agenda items. (Pause.) I would like you to consider finding some way of planning your schedule that lets you get to these meetings on time. That way we can be more productive at the meetings and we can all keep to our tight schedules."

Chapter 6

– **Don't use labels**

Be clear, specific and unambiguous. Words like "immature," "unprofessional," "irresponsible," and "prejudiced" are labels we attach to sets of behaviors. Describe the behavior and drop the labels. For example, say, "You missed the deadline we had all agreed to meet" rather than, "You're being irresponsible and I want to know what you're going to do about it!"

– **Don't exaggerate**

Be exact: To say, "You're always late for deadlines" is probably untrue and, therefore, unfair. It invites the feedback receiver to argue with the exaggeration rather than respond to the real issue.

– **Don't be judgmental**

Or at least don't use the rhetoric of judgment. Words like "good," "better," "bad," "worst," and "should" place you in the role of a controlling parent. This invites the person receiving your comments to respond as a child. When that happens, and it will most of the time, the possibility of constructive feedback is lost.

– **Speak for yourself**

Don't refer to absent, anonymous people. Avoid such references as, "A lot of people here don't like it when you...." Don't allow yourself to be a conduit for other people's complaints. Instead, encourage others to speak for themselves.

– Talk first about yourself, not about the other person

Use a statement with the word "I" as the subject, not the word "you." This guideline is one of the most important and one of the most surprising. Consider the following examples regarding lateness:

1. "You are frequently late for meetings."
2. "You are very prompt for meetings."
3. "I feel annoyed when you are late for meetings."
4. "I appreciate your coming to meetings on time."

Statements 1 and 2 are "you" statements. People become defensive around "you" statements and are less likely to hear what you say when it is phrased this way. Statements 3 and 4 are "I" messages and create an adult/peer relationship. People are more likely to remain open to your message when an "I" statement is used. Even if your rank is higher than the feedback recipient, strive for an adult/peer relationship. Use "I" statements so that the effectiveness of your comments is not lost.

– Phrase the issue as a statement, not a question

Contrast "When are you going to stop being late for meetings?" with "I feel annoyed when you are late for meetings." The question is controlling and manipulative because it implies, "You, the responder, are expected to adjust your behavior to accommodate me, the questioner." Most people become defensive and angry when spoken to in this way. On the other hand, the "I" statement implies, "I think we have an issue we must resolve together." The "I" statement allows the receiver to see what effect the behavior had on you.

Chapter 6

– **Restrict your feedback to things you know for certain**
Don't present your opinions as facts. Speak only of what you saw and heard and what you feel and want.

– **Help people hear and accept your compliments when giving positive feedback**
Many people feel awkward when told good things about themselves and will fend off the compliment. ("Oh, it wasn't that big a deal. Others worked on it as much as I did.") Sometimes they will change the subject. It may be important to reinforce the positive feedback and help the person hear it, acknowledge it, and accept it.

Know how to receive feedback

There may be a time when you receive feedback from someone who does not know feedback guidelines. In these cases, *help your critic refashion the criticism* so that it conforms to the rules for constructive feedback. ("What did I say or do to dissatisfy you?") When reacting to feedback:

– **Breathe**
This is simple but effective advice. Our bodies are conditioned to react to stressful situations as though they were physical assaults. Our muscles tense. We start breathing rapidly and shallowly. Taking full, deep breaths forces your body to relax and allows your brain to maintain greater alertness.

– **Listen carefully**
Don't interrupt. Don't discourage the feedback-giver.

– Ask questions for clarity

You have a right to receive clear feedback. Ask for specific examples. ("Can you describe what I do or say that makes me appear aggressive to you?")

– Acknowledge the feedback

Paraphrase the message in your own words to let the person know you have heard and understood what was said.

– Acknowledge valid points

Agree with what is true. Agree with what is possible. Acknowledge the other person's point of view ("I understand how you might get that impression") and try to understand their reaction.

Agreeing with what's true or possible does not mean you agree to change your behavior. You can agree, for instance, that sometimes you jump too quickly to a conclusion without implying that you will slow down your conclusion-making process. Agreeing with what's true or possible also does not mean agreeing with any value judgment about you. You can agree that your reports have been late without thereby agreeing that you are irresponsible.

– Take time to sort out what you heard

You may need time for sorting out or checking with others before responding to the feedback. It is reasonable to ask the feedback-giver for time to think about what was said and how you feel about it. Make a specific appointment for getting back to him or her. Don't use this time as an excuse to avoid the issue.

Chapter 6

Summary

In this chapter we have discussed some of the human dynamics that underlie the work of teams. For better or for worse, when people work together, more than the task itself occupies their energies. In this chapter we have discussed a variety of non-task issues and concerns, while at the same time suggesting ways to prevent and cope with them. Frequently the difference between teams that achieve their goals, and teams that break down before they get there is that the successful teams have gained mastery over the "people issues" covered in this chapter. In Chapter 7, we will be exploring what to do if, in spite of your efforts at prevention, serious problems emerge as the team strives to achieve its goals.

Chapter 7
Dealing With Conflict

It would be nice to say that if you follow the advice in this handbook, you will never run into problems. But we all know that simply isn't true. Sometimes things go wrong, and as a result, the work suffers. Miscommunications happen. Quarreling breaks out in the ranks. The excitement when hard work pays off dissolves into frustration and anger when progress stops because of disagreements or confusion. It's not easy to know when a problem your team is having is something that is normal and will pass, and when it's something that needs special attention. This chapter describes some common team problems that usually need attention and offers advice on what to do about them.

I. The Value of Conflict

Whenever people work together, conflict is likely. Since many people associate conflict with stress, tension, and anger, it's not surprising that conflict is often viewed as a disease that should be stamped out. However, conflict can actually be of value to a working team. It can help a team by increasing the energy level, and by providing greater creativity through a diversity of viewpoints. It can also add depth to discussions; members are challenged to elaborate their ideas so that others understand them better. Another benefit is that more effective solutions result because more diverse perspectives are taken into account. Conflict that is part of critically examining ideas is necessary for good decisions.

The Danger of Too Much Agreement

Even though conflict and disagreement can be beneficial to a team, many people seem to fear and avoid it. In fact, for many, the definition of a good team might be one with no conflicts among its members. When team members want to get along above all else, there is a danger that

What You Will Find Here

In this chapter we explore:

Chapter 7

"groupthink" can occur. In groupthink, everyone goes along with a proposal even when they secretly have reservations about it. The danger, of course, is that groupthink can lead to very bad decisions, since the decisions are not thoroughly examined and tested against reality. Sometimes members of a team think it is so important for everyone to agree that they pressure anyone who suggests an alternative viewpoint to withdraw their idea from the discussion. *If too much agreement is a risk for your team,* stirring up a little controversy may be just the right thing for a leader to do.

II. Understanding Your Responses to Conflict

Avoiding groupthink requires team members to be able to constructively disagree with one another. To do this involves understanding and believing the following:

- Conflict is natural and can be valuable
- Conflict can be a source of energy
- Conflict is a result of real differences
- Different perspectives are often necessary for breakthrough thinking
- One's views and habits in handling conflict are important determinants of the outcomes of a conflict
- Mastering skills in managing conflict takes lots of practice

Groupthink

When team members want to get along above all else, there is a danger that "groupthink" can occur. This means that critical information is withheld from the team because individual members censor themselves, deciding that their concerns are not worth discussing. Ideas are accepted without careful consideration of the pros and cons. Sometimes members pressure anyone who suggests an alternative viewpoint to withdraw their idea from the discussion. Also, some members might see themselves as maintaining the team's "togetherness" by protecting the team from outside information that might challenge the team's thinking.

How to recognize groupthink

- Once a position is outlined, especially by someone with power or authority on the team, everyone focuses on why the position is the right one. No one raises objections. There is an insufficient examination of risks or weaknesses.

- No alternatives are offered.

- If different perspectives are offered, they are quickly dismissed.

- Options that were rejected during discussion are never brought up again for reevaluation.

- Information that might challenge the team's thinking is not actively sought (the team thinks it knows all it needs to know).

Conditions for groupthink

Irving Janis, who originally developed the theory of groupthink to explain some disastrous presidential decisions, identified the following conditions that encourage groupthink.

- The team has a high level of agreement and cohesiveness among its members. Team members are very similar to one another. There is little diversity in background, experience, or beliefs.

- The team is isolated from sources of information that might contradict its emerging opinions.

- The team leader states his or her opinions early in the discussion rather than waiting until the team has developed some of its own thinking.

- The team leader encourages members to agree with the leader's position instead of encouraging critical discussion of all options.

- The team does not have methods or procedures that require data collection and reality checking of options, and therefore the team chooses a closed-minded path that is relatively free of criticism and conflict.

How to prevent groupthink

Have the team agree to follow the scientific method. Gather data to help understand the nature and potential causes of the problem before jumping to solutions.

Have a group norm of brainstorming a list of alternatives before discussing any course of action in detail. (◀See Chapter 4, pp. 4-13 and 4-14, on the exploratory phase of discussion.)

Team leaders or members with positions of power should not state their opinions and positions at the beginning of discussion.

Invite outside experts to share their knowledge with the group. Actively search for information that does not support the preferred course of action or the evolving decisions.

Develop a list of criteria against which to evaluate all the options.

Once an option is selected, ask the team to brainstorm everything that could go wrong with that choice. Discuss ways of assessing risks and preventing potential problems that have been identified. Decide whether or not additional information is needed.

Once a solution has been selected, require the team to develop a second solution to the problem. Often the second solution is more creative and robust than the first one developed.

Chapter 7

Common Responses to Conflict

- Avoiding
- Smoothing
- Forcing
- Compromising
- Problem solving

Common Responses to Conflict

How conflict affects the team depends on how members respond to it. Different people use different strategies for handling conflicts. Often these strategies are habitual, and often we are unaware of what our habitual responses are. In order to choose an appropriate strategy it is important to understand the responses that come to us naturally as well as to be aware of new behaviors that may be valuable to adopt.

In assessing your response to conflict, ask yourself two questions. First of all, how important to you is the opinion, goal, or perspective under discussion? Secondly, how important to you is it to maintain good relationships with the people with whom you are in conflict? The balance between these two issues is played out in the following common responses to conflict:

1. **Avoiding** the conflict. This strategy involves avoiding both the issues that are likely to lead to conflict, and the people with whom you are likely to be in conflict. Fundamentally this strategy is based on a belief that it is easier to avoid conflict than to face it.

2. **Smoothing** over the conflict. This strategy focuses on minimizing the conflict so that group relationships will not be strained. Underlying this strategy is the belief that discussing conflicts damages relationships rather than strengthens them. This approach sacrifices personal opinions and goals out of fear of losing the relationship.

Both avoiding the conflict and smoothing it over are ways of suppressing conflict. Tactics include:
- Denying that there is a problem
- Smoothing over the issue or problem
- Changing the topic or focus to avoid the issue or problem
- Ignoring the feelings you have about the issue or problem

The problem with suppressing or avoiding conflict, however, is that when you simply "put a lid on it," it tends to simmer under the surface and undermine the work of the team.

3. **Forcing** the conflict. This strategy attempts to overpower others and force them to accept your position. In this strategy personal opinions and goals are very important and relationships with others are less important. This is a competitive, win-lose approach to conflict. Forcing escalates a conflict that already exists and increases the likelihood of conflict emerging later. Some typical tactics in this category are:

   – Attacking others' ideas
   – Using your expertise, position, or experience to overpower others

4. **Compromising**. This strategy tries to get others to give up some of what they want in exchange for giving up some of what you want. The idea here is that everyone gives up something and everyone gains something. This can be a lose-lose strategy because no one achieves their goal. Everyone gives up something and might resent doing so. The underlying assumption in compromise is that everyone should accept less than they want because that is the best they can hope for. Sometimes compromise may be the best tactic to use, but usually that is after problem solving has not worked.

5. **Problem solving** through the conflict. This is a win-win approach. Both personal goals and group relationships are highly valued. The purpose of the approach is to find the path forward that meets everyone's goals, and, by doing so, preserve group relationships.

Chapter 7

Problem solving includes strategies aimed at taking diverse viewpoints into account, clarifying the issues, clearing the air constructively, and enabling everyone to move forward together. Some typical tactics in this category are:

- Stating your views about the issue or problem in clear, non-judgmental language

- Clarifying the core issue(s) by sorting out areas of agreement from areas of disagreement

- Listening carefully to each person's point of view

- Periodically checking your understanding of the disagreement by stating the core issues in your own words

- Using techniques such as circling the group for comments and having some silent "thinking" time when emotions run high

One reason to become aware of your habitual responses to conflict is that the awareness opens you to having a choice about how to respond. For example, once you are aware that you always try to smooth over potential conflicts, you can try to understand why that is your habitual choice. What feelings and assumptions are behind the habit? You can experiment with other behaviors to broaden your repertoire. The problem with habits is precisely that—they are habits. That means we will tend to use habitual behaviors whenever conflict emerges, or whenever we think it might emerge, regardless of whether our habitual behaviors are appropriate, or whether they are likely to meet our needs. Becoming aware of habits and learning a range of behaviors to use in conflict situations allows us to choose the behaviors that are most likely to meet our goals in that situation.

Chapter 7

III. Guidelines for Managing Group Problems

Regardless of how well we try to manage conflict, sometimes disagreements can become highly emotional. Members polarize; legitimate differences of opinion become win-lose struggles, and progress is stopped. Occasionally an individual's behavior may disrupt the team, or the entire team behaves in ways that prevent work from getting done. In these cases, the problem should be dealt with so the team can get back to work.

Dealing With Group Problems

Generally, the best way to deal with problems is to do the following:

- **Anticipate and prevent problems whenever possible**
  As noted in Chapter 6, most problems can be anticipated or prevented if a group spends time developing itself into a team: getting to know each other, establishing ground rules, and discussing norms for group behavior. If you do this when your team starts, you will save time, and prevent hassles, frustrations, and animosities.

- **Think of each problem as a group problem**
  A natural tendency is to blame individuals for causing problems. Remember, most problems are attributable to the system, not the individual. The truth is that many problems arise because the group lets them happen or even encourages them in some way. Examine each problem in light of what the group does to encourage or allow the behavior and what the group can do differently to encourage more constructive behavior. Assume that the problem continues to exist because it somehow benefits the group. What could that

 **Dealing With Group Problems**

- Anticipate and prevent problems whenever possible

- Think of each problem as a group problem

- Neither overreact nor underreact. A leader's range of responses typically includes:
  – Do nothing (nonintervention)
  – Off-line conversation (minimal intervention)
  – Impersonal group time (low intervention)
  – Off-line confrontation (medium intervention)
  – In-group confrontation (high intervention)
  – Expulsion from the group (**Rarely Use This Option**)

Chapter 7

hidden benefit be? How have group members contributed to the continuation of the problem?

- **Neither overreact nor underreact**

  Some behaviors are only fleeting disruptions in the team's progress. These are usually not a problem and sometimes even give a needed break in the activity. Other behaviors are very disruptive and impede, halt, or reverse the team's progress towards its goals. Some behaviors are chronic, occurring over and over again. The team leader should respond appropriately to the seriousness of the problem, ignoring fleeting disruptions, and confronting chronic or serious disruptions directly. Experienced leaders develop a range of responses to typical problems. This way they can "crank up" the response as a problem gets more disruptive and the team realizes the seriousness of the situation.

  ### A leader's range of responses typically includes:
  #### – Do nothing (nonintervention)

  Ignore the offensive behavior, particularly if it is not a chronic problem or doesn't seem to inhibit the group. Sometimes the leader need not intervene because other group members will deal with the offending behavior. In such cases, the leader is available to facilitate the discussion that is provoked when one member confronts another.

  #### – Off-line conversation (minimal intervention)

  Talk to the disruptive members outside the group meeting, asking them what would increase their satisfaction with the group. Give constructive feedback.

– Impersonal group time (low intervention)

At the start of a meeting, talk about general group process concerns without pointing out individuals, perhaps by going through a list written on a flipchart. Include the disruptive behavior on the list. During the critique at the end of the meeting, the group evaluates itself on each item on the list. It is usually difficult to deal with problems without referring to the offenders. Sometimes not referring to the specific offenders is awkward and phony. One way to get around this is to describe the context of the problem (such as, "Every time we talk about subject X, we get sidetracked"). Focus attention on how the group encourages the problem and what the group can do to discourage it. This approach treats all problems as group process problems rather than offenses by individuals.

– Off-line confrontation (medium intervention)

Off-line confrontation is similar to off-line conversation except the leader is more assertive. Use it when other attempts have failed, especially when the disruptive behavior continues even when the group has tried to change. Sometimes this confrontation may lead to an informal "contract" regarding agreed-upon changes in the leader's and member's behavior. (For example, "I know you don't get along with Joe and I will do everything I can to avoid pairing you up on assignments. For your part I want you to stop being critical of him during team meetings.")

Chapter 7

– In-group confrontation (high intervention)

As a last resort, after other approaches have failed, the leader may deal with the offending behavior in the presence of the group. This disrupts the group's other business and exposes an individual's behavior to open critique in the group. This tactic can be effective; it can also be disastrous. The leader must prepare carefully for this intervention: how to word the confrontation, what reactions to anticipate, how to avoid defensiveness or hostility in the offending member. Use constructive feedback techniques, expressing feelings as "I statements" (◀see p. 6-24). The purpose of high intervention is to change the offensive behavior, not to punish the offending member.

– Expulsion from the group (very high intervention)

We believe that you should rarely kick anyone off a team. We recommend against expulsion for several reasons. It can create a stigma that remains with the team and with the expelled member for a long time. The costs of expelling a member include ill will, creating an adversary, and creating an unfavorable impression of the team among others in the organization.

What can a team leader do when highly disruptive behavior continues? One of the best strategies is to talk privately with the offending team member, pointing out that disruptive behavior seems inconsistent with a commitment to help the team succeed. If the person would rather not attend meetings, find other ways to allow his or her input into the team's work.

Conflict Intervention

As a team leader or coach, you may need to intervene in a conflict if team members cannot manage it themselves. Here are some questions to help you think through your decisions to intervene:

- Do you have enough credibility to intervene?
- Can you remain neutral?
- How much time, energy, and skill is needed for success? Do you have these resources?
- Can you select one issue or element of the conflict which might be manageable?
- Is the timing right?
- Is not intervening riskier than intervening?

Tactics for conflict intervention

To make an intervention effective, you must carefully structure the environment in which it takes place. To do this:

- Select neutral territory
- Make sure the setting is informal
- Make sure all appropriate people are present
- Set an agenda and ground rules; stick to them
- Manage the time carefully
- Use active listening and constructive feedback skills throughout the intervention

Chapter 7

Once the meeting is underway, referee the process conscientiously, and limit the participants to short, equal exchanges. When the exchanges are complete, try to restate the views and issues in neutral terms. This helps all participants hear and understand the key elements of the conflict. Try to help uncover the core issue in the conflict, and move the participants toward a resolution.

Controlling conflict triggers

Sometimes a conflict is severe enough that it requires specific action on the part of a team leader or coach to steer the team off dangerous ground toward more productive territory.

Using triggers, such as highly emotional language, sarcasm, ignoring someone, or attacking someone's values, escalates conflict. One way to suppress or contain a conflict is to try to control the triggers. One example of this would be to avoid a topic, or to be careful to use neutral language when discussing a topic to avoid triggering someone else's emotions about the issue. Or, if someone else has made an inflammatory statement, you could reframe it more neutrally for the team.

On the other hand, when you want to bring a conflict into the open for resolution, you might use a trigger so that members can explore their differences in a constructive way (for example, stating a difference in values to bring out a range of perspectives).

IV. Ten Common Problems and What to Do About Them

One way to deal with team problems, particularly those arising from unspoken issues, such as competing loyalties to the team and work groups, is to talk about them. Most problems, though, require a more structured solution. The following examples show how to use the guidelines for constructive feedback (◄see p. 6-24) and working through common team problems.

1. Floundering

Teams commonly have trouble starting and ending a project, or even moving between different project stages. They flounder, wondering what actions to take next. At the beginning, they sometimes suffer through false starts and directionless discussions and activities. As the team progresses, team members sometimes resist moving from one phase or step to the next. At the end, teams may delay unnecessarily, postponing decisions or conclusions because "We need something else. We're not ready to finish this yet."

Problems at the beginning suggest that the team is either unclear about or overwhelmed by its task. Start-up problems may also indicate team members are not yet comfortable enough with each other to engage in real discussion and decision making.

Floundering when trying to make decisions may indicate that the team's work is not really the product of consensus, and that in fact, some members are reluctant to say they don't support the team's conclusions.

 **Ten Common Problems**

- Floundering
- Overbearing participants
- Dominating participants
- Reluctant participants
- Unquestioned acceptance of opinions as facts
- Rush to accomplishment
- Attribution
- Discounts and "plops"
- Wanderlust: digression and tangents
- Feuding team members

Chapter 7

Floundering after completing one phase of a project or task could mean the team does not have a clear plan and does not know what steps to take next. Floundering at the end of a project usually indicates that the team members have developed a bond and are reluctant to separate. Or, perhaps, they are reluctant to expose their work to review and possible criticism from outsiders.

How a team leader can deal with floundering

- "Let's review how this project is being run." Review your improvement plan (Chapter 5), or create a plan if you don't already have one. Use a planning grid (◀see p. 4-32) to stimulate discussion.

- "Let's review our mission and make sure it's clear to everyone."

- "Let's go over our work plan and see what we have to do next."

- "What do we need to do so we can move on? What is holding us up?" (Data? Knowledge? Assurances? Support? Feelings?)

- "Are we getting stuck because we have previous business that is unfinished? Does anyone feel we have missed something or left something incomplete?"

- "Let's reserve time at the next meeting to discuss how we will proceed. Meanwhile, I suggest that each of us writes down what we think is needed to move to the next stage."

Overbearing Participants...

Seem to hold an unusual amount of influence in a team, often because they have a higher rank in the company or in-depth technical knowledge.

2. Overbearing Participants

Some members wield a disproportionate amount of influence in a team. These people usually have a position of authority or an area of expertise on which they base their authority. Teams need authorities and experts because these are important resources. Most teams benefit from their participation. But the presence of an authority or an expert is detrimental when the person:

- **Discourages or forbids discussion encroaching on his or her area of authority or expertise**. ("You need not get involved in those technicalities. We are taking care of that. Let's move on to something else.")

- **Signals the "untouchability" of an area** by using technical jargon or referring to present specifications, standards, regulations, or policies as the ultimate determinants of future actions. ("What you don't understand is that PP85271 requires a bimordial interface between the cragstop and any abutting AC135.")

- **Regularly discounts any proposed activity by declaring that it won't work**, or cites instances when it was tried unsuccessfully in the past. Other members soon get the message that their suggestions will be seen as trite or naive. ("We tried that in Johnstown in 1968. It was a disaster! Steer clear of that solution.")

How a team leader can deal with overbearing participants

- Reinforce the agreement that no area is sacred; team members have the right to explore any area that pertains to the project.

- Get the overbearing participant to agree (before the project starts, if possible) that it is important for all members to understand the process and operation. The expert may occasionally be asked to instruct the team, to share knowledge or a broader perspective.

Chapter 7

Dominating Participants...

Like to hear themselves talk, and rarely give others a chance to contribute.

- Talk to the expert off-line, and ask for cooperation and patience.
- Enforce the primacy of data and the scientific approach. ("In God we trust. All others must have data!")

3. Dominating Participants

Some members, with or without authority or expertise, consume a disproportionate amount of "air time." They talk too much. Instead of concise statements, they tell overlong anecdotes and dominate the meeting. Normal moments of silence that occasionally occur are an invitation for the dominator to talk. Their talk inhibits the team from building a sense of team accomplishment or momentum. Other members get discouraged and find excuses for missing meetings.

How a team leader can deal with dominating participants

- Structure discussion on key issues to encourage equal participation. For example, have members write down their thoughts and share them around the table.
- List "balance of participation" as a general concern to critique during the meeting evaluation.
- Practice gatekeeping: "We've heard from you on this, Joe. I'd like to hear what others have to say."
- Get the team to agree on the value of balanced participation and the need for limits and focus in discussions.

Reluctant Participants...

Feel shy or unsure of themselves and must be encouraged to contribute.

4. Reluctant Participants

Many teams have one or two members who rarely speak. They are the opposites of the dominators. When invited to speak, these "underbearing" members commonly say, "I am participating; I listen to everything that's said. When I have something to say, I'll say it."

Each of us has a different threshold of need to be part of a team ("tribal" instincts versus "loner" instincts) and a different level of comfort with speaking in a group (extrovert versus introvert). There is nothing right or wrong about being tribal or a loner, extroverted or introverted; these are just differences among people. Problems develop in a team when there are no built-in activities that encourage the introverts to participate and the extroverts to listen.

How a team leader can deal with reluctant participants

- As with dominating participants, structure discussion to encourage equal participation.

- When possible, divide the task into individual assignments and reports.

- Act as a gatekeeper: "Does anyone else have ideas about this?" (asked while looking at the reluctant participant); more directly, "Sam, what is your experience with this area?"

5. *Unquestioned Acceptance of Opinions as Facts*

Some team members express personal beliefs and assumptions with such confidence that listeners assume they are hearing a presentation of facts. This can be dangerous, leading to an unshakable acceptance of various "earth-is-flat" assertions.

Most team members are reluctant to question self-assured statements, such as "customers want it that way," from other members. Besides not wanting to be impolite, they think they need to have data before they challenge someone else's assertions. Worse yet, the skeptic could be wrong and lose face with the team.

There is an ancient axiom of debate that says if a speaker presents something as fact without legitimate supporting evidence, the listener need not have evidence to respond with skepticism.

How a team leader can deal with unquestioned acceptance of opinions as facts

- "Is what you said an opinion or a fact? Do you have data?"
- "How do you know that is true?"
- "Let's accept what you say as possible, but let's also get some data to test it."
- "Let's have the team agree on the primacy of the scientific approach."

Rush to Accomplishment...

Is common to teams being pushed by one or more members who are impatient for results and unwilling to work through the necessary steps of the scientific approach.

6. Rush to Accomplishment

Many teams will have at least one "do something" member who is either impatient or sensitive to pressure from managers or other influential people or groups. This type of person typically reaches an individual decision about a problem and its solution before the group has had time to consider different options. They urge the team to make hasty decisions and discourage any further efforts to analyze or discuss the matter. Their nonverbal behavior, direct statements, and "throw away" expressions constantly communicate impatience.

Too much of this pressure can lead a team to a series of random, hasty decisions. Like hunters shooting at dim targets in a heavy fog, they are satisfied that they're "doing something" and pray that at least one shot will hit the target.

Teams must realize that results do not come easily, and rarely can they make significant gains overnight. Quality takes patience.

How a team leader can deal with a rush to accomplishment

- Remind team members of their prior agreement that the scientific approach will not be compromised or circumvented.
- Make sure the team leader is not among those exerting the pressure.
- Confront the rusher using the techniques of constructive feedback. Give examples of rushing and describe the effect of this impatience on the team's work.

7. *Attribution*

As individuals and teams, we tend to attribute motives to people when we disagree with or don't understand their opinion or behavior. Through attribution we try to bring order and meaning into apparent disorder and confusion.

However, attribution is a substitute for the hard work of seeking real explanations. It also creates resentment: it is perfectly normal to bristle when someone else tells you that they know what makes you tick or tries to explain your motives.

Within a team, attribution can lead to hostility when aimed at another team member ("He's just trying to take the easy way out"). When aimed at individuals or teams outside of the team, attribution can lead to misguided efforts. ("They won't want to get involved. They're just waiting 'til they can collect their pension.")

How a team leader can deal with attribution

- Reaffirm prior agreement on the primacy of the scientific approach.
- Identify and respond to a statement of attribution: "That may well explain why they behave the way they do. But how do we know? What has anyone seen or heard that indicates this? Can we confirm that with data?"
- If the attribution is from one member to another, don't let it go by without checking it out: "Jim, I heard Sally describe your approach as 'catering to the other side.' How would you describe it?"

Discounts and "Plops"...

Arise when team members fail to give credit to another's opinions. They are likely to ignore this person's contributions.

8. Discounts and "Plops"

We all have certain values or perspectives that are important to us at conscious or unconscious levels. When someone else ignores or ridicules these values, we feel discounted. Being discounted can cause hostility on a team, especially if it happens frequently.

For instance, there will be times on every team when someone makes a statement that "plops." No one acknowledges it, and the discussion picks up on a subject totally irrelevant to the statement, leaving the speaker to wonder why there was no response.

Discounts happen for many reasons. Perhaps the discounted member said something irrelevant to the team's discussion, or did not clearly state the idea. Perhaps the rest of the team missed the meaning in the statement. No matter what the reason, every member deserves respect and attention from the team. Teams must help discounted members identify and articulate what is important to them.

How a team leader can deal with discounts and plops

- Include training in active listening and other constructive behaviors early in the team's life.

- Support the discounted person. "Nancy, it sounds like that is important to you and we aren't giving it enough consideration"; "I think what Jerry said is worthwhile and we should spend time on it before we move on"; "Bill, before we move on is there some part of what you said that you would like the group to discuss?"

- Talk off-line with anyone who frequently discounts, puts down, or ignores previous speakers' statements. Use the guidelines for constructive feedback (◄ see p. 6-24).

Chapter 7

Wanderlust...

Happens when team members lose track of the meeting's purpose or want to avoid a sensitive topic. Discussions then wander off in many directions at once.

9. Wanderlust: Digression and Tangents

The following scenario will probably sound familiar to anyone who has sat in on meetings: A team describing breakdowns in a work process is told of how one worker solved the problem. This reminds someone of how that same worker solved a problem in another process, which reminds someone else of an incident between that worker and his supervisor, which leads to a discussion of whatever happened to that supervisor, which leads to a discussion of retirement condominiums in Florida, and on and on. When the meeting ends, the team wonders where the time went.

Such wide-ranging, unfocused conversations are an example of wanderlust, our natural tendency to stray from the subject. Sometimes these digressions are innocent tangents from the conversation. But they also happen when the team wants to avoid a subject that it needs to address. In either case, the meeting facilitator is responsible for bringing the conversation back to the meeting agenda.

How a team leader can deal with wanderlust

- Use a written agenda with time estimates for each item; refer to the topic and time when the discussion strays too far.
- Write topics or items on a flipchart and post the pages on the wall where all members can refer to them throughout the discussion.
- Direct the conversation back on track: "We've strayed from the topic, which was ____. The last few comments before we digressed were ____."
- "We've had trouble sticking to this point. Is there something about it that makes it so easy to avoid?"

Feuding Team Members...

Can disrupt an entire team with their disagreements. Usually these feuds pre-date the team and are best dealt with outside team meetings.

10. Feuding Team Members

Sometimes a team becomes a field of combat for members who are vying with each other. Usually, the issue is not the subject they are arguing about but rather the contest itself. Other members feel like spectators at a sporting match, and fear that if they participate in any disagreement between the pair, they will be swept into the contest on one side or the other. Usually these feuds predate the team, and in all likelihood will outlast it, too. The best way to deal with this situation is to prevent it by carefully selecting team members so that adversaries are not on the same team. If that is impossible, then bring the combatants together before the first meeting to work out some agreement about their behavior.

How a team leader can deal with feuding team members

- When confrontations occur during a meeting, get the adversaries to discuss the issues off-line. Offer to facilitate the discussion.

- Push them to some contract about their behavior ("If you agree to X, I will agree to Y") or ground rules for managing their differences without disrupting the team.

Chapter 7

Summary

When people work together on a project, it is unreasonable to suppose that everything will go smoothly. For that reason it is best to be prepared for what might go wrong. Allow team members to get to know each other early in the process. Establish and discuss ground rules for behavior before the work begins. It is also important to develop strategies dealing with the things that are most likely to go wrong, including coping with conflict and defusing serious conflicts. Being prepared to deal with difficulty makes a team's work go more smoothly and efficiently.

Appendices

Appendix A
Quality Leadership

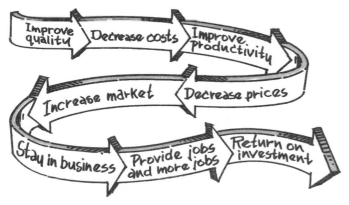

The Quality Revolution: Its Impact and Legacy

The quality movement has had a profound impact on business management around the world. Management consultants Dr. W. Edwards Deming, Dr. Joseph Juran, and others taught that improving systems and quality were the keys to a company's success. Quality was to be achieved by giving customer concerns top priority, and by studying and constantly improving key work processes so that the final product or service met or exceeded customer expectations. As processes improve, productivity goes up, and inefficiency goes down. Customers get better and better products at lower and lower prices. Customers who receive high quality products or services at a fair price tell others, causing demand to increase. Dr. Deming summarized this cycle in what has come to be called the Deming Chain Reaction.

The principles and methods of quality are slowly permeating our organizations, even those that have not formally adopted a "Quality Leadership" approach. A customer focus is being promoted almost everywhere, in speech if not in action. More decisions are being made today on the basis of data instead of guesswork. Many organizations are putting new emphasis on the continuous improvement of processes. There is an increased focus on *how* work gets done, as well as on *what* is done.

In many places, relationships between managers and other employees are being restructured: a manager's job becomes helping people do the best job possible, foreseeing and eliminating barriers that prevent employees from providing quality products and services all the time. More employees are learning how to use the knowledge and insight they've gained from being on the job day after day.

In spite of these positive changes, however, there are still many lingering problems. To get a better idea of where we are, it helps to look back at where we've been.

I. Management by Results

American managers are generally a tough lot who have accomplished a great deal. Their efforts have helped build one of the strongest economies the world has known. Yet the strength of many organizations is still shackled. Trapped in an outdated style of running organizations, managers are unable to unleash the full potential of their employees. Many organizations are thus failing to keep up with the developing needs of their customers, and thus are losing them.

Many managers still do business, at least in part, through a management approach that is sometimes called Management by Results. It is still practiced in many organizations, and still taught in many business schools.

CONVENTIONAL ADMINISTRATIVE STRUCTURE

Management by Results has its own logic and consistency. As shown (right), it emphasizes a chain of command and a hierarchy of objectives, goals, and accountability. Traditional organizational charts therefore portray a chain of accountability where objectives are translated into work or sales quotas. The performance of all employees is guided and judged according to these numerical goals, which are the heart and driving force of this management practice.

The shortcomings of Management by Results are rooted in the use of goals to reward and punish. Management by Results pays little, if any, attention to the processes and systems which define the real capabilities of the organization. So these goals and quotas wind up being arbitrary, leading employees, supervisors, and managers to play games. "Looking good" soon overshadows a concern for the organization's long-term success. Too often, they lose sight of the larger purpose of the work they do.

In short, use of numerical goals to judge and reward performance fosters a host of problems.

Short-term thinking

In a system of numerical objectives, standards, and quotas, rewarded efforts are measurable and short-term. The near horizon gets attention and countable results get priority even though the company's survival may depend on unmeasurable activities undertaken to reach long-term goals. Top managers impose goals on lower managers, who impose goals on others. Employees struggle to meet their goals, forced to ignore how what they do distorts efforts at some other time or place in the organization. Everyone struggles to survive distortions inherited from other times or places, and the cycle becomes self-reinforcing. Employees are too busy meeting quotas to care about what happens to customers.

In this climate, meeting short-term, measurable goals reflects well on an individual and reinforces the legitimacy of the goals themselves. When goals are met, the entire company can boast of its performance. But this attitude wreaks havoc with quality and employee morale along the way.

Internal conflict

Systems of numerical controls cause internal conflict. The controls that direct one unit's short-term gain more often than not contradict the goals given to another unit.

For example, when salespeople are exhorted to boost business, they make promises other areas can't keep. Designers rush new products into production too quickly. Purchasing buys materials that people can't use. The conflicts between departments lead to finger pointing, blame games, and an endless series of excuses ("If it weren't for them..."). Each group struggles to meet the goals independently of other groups. Turf wars flourish.

Fudging the figures

Frequently, imposed measurable goals are unattainable; they lie beyond a system's real capability. But since people or departments lose status if they fail to reach the goals, they make it look like they are conforming. They are encouraged by the system to fudge figures, alter records, or just "play the game"—to work around the system instead of improving it. This charade fosters guarded communication and dishonesty. The greater the stress on reaching the goals, the more likely it is that reports and numbers will be given a face-lift.

Greater fear

The worst fallout from Management by Results is fear—fear of what will happen if orders are not followed exactly, of not getting a raise or a promotion, of being out of favor or losing a job. Fear is the prime motivator in a Management by Results system. The more rigid and unrealistic the controls, the deeper the fear.

Blindness to customer concerns

Management by Results encourages a company to look inward, rather than outward at the world in which the customer operates. Accomplishment comes from meeting a numerical goal, rather than in providing a product or service that works and satisfies the customer.

These problems compound each other, each disguising the true shape of the organization. People think they are doing a good job—and they are by the organization's internal standards. These are driven by the logic of Management by Results. The result is a Titanic-like false sense of security. When people finally realize that the indicators of control may be focused on the wrong thing, it's too late. The ship is going down and "Nearer My God To Thee" is heard from the afterdeck.

II. Quality Leadership

Managers often say, "I agree there are serious problems with Management by Results, but what is a better alternative?" The alternative, we believe, is Quality Leadership.

The Principles of Quality Leadership

Because many of the elements of Quality Leadership have appeared separately, most people fail to recognize how the total package differs from anything they have seen before. Quality Leadership combines old ingredients in a powerful new way. The integration of the characteristics described in the following paragraphs distinguishes Quality Leadership from its predecessors.

Customer focus

Quality Leadership starts with the customer. An organization's goal is to be high value-added to customers. If we are continually developing better and better ways to provide value, at lower and lower cost, we will do well as customers boast of our quality, service, and cost. (Note: In some government organizations, such as the Air Force, the concept of mission may be more appropriate than that of customers. If so, the focus should be on the mission.) Many organizations also need to integrate customer information with stakeholder needs (e.g., regulatory requirements, taxpayer concerns, or community needs).

Obsession with quality

Quality is many faceted, but the essence is value and reliability at a reasonable price. In Quality Leadership, everyone in the organization becomes obsessed with quality. Quality is relentlessly pursued through products and services that delight the customer, and through efficient and effective methods of execution.

Recognizing the structure in work

Work is not haphazard. All work has structure. The structure may be hidden behind inefficiency and rework, but it can and must be studied, measured, analyzed, and improved. Employees should monitor many variables inside and outside the organization

---

in order to understand what is happening in their work processes.

These measures (not to be confused with the numerical goals of Management by Results) guide the search for better performance, and are recognized as a means rather than an end. They lead the way to a deeper understanding of the organization, and are not used as criteria for judging individuals.

Freedom through control

In Quality Leadership there is control, yet there is freedom. Use of the best-known method for any given process provides control. Employees standardize processes and find ways to help everyone follow the standard procedures. They reduce undesirable variation in output by reducing variation in the way work is done. As these changes take hold, they are freer to spend time finding still better methods of work rather than fire fighting.

Unity of purpose

There is a unity of purpose throughout the organization in accord with a clear and widely understood vision. This environment nurtures commitment from all employees. Rewards go beyond benefits and salaries to the joy that comes from doing excellent work.

Looking for faults in systems

Quality Leadership recognizes—as Dr. Joseph M. Juran and Dr. W. Edwards Deming have maintained since the early 1950s—that at least 85% of an organization's failures are the fault of management-controlled systems. Individual employees can control fewer than 15% of the problems. Therefore, the focus is on constant and rigorous improvement of every system, not on blaming individuals for problems.

Teamwork

Where once there may have been barriers, rivalries, and distrust, the organization now fosters teamwork and partnerships with the workforce and their representatives. This partnership is not a pretense or a new look to an old battle. It is a common struggle for the customers, not separate struggles for power. The notion of a common struggle for quality also applies to relationships with suppliers, regulating agencies, and communities.

Continued education and training

In a quality organization everyone is constantly learning. Management encourages employees to constantly elevate their level of technical skill and professional expertise. People gain an ever greater mastery of their jobs and learn to broaden their capabilities. Management leads by example.

The 85/15 Rule

There is a widely held belief that an organization would have few, if any, problems if only workers would do their jobs correctly. As Dr. Joseph M. Juran pointed out years ago, this belief is incorrect.

In fact, the potential to eliminate mistakes and errors lies mostly in improving the systems through which work is done, not in changing the workers.

This observation has evolved into the rule of thumb that at least 85% of problems can only be corrected by changing systems (which are largely determined by management) and less than 15% are under a worker's control—and the split may lean even more towards the system.

For example, a customer service representative cannot do a top quality job when working with faulty knowledge or tools; a surgical nurse cannot do a good job with gloves that do not fit.

Even when it does appear that an individual is doing something wrong, often the trouble lies in how that worker was trained, which is a system problem.

Once people recognize that systems create the majority of problems, they stop blaming individual workers. They instead ask which system needs improvement, and thus are more likely to seek out and find the true source of improvement.

W. Edwards Deming

Though Quality Leadership is often seen as foreign, its roots are American. Many of the ideas originated with Dr. W. Edwards Deming, the American statistician who helped Japanese industry recover after World War II. His teachings continue to be of interest to business leaders.

Over the years, Dr. Deming developed 14 Points that describe what is necessary for a business to prosper today. They contain the essence of his teachings. Read them, think about them, talk about them with your co-workers or with people who understand them. And then come back to think about them again. Soon you will start to understand their significance and how they work together. Understanding the 14 Points can shape a new attitude toward work and the work environment that will foster continuous improvement.

Deming's 14 Points

1. Create constancy of purpose toward improvement of product and service.

2. Adopt the new philosophy. We are in a new economic age. Western management must awaken to the challenge.

3. Cease dependence on inspection to achieve quality.

4. End the practice of awarding business on the basis of price tag. Instead, minimize total cost.

5. Improve constantly and forever the system of production and service, to improve quality and productivity, and thus constantly decrease costs, improve profit.

6. Institute training on the job.

7. Institute leadership (see Point 12). The aim of leadership should be to help people and machines to do a better job.

8. Drive out fear, so that everyone may work effectively for the company.

9. Break down barriers between departments. Optimize the company as a system.

10. Eliminate slogans, exhortations, and targets for the workforce.

11. (a) Eliminate work standards (quotas). (b) Eliminate management by objective. Eliminate management by numbers, numerical goals.

12. (a) Remove barriers that rob the hourly worker of his right to pride of workmanship. (b) Remove barriers that rob people in management and in engineering of their right to pride of workmanship. This means, *inter alia*, abolishment of the annual or merit rating.

13. Institute a vigorous program of education and self-improvement.

14. Put everybody in the company to work to accomplish the transformation.

(For information on W. Edwards Deming, Joseph Juran, and 4th Generation Management, see Appendix D.)

III. Starting a Quality Effort

The principles of Quality Leadership are easy to understand, but putting them into practice can be difficult. It requires effort on many fronts.

Some people seem to think the route to Quality Leadership can be traveled solely by project teams. While project teams are a crucial tool for quality improvement they are only one dimension of the total package. Organizations must adopt other practices if they are to practice Quality Leadership.

We have identified six dimensions to pursue in the early phases of adopting Quality Leadership. They are displayed in a cause-and-effect diagram (next page).

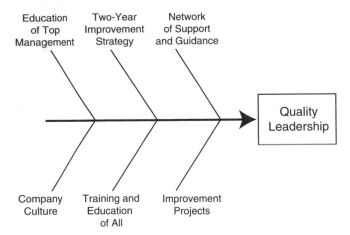

Education of Top Management · Two-Year Improvement Strategy · Network of Support and Guidance · Company Culture · Training and Education of All · Improvement Projects → Quality Leadership

A two-year strategy addresses these questions:

- In which parts of the organization should the changes start? Which potential projects are the most critical to success?

- What resources, financial and personnel, will be needed to sustain initial education, training, and projects? Who will provide guidance and technical assistance to managers, supervisors, project teams, and others?

- Who will coordinate logistics and company-wide communication? What systems must be developed for deploying resources, maintaining an information clearinghouse for publications, conferences, and seminars on Quality Leadership, sharing successes and lessons learned, and a thousand other details?

1. The education, reeducation, and active leadership of top management

The most frequent cause of failure in any quality improvement effort is uninvolved or indifferent top and middle management. Therefore, the active leadership and participation of managers, beginning at the top, is essential.

Quality can't be delegated to others. Managers must lead the change effort to ensure long-lasting success. They must become leaders and coaches. They must focus on preventing and eliminating problems. Only this will lead to constant improvement.

Managers should understand the principles Dr. Deming espoused (see "Deming's 14 Points," p. A-5). They need to understand and use approaches for stabilizing and improving processes. They need to understand variation and know how to use data effectively. When top managers feel these concepts deep in their bones, quality will become the new leadership method.

2. A multiyear strategy for starting and implementing a quality improvement philosophy

Companies commonly make the mistake of involving too many people too soon. It is easy to plant a big garden; hard to tend it. Don't begin a bigger effort than you can realistically support and maintain. Plan to start with at least a two-year strategy.

3. A network of coordination, guidance, and technical support

Identifying and developing resource people within the organization is a need you should start meeting early on. It may be necessary to recruit technical resources from the outside as well. (In this book we refer to these technical specialists as coaches or "quality advisors."

These specialists and advisors coach managers and supervisors about how to lead differently.

4. A company culture supportive of Quality Leadership

The notion of culture in a company is complex and elusive. In general, culture refers to the everyday work experiences of the mass of employees. We urge managers to address these questions: How do employees experience their jobs? What gets in the way of employees' pride in their work and their work groups? Do they feel valued and trusted by the company? Do they see serving customers as a priority?

Sometimes a simple change of policy or management practice can have a positive influence on these attitudes. Managers must review the company's policies and practices and change those that are contrary to Quality Leadership and a supportive environment.

5. Training and education

All employees must understand their jobs and their roles in the company—and how these roles change as quality improves. Such understanding goes beyond the instructions given in manuals or job descriptions. Employees need to know where their work fits into the larger context: how their work is influenced by workers who precede them and how their work influences workers who follow. They must learn new skills for improving work.

6. Carefully selected improvement projects

Having teams work on carefully selected improvement projects is a useful vehicle for moving Quality Leadership forward. Project teams can tackle larger issues than individuals can. Their access to technical support and guidance from people versed in data-based approaches, project management techniques, and group leadership skills enhances their ability to find lasting solutions to problems.

Early projects must be carefully selected to ensure the greatest chance of success on issues critical to the organization. Often teams are asked to tackle projects that are too large or diffuse for them to handle. This leads to frustration and only dampens enthusiasm for the needed changes.

IV. The Role of Project Teams

Though project teams are only one dimension of Quality Leadership, they are, nevertheless, an important one. The success or failure of projects will have great impact on the company because their success or failure will be highly visible. Therefore, it is important to understand clearly where project teams fit into the overall quality effort and to know how to use them properly.

Whether you are involved in a pioneer project, or one that is part of a later expansion, your project is part of something very big, very long-lasting, and very important to your company. As mentioned above, the main agenda of quality projects is to deal with an issue that managers have identified as important to the organization. To do this, members use the tools and skills described throughout this book. But project teams, especially initial teams, have an additional agenda. They are an instrument of widespread education, a purpose equally important in the long run as their improvement work.

The first project teams are a classroom through which the entire company learns lessons such as:

How to blend teamwork and scientific methods

Project team members learn how to work as a team and how to make improvements using scientific tools and other techniques. The team leader also learns how to plan and manage a project, conduct effective meetings, and facilitate group processes. They all carry these skills beyond the project.

Where guidance teams fit in

Through regular meetings with the project team, the managers guiding the project also learn about the scientific approach to improvement. In addition, they learn how to coach and inquire about progress. They begin to understand both the exciting, successful side of projects and the tedious, confused, and unsuccessful stages.

Moving decisions downward

In most organizations, decisions are made two or three hierarchical levels above where they should be made. Projects provide an opportunity to empower those who do the work everyday with authority to decide on changes.

Making improvements is not easy

Everyone in the company learns that the achievement of ever-improving quality is not easy. Managers learn they need to be both supportive and persistent.

How to develop internal experts

Most companies develop a network of individuals trained to provide technical assistance to project teams and other improvement efforts. In this book we refer to these specialists as "Quality Advisors." Early projects provide an opportunity for Quality Advisors to improve their coaching and consulting skills.

How to expand the effort

Other people inside and outside the company learn from the project team's work through presentations and by participating in the changes resulting from the team's effort. To aid this process, project teams are typically asked to make presentations to people inside and outside the company: key customers, suppliers, other departments or facilities, regional and national meetings, and so on.

The project team's importance in this reeducation of all employees cannot be underestimated. Teams should constantly record their progress with clear, attractive visual displays. They should plan carefully any meetings with other groups in the company, paying attention to what is said and how, and addressing the above-mentioned lessons as well as the bottom-line results of the project.

Appendix B

Storyboard Example

Project

Purpose: Reduce the amount of time it takes to process credit vouchers by 50%.

Reason selected: Customers have been extremely dissatisfied with the amount of time it takes to resolve credits. They like our product but have problems doing business with us.

Current Situation

A frequency plot shows that it can take up to 170 days or more for a credit voucher to be processed. The overall median is 55 days, but it looks like there are really two clusters, one that takes about 30 days on average, and one that takes about 140 days on average.

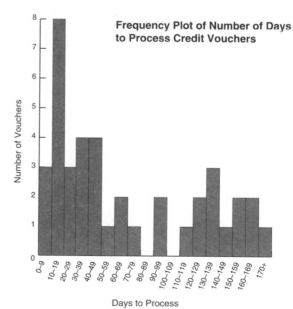

Frequency Plot of Number of Days to Process Credit Vouchers

Current Situation, cont.

There are 12 basic steps in the credit voucher process.

Basic Flowchart of Credit Voucher Process

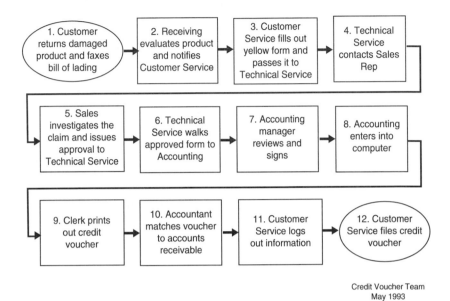

1. Customer returns damaged product and faxes bill of lading
2. Receiving evaluates product and notifies Customer Service
3. Customer Service fills out yellow form and passes it to Technical Service
4. Technical Service contacts Sales Rep
5. Sales investigates the claim and issues approval to Technical Service
6. Technical Service walks approved form to Accounting
7. Accounting manager reviews and signs
8. Accounting enters into computer
9. Clerk prints out credit voucher
10. Accountant matches voucher to accounts receivable
11. Customer Service logs out information
12. Customer Service files credit voucher

Credit Voucher Team
May 1993

Tracking a number of vouchers through the entire process showed that the hands-on time needed was only 60 minutes. This is obviously much shorter than the median 55-day cycle time shown in the original frequency plot.

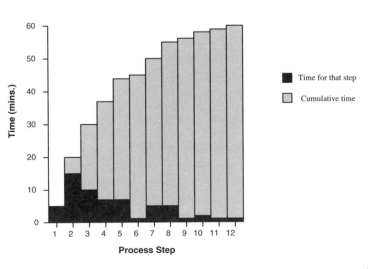

Hands-on Time for Credit Voucher Process
(both time per step and cumulative time)

■ Time for that step
□ Cumulative time

Cause Analysis

Work-flow Diagram of Credit Voucher Process

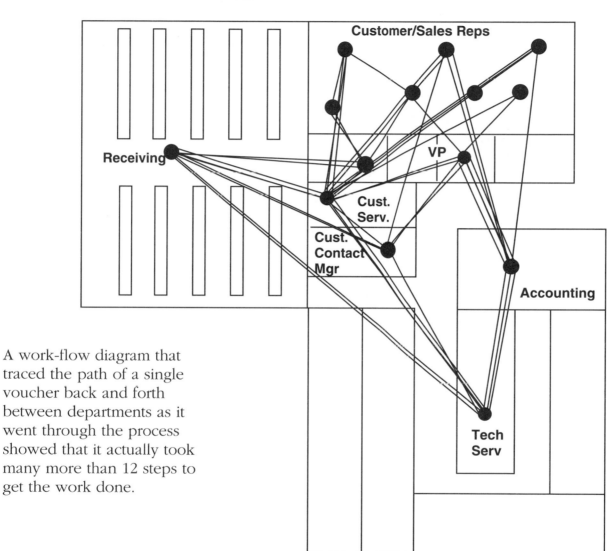

A work-flow diagram that traced the path of a single voucher back and forth between departments as it went through the process showed that it actually took many more than 12 steps to get the work done.

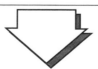

Cause Analysis, cont.

Why was there so much back and forth between departments just to get through the process?
A deployment flowchart that showed the decision steps and handoffs between people revealed that there were **nine pathways** through this one process. Furthermore, everyone had a different idea about which types of vouchers should follow which pathways. The types of vouchers that produced the greatest confusion were those that had the much longer processing times (over 150 days).

Why were there so many delays in the process?
The team discovered many vouchers sat around on desks in many of these steps. No one treated the vouchers as a high priority.

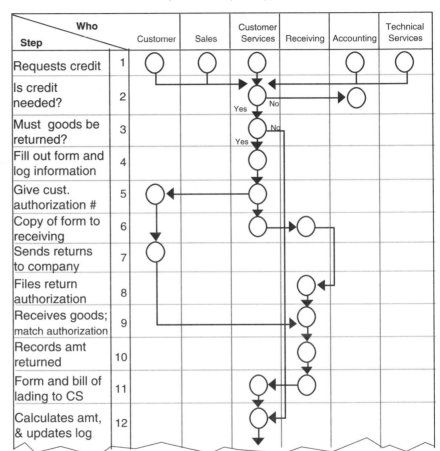

Deployment Flowchart of Credit Vouchers Process
(first 12 steps only)

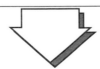

Solutions

The team came up with a brief list of countermeasures.
1. Categorize vouchers based on what types of information/approvals are needed.
2. Eliminate unnecessary approval steps in Technical Services and Accounting.
3. Clarify what signatures/approvals are needed for other vouchers.
4. Emphasize to all employees the importance of processing credit vouchers as soon as possible. Change the mindset from processing vouchers "as time permits" to "do it today."
5. Create a single, shared database that can be accessed by every department so there will be a central place to find information about any given voucher.

The first four solutions all met the criteria of being easy and inexpensive to do, so all of them were tried on a small scale for 30 days. The Information Systems group worked with the team on testing the feasibility of the last idea because, although it was more complex and expensive, it addressed several key organizational needs in addition to the voucher problem.

Results

After the changes were put in place, the time to process invoices dropped dramatically from an average of about 55 days to an average of about 3 days. Also, there were no longer two "humps" in the distribution because the vouchers no longer sat idle waiting for approvals.

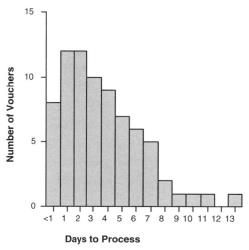

Frequency Plot of Days Needed to Process Vouchers
(after changes)

Number of Vouchers

Days to Process

Standardization

While additional work was being done to reduce the processing time even further, the team took the following steps to make sure the current gains were maintained:
- Developed a new flowchart of the process, which was introduced to all staff during a cross-departmental meeting
- Developed a training program on how to use the new database; established who had responsibility to update and maintain the database
- Designated the Customer Service manager to maintain current data on "time to resolve credits" and take appropriate actions as necessary

Future Actions

- Continue working on process improvements with a target turnaround time of 3 days.
- Need to work to reduce the number of vouchers. Current data shows there are about 85 vouchers per month, many of which result from defective product. See if these defects can be reduced.

A time plot of vouchers per month shows that there have been between 30 and 203 vouchers issued per month (with a median of 85).

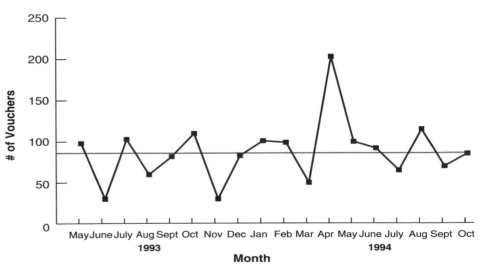

Time Plot of # of Vouchers per Month

Appendix C
Team-Building Activities

Some companies think the team-building dimension of a project is as important as process improvement. This appendix includes a sampling of exercises and activities you can use to help new team members get to know one another and to help the whole team become more familiar with the processes they may be focusing on.

This appendix begins with a collection of warm-ups, brief 2- to 15-minute activities used at the beginning of meetings to free members from outside distractions so they can focus on the meeting. A selection of exercises fills the remainder of the appendix. These exercises help teams work through common group issues, provide for team members' needs, prevent problems, and explore dimensions of their work. They require more time than warm-ups and are appropriate during the first months of a team's efforts.

The activities we present are meant to be guidelines, perhaps inspiring you to create variations more suited to your team. All instructions are written for the team leader.

I. Warm-Ups

Team members come into meetings with a lot of distractions. Just as it is important to stretch muscles before physical exercise, people should stretch their minds before each meeting. A warm-up activity allows a team to leave behind concerns and ease into the meeting, to gradually focus on its task.

Warm-ups are also just plain fun. They signal a lightening up and give members permission to talk to people they might not normally talk to about things they usually don't talk about. They also encourage a little spontaneity and a bit of adventure. For example, some warm-ups ask participants to talk about something important to them. When team members begin talking about their interests or feelings, they start letting go of their roles, and can meet each other as equals.

The warm-ups here have been used successfully in many types of teams, but that does not mean they are appropriate for every team. The meeting facilitator should ask two questions when choosing a warm-up: Does this warm-up challenge team members to a new experience without making them too uncomfortable? And, will I be reasonably comfortable leading this exercise?

When using a warm-up for the first time, you should describe the warm-up to the team and then be the first to do it. This shows team members how to do it and demonstrates that you are not asking them to do something you are unwilling to do yourself. After leading the warm-up, ask who is willing to go next. Then look around the team and wait for a volunteer to go next.

Team Member Introductions

Going around the table, have team members introduce themselves to the group. Everyone tells: name; job; the thing I like best about my job, a recent success in my work, or what I currently find most challenging in my job; and how I got to be on this team. This activity is especially appropriate at the first team meeting.

Paired Introductions

Pair up members who don't know each other well. Have them get acquainted by asking each other questions such as:

- What is your name?
- What is your job?
- How long have you been at the company?
- What got you started here?
- What do you like best about your job?
- How did you become part of this team?
- What is your favorite weekend recreation? Hobby?

Before the meeting, the team leader and quality advisor choose which questions to present, write them on flipcharts, and post the pages where all members can see. Optional: You can follow the paired introductions by having partners introduce each other to the rest of the group.

Flipchart Introductions

Few team members will have had experience writing on flipcharts in front of a group. But they will have to write on flipcharts during meetings, and may be asked to make presentations from time to time. This activity gives members experience using a flipchart for discussing ideas, and helps them get better acquainted.

Each member takes a turn at the flipchart talking about and writing down the answers to one or more of the following topics (selected in advance by the team leader):

- Tell us the name of your hometown, and describe three or four characteristics that you find most memorable.
- Explain an achievement or something you've accomplished in the past six months.
- Draw a work-line with its ups and downs, highlights and disappointments, from your first job to the present. Describe the major events on the line.

First Job

Working in pairs or with the whole group, members talk about one of their first jobs. Since members are learning about quality, each of them may want to talk about:

- What parts of the job didn't make sense then (and still don't make sense)
- What impression I had of the owners or managers, and what I learned from them
- What I learned about the "working world" from that job

Background

Have members list background information they would like to know about each other, such as hobbies, pets, years living in the area, hometown, etc. List these items on a flipchart. Then have team members take turns answering these questions.

Superlatives

Ask members to study the composition of the group and silently decide on a superlative adjective (youngest, tallest, baldest, grandmotherliest) that describes themselves in contrast to the others. Then go around the table sharing adjectives.

Hopes and Concerns

Have team members reflect on their hopes for this team or this project, as well as their concerns about the outcome. Encourage them to think as broadly as possible. They may write down their answers if they want.

After individual reflection, divide the group into pairs, and have partners share answers. Then have each pair share answers with the group. Record all responses on flipcharts.

When all pairs have taken their turn, have the entire group discuss what the team or organization can do to make the hopes come true, and what can be done to prevent anything negative from happening.

"What I Want for Myself Out of This"

Once team members clearly understand the purpose of the project, it is useful to explore what each individual would like to achieve over and above the team goals.

Allow members three to five minutes to list personal goals for their participation. What do they want to learn or do, and why? Suggest they consider personal goals such as getting to know new people, learning about other aspects of the operation, feeling good about themselves as employees, learning new skills, and other non-task goals.

Have each one read the list to the group. You may choose to just listen, discuss the ideas among the team, or record and save them.

Member Mapping

In preparation for this activity, find or draw a map of the building or work area the team is studying. Post it on the wall before the meeting. Then have members initial (or otherwise mark) their job stations or areas where they work. After everyone has taken a turn, the team studies the map. Are there any patterns? How do members' roles interact? Are significant parts of the operation unrepresented or overrepresented in this team? What else does this map show?

Group Conversation

Prior to the meeting, make a list of incomplete sentences, "conversation starters." You may use the list below, devise your own, or use a combination. Either post the list on a flipchart or write it on one sheet of paper that can be passed around the table.

Possible conversation starters include:
- Anybody will work hard if...
- People who run things should be...
- I would like to be...
- One thing I like about myself is...
- Nothing is so frustrating as...
- The teacher I liked best was a person who...
- Ten years from now, I...
- Every winning team needs...
- I take pride in...
- If you want to see me get mad...
- A rewarding job is one that...

Go around the table and have one team member at a time start a conversation on one topic, focusing on what this person has witnessed or experienced rather than on abstract principles. The whole team discusses the idea; when that conversation is done, the next person selects a new topic.

Alternatively, break the group into pairs or threes and distribute copies of the list to each group. Have these small groups do this exercise for 10 to 15 minutes. Each group then reports back to the entire team.

Drawing a Shop or Office...

Often helps team members come up with creative solutions to problems caused by the physical limitations of their work spaces.

If I Were Still at My Job...

As a way to get to know each other's jobs, have members say what they would be doing if they weren't in the team meeting. Allow them to go into detail; other members can probe for more information. (Alternately, this can be a quick go-around of short, one-sentence explanations.)

After everyone's job has been discussed, turn the tide and suggest that members forget about their usual job responsibilities until the meeting ends. Create an image of leaving the job outside the meeting room door as if hung on a coat rack; members can retrieve them when they leave the meeting.

Draw a Shop or Office

Distribute paper and markers, and give each member 5 to 10 minutes to draw an ideal shop floor, waiting room, office, meeting room, or other appropriate environment. Tape the pictures on a wall and invite everyone to walk through the "gallery" to view the drawings. Discuss the pictures, clarifying and elaborating on the ideas represented. Guide the discussion to issues of quality, productivity, problems in the operation, etc.

Team Name

Ask each person to write down as many names as possible for the team, at least five. Have members read their lists while you jot down the ideas on a flipchart. Add other ideas as they come up. Discuss the suggestions and choose a team name.

Common Denominators

Pair up members who don't know each other well. Have them search for traits they have in common that make them *unique* from other team members. For example, acceptable answers would be that both can wiggle their ears, have sons born on the same day, or will travel to California for the first time this July. However, saying both are human beings or are participating on this team would not make them *unique* since all members share those traits. The answers may not be stated negatively. They cannot say, for example, that neither has ever broken a leg.

If there is time, form new pairs and repeat the exercise. At the end, have members share answers with the whole team.

Footnote: One other warm-up (the "Check-In") was given in Chapter 4, p. 4-43. "Superlatives" and "Background" are adapted from *A Handbook of Structured Experiences for Human Relations Training, Volume IV.* J. William Pfeiffer and John E. Jones, editors. LaJolla, CA: University Associates, Inc., 1975. "Group Conversation" is adapted from Volume II of the same series (1973). This annual publication is an excellent source of various group activities.

II. Team-Building Exercises

Teams can benefit from exercises and activities that help members develop good working relationships. These activities help members develop agreements about how to work together as a team. They can be used by members to identify their current team strengths, as well as to identify skills they want to develop further. Some of these activities also help team members learn more about the problem or process they are working on.

Many of these activities are best used early in the team's life. For example, The Responsibility Matrix, Discussing Your Mission, and Questions to Ask About a Process are all useful in establishing an understanding of the team's work. Other activities can be used whenever the team leader or team finds it appropriate. Some, such as Meeting Skills Checklist and Observing Group Process, can be used periodically throughout a team's life.

Though longer than warm-ups, most of these exercises can be done in a single team meeting. Some may require the entire meeting. The instructions for the exercises are written for the team leader or meeting facilitator.

The first four exercises in this section focus on understanding and reaching agreements about how the team works together. The last three exercises can be used to help the team better understand its problem or process.

Exercise 1
The Responsibility Matrix

Time: 1 to 1.5 hours

Overview

In Chapters 3 and 4 we identified tasks to be performed in preparing for a project and running meetings. The responsibility for many of these activities belongs to the team leader, quality advisor, or a designated team member. However, the team will run into many tasks that do not clearly belong to any one person or role. This exercise helps the team identify and assign the responsibility for these tasks.

Instructions

1. Identify tasks

Have the team list activities not clearly assigned to a person or group of people. Use the following examples to spur your own discussion (some of these may already be assigned in your team). Aim for a list of no more than 20 items.

Meeting responsibilities
- Sending out meeting material, agendas, and minutes
- Setting up the meeting room; cleaning up after meetings
- Taking minutes
- Facilitating meetings
- Arranging meetings with the sponsor or manager
- Helping the group when it's stuck
- Maintaining files
- Leading warm-ups
- Leading the meeting evaluation
- Containing digression; managing participation; using other discussion skills

Project responsibilities
- Gathering data
- Plotting charts
- Maintaining files
- Communicating with others affected by the team's work

Education/Training responsibilities
- Teaching methods of collecting and analyzing data
- Teaching work planning skills
- Teaching meeting management skills

2. Create a matrix

Set up one or two flipchart pages to correspond to the matrix shown on the next page. Then list the tasks you identified in the TASK column.

3. Work through the matrix

Work through the matrix one task at a time, having each member mark (with an X or initials) the column representing the group or person he or she thinks is responsible for that task. (Note: Have each member use a different color marker when marking the columns to simplify later discussion.) Do this for every task listed.

4. Discuss the answers

Discuss the answers, again working through the matrix one task at a time. Do not move to the next item until the team has reached consensus on which person or group is responsible for that task. You can decide to rotate a responsibility between people or groups, but you must clearly set down procedures for how and when to switch.

Exercise 1: The Responsibility Matrix, continued

Sample Matrix

Instructions: Copy this form onto flipcharts. Enter tasks in the left column, then have team members mark who they think is responsible for each task. Discuss the answers as a group, and make final decisions regarding the responsibilities.

TASK	WHO			
	Team Leader	All Team Members	Quality Advisor or Coach	Sponsor or Manager

Exercise 2
Meeting Skills Checklist
Time: 30 to 45 min.

Overview

Having team members evaluate their meeting *skills* is an excellent alternative to evaluating the meeting itself. This exercise may precede or follow activities involving role behavior, such as the Responsibility Matrix (p. C-11).

Use this exercise after the team has had four or five meetings and has begun to establish patterns and routines of behavior.

Instructions

1. Preparation
Make enough copies of the "Meeting Skills Checklist" to distribute to the team. On a flipchart, draw 21 rows and 4 columns: Label the first column "Behavior" and the last three "Never," "Occasionally," and "Often," in sequence. Number each row and copy keywords from the corresponding sentences provided (unless you want to copy down the entire sentence).

2. Fill out forms
Hand out copies of the checklist and have each member individually complete one.

3. Compile answers
Transfer individual ratings to the previously prepared flipchart that duplicates the checklist. Have each member enter a checkmark or initials on the line under the appropriate column.

4. Discuss the answers
Any surprises? Which areas seem to be weakest? What can you do to help yourselves and each other? Should you do this exercise in the future to see whether there is a shift? When?

> **Note:**
> Team members can also use this checklist on their own so they can work to improve the skills each is weakest in.

Exercise 2: Meeting Skills Checklist, continued

Instructions: Either photocopy this page and the next page or create your own version. Have team members work through it first individually and then as a team.

Behavior	Never	Occasion-ally	Often
1. I suggest a procedure for the group to follow or a method for organizing the task.			
2. I suggest a new idea, new activity, new problem, or a new course of action.			
3. I attempt to bring the group back to work when joking, personal stories, or irrelevant talk goes on too long.			
4. I suggest, when there is some confusion, that the group make an outline or otherwise organize a plan for completing the task.			
5. I initiate attempts to redefine goals, problems, or outcomes when things become hazy or confusing.			
6. I elaborate ideas with concise examples, illustrations.			
7. I suggest resource people to contact and bring in materials.			
8. I present the reasons behind my opinions.			
9. I ask others for information and/or opinions.			
10. I ask for the significance and/or implications of facts and opinions.			
11. I see and point out relationships between facts and opinions.			
12. I ask a speaker to explain the reasoning that led him or her to a particular conclusion.			

Exercise 2: Meeting Skills Checklist, continued

Behavior	Never	Occasion- ally	Often
13. I relate my comments to previous contributions.			
14. I pull together and summarize various ideas presented.			
15. I test to see if everyone agrees with, or understands, the issue being discussed or the decision being made.			
16. I summarize the progress the group has made.			
17. I encourage other members to participate and try to unobtrusively involve quiet members.			
18. I actively support others when I think their point of view is important.			
19. I try to find areas of agreement in conflicting points of view (e.g., "How could we change our solution so that you could support it?" or "It sounds to me that we all agree to X, Y, and Z").			
20. I use appropriate humor to reduce tension in the group.			
21. I listen attentively to others' ideas and contributions.			

Exercise 3
Disruptive Group Behavior

Time: 1.5 to 3 hours

Overview

In this exercise, the team agrees on methods for dealing with group problems that members choose to discuss. Through this exercise the team develops a common understanding of acceptable team behavior. Team members decide how far a leader or facilitator can go in dealing with a problem, and how much disruptive behavior they will allow. Each member thus knows, and even helps determine in advance, the consequences of disruptive behavior.

This exercise is particularly effective when used after the second or third meeting, when members know at least a little about each other. It can also be used when disruptive patterns begin to develop in the team activities. This way, the team is involved in its own self-government from the beginning, an important value to establish early on.

Note: This exercise was developed by John Criqui when he was the statistical coordinator for Microcircuit Engineering Corporation of Mount Holly, New Jersey. Criqui has had great success in using this exercise to help project teams develop a greater awareness of acceptable group behavior.

Instructions

1. Preparation
Have a flipchart or chalkboard available, and pencil and paper for each member.

2. Introduce the exercise
The goal is to focus the team on behavior that interrupts group activities or hinders the team's progress. While people may witness the same behavior and interpret it differently—some seeing it as a problem and others not—usually they can agree on whether it is *disruptive*, that is, whether it interrupts work the group is doing. Introduce this exercise as a tool used to establish guidelines for conducting business at meetings and to develop methods for dealing with disruptive behavior.

3. Brainstorm
Direct the team to brainstorm about behaviors that could disrupt meetings or other team activities. Remind the team that in brainstorming there are no right or wrong answers. Do not critique responses. Crazy or silly answers are OK and can help the process. (You may even encourage these responses.)

Start with each member taking a turn giving one response at a time (about two to three rounds) until ideas start to snowball. Record the ideas on a flipchart or chalkboard as they are given. Do not change the wording. Include everything from minor disruptions (noisily flipping through a stack of paper) to major disruptions (holding side conversations, walking out of the room). Continue until all ideas have been exhausted. (◀See p. 4-14 for more instructions on brainstorming.)

4. Select one behavior
Reduce the brainstormed list to the two or three most important types of disruptive behavior. This can be accomplished through multivoting (◀described on p. 4-15). Take a vote to decide which to discuss first.

5. Discuss types of responses to disruptive behavior
Introduce the group to the concept of graded intervention—the response to a problem can be anything from no action to confrontation in a meeting. Focus only on three levels: preventive measures, minimal intervention, high intervention. (These are adapted from material in Chapter 7.)

Exercise 3: Disruptive Group Behavior, continued

6. Discuss possible responses to this behavior

Write the type of disruptive behavior at the top of a flipchart or chalkboard. Divide the rest of the page or board into three columns and label each in order:

#1 Preventive Measures
#2 Minimal Intervention
#3 Higher Intervention

Start with column 1, Preventive Measures. Have the team brainstorm possible ways to prevent the disruptive behavior. Record the ideas in the appropriate column. When the list for this column is complete, discuss the pros and cons of each idea. This discussion is extremely important. As the members discuss the brainstormed interventions, they are sorting out their values on such issues as "How much response to a problem is too much response?" Often after discussions of this type the team implicitly agrees on what behaviors are acceptable or unacceptable in the group. Reach consensus on which ideas best represent the team position on preventing this behavior.

Repeat this process for Minimal Intervention (column 2) and then Higher Intervention (column 3), each time reaching a consensus on the group's position about dealing with the behavior at that level of intervention.

7. Review the team decisions

After all columns have been discussed, summarize the team's position on this disruptive behavior. Ask members if the summary is accurate. Discuss and revise the answers until the team is satisfied.

Suggested format for flipcharts:

Problem being discussed:		
Preventive Measures	Minimal Intervention	Higher Intervention

8. Repeat for another disruptive behavior

Return to Step 5 and repeat the process on another type of disruptive behavior.

9. Critique

When the team has discussed the two or three behaviors chosen in Step 4, review the entire exercise.

Example Output From Team Discussion

Results from a team that discussed problems between feuding members.

Preventive Measures	Minimal Intervention	Higher Intervention
Leader:	**Leader:**	**Leader:**
Most feuds predate the team. One way to prevent disruptions is to know about the feud in advance and leave one of its members off the list of team appointment candidates.	Talk to the feuding parties, either alone or together, but outside of the group. "When you two go at each other, I feel angry. It wastes the group's time and makes it difficult for anyone in the group to participate in the discussion without appearing to choose sides."	Set aside a meeting (with or without the combatants) in which the team discusses what to do about the problem. Ask the feuders to suggest ways to intervene. Agree on a process or mechanism to end the feuding (if not the feud).
If this is impossible, then the feuding parties should be brought together prior to any meeting of the team so they can decide how they might work together on this team.		Alternatively, when the behavior appears, the facilitator may say: "Mr. Hatfield, state in one sentence the point you're trying to make on this issue without reference to anyone who might disagree with you... Mr. McCoy, do likewise." Then let the others on the team give their one-sentence statement. Record all the sentences on a flipchart and start from there.
Agreement to the scientific approach will force them to substantiate their conflicting opinions with data.		

Exercise 4
Observing Group Process

Time: Duration of the meeting

Overview

In this exercise, the team leader, coach, or an individual team member observes a team meeting in order to better understand how the team is interacting. The observer does not participate in the meeting. She or he simply watches for specific behaviors during discussions and takes notes on forms like those provided on the next few pages. At the end of the meeting, or during some designated discussion time, the observer may report his or her observations. Then the whole team can discuss the observations.

Observing how the team works can serve several purposes. It can help identify patterns of interaction that may become problems in the team if they persist. For example, you might notice that no one disagrees with the team leader; or that decisions are never clearly stated during the meeting; or that three members contribute lots of ideas and information but no one asks what the quieter members think. Observation can help team members distinguish between the content of a discussion and the methods used during the discussion. Observation also gives members an opportunity to notice examples of skills which they are trying to develop. For example, a member who has never summarized ideas can observe what others say when they summarize for the team.

The instructions are in two parts. First are general instructions for observing teams. Then there are specific instructions for each type of observation form.

General Instructions

1. Preparing to observe a team

a. **Be clear about the purpose of observing the meeting**. If the team leader or the team has asked you to observe, understand what they want to learn from the observation. If you are volunteering, understand what you hope to learn or are curious about.

b. **Decide how many observers**. You may use one or two observers for a meeting. If you use two, each can observe for half of the meeting (approximately 30 minutes).

c. **Choose an appropriate observation form**. The following pages contain several forms and checksheets to use when observing a group. Select the form that best fits your purpose in observing the team.

d. **Decide when and how to share the observations.** Observers are allowed to report only during a predetermined meeting evaluation time. You may include a discussion of the observations during the regular meeting evaluation time (usually at the end of the meeting), or designate a special time to discuss the observer's feedback. Decide in advance whether team members should share their observations of the meeting before or after the observer reports. In either case, leave time for the whole team to discuss the observer's information. The observer should also be prepared to share what it was like to observe. What were the challenges of the task?

Exercise 4: Observing Group Process, *continued*

e. Review the following guidelines for observing a team:

- **Sit apart from the group.** The observer sits apart from the rest of the team in a chair obviously separate from the group. It helps to be able to see as many team members as possible.

- **Do not participate in the meeting content.** The observer **does not** participate in discussions. The observer ignores the topics discussed (the content) and pays attention to the discussion methods and interactions among members (the process). Observers may join the team when their turn at observing is over and may then contribute to the discussion.

- **Do not share observations with the team during the meeting.** Observers must reserve their observation comments for the scheduled meeting evaluation time.

- **Record your observations, not your judgments or evaluations.** Stick to noticing behaviors and verbatim comments. Set aside your interpretations and judgments. For example, note that after John told a joke, the team continued laughing and joking for 10 minutes before returning to the task, instead of noting that John distracted the group.

2. Observing a team

- **a. Practice observing the team.** At the meeting, watch the team for about 10 minutes without taking notes. Practice ignoring **what** they say; pay attention only to how members are interacting.

- **b. Observe and take notes.** Once you've gotten used to watching the team, begin taking notes on the form you have chosen. If your form doesn't work for you, feel free to change it. Remember that observation takes practice. Some kinds of

observation may be difficult to do at first. This means your data may not be very reliable at first because you may miss a lot of the interaction as you get used to the observer role. Still, the information captured is usually both useful and interesting to the team. Most teams enjoy discussing data about their meetings as long as the data is not presented judgmentally.

c. Report the observations.

- **Show the team the form used.** If the team is unfamiliar with the form used to record the observations, explain it before describing the observation data. This will help the team better understand what they are about to hear.

- **Report only what you saw and heard.** Avoid reporting what you thought was going on in people's minds. Be descriptive, not judgmental. Follow the guidelines for giving useful feedback on pp. 6-23 to 6-30.

- **Be organized.** Report categories of observations; or recurring patterns of behavior; or a chronological sequence of what happened in the meeting.

d. Discuss the observations. Invite questions and comments on the observations. Remember that the data collected can have many interpretations. Did team members' observations differ from those of the observer? Also remember that a pattern observed in one meeting does not mean a problem exists.

Meeting Observation Form 1: Examples of Contributions

Instructions: This form helps you notice what kinds of comments people make. Make notes below whenever you observe examples of each type of behavior. Be as specific as possible in capturing what was said. The purpose is to collect examples of the behaviors below. Feel free to use only part of the form or to change some categories. The first three types of comments on each page help the team get the task done; the last two categories help members get along together.

---

1. Suggests methods or procedures. Suggests ways of doing things; steps to move the discussion forward; use of methods such as brainstorming, circling the group for opinions, multivoting, etc.

---

2. Seeks information or opinions. Draws out relevant information, opinions, ideas, suggestions, or concerns from team members. Asks questions to invite others' ideas.

---

3. Gives information or opinions. Shares relevant information, opinions, suggestions, and concerns.

---

4. Encourages others. Is friendly, warm, and responsive; uses eye contact and "uh-huhs" to support others' participation.

---

5. Reduces tension. Reduces tension by using humor appropriately; gets the group to laugh; admits errors.

---

continued...

Meeting Observation Form 1: Examples of Contributions, continued

6. **Clarifies and elaborates ideas.** Clears up confusion; gives examples; points out issues and alternatives; shares interpretations of what's been said; builds on what others have said.

7. **Summarizes.** Pulls together what's been said; organizes related ideas; integrates different ideas; offers conclusions for the team to consider.

8. **Checks decisions.** Notices when the group is making a decision and states the decision for the group; checks to be sure the decision method (vote, seek consensus, delegate to subgroup) is acceptable; checks to be sure decision has been well thought out.

9. **Resolves disagreements.** Works out disagreements; looks for ways to address objections and concerns; incorporates others' ideas into proposals.

10. **Notices group feelings.** Senses and expresses team feelings and moods; is aware of significant shifts in tone and helps team be aware of shifts also.

Meeting Observation Form 2: Patterns of Contributions

Instructions: This form helps you see what kinds of contributions team members make during a discussion. Usually each member's contributions will cluster in a few categories. For example, one member will offer lots of ideas and provide summaries during the discussion, while another will ask questions and draw out quiet members. Data from this type of observation can help a team appreciate the different strengths members bring to the group. It can also help a team identify areas where they need to build skills to keep the team functioning well. Copy the form below or make a version of your own. Enter the names of team members across the top. Enter hash marks or comments in the appropriate boxes when you see one of the behaviors listed. The behaviors listed on this page tend to address relationships within the team. The behaviors listed on page C-24 help move the team's task forward.

Behaviors	*Team Member Names*				
Encourages others. Is friendly, warm, and responsive; uses eye contact and "uh-huhs" to support others' participation.					
Reduces tension. Reduces tension by using humor appropriately; gets the group to laugh; admits errors.					
Resolves disagreements. Works out disagreements; looks for ways to address objections and concerns; incorporates others' ideas into proposals.					
Notices group feelings. Senses and expresses team feelings and moods; is aware of significant shifts in tone and helps team be aware of shifts also.					

continued...

Meeting Observation Form 2: Patterns of Contributions, *continued*

Behaviors	*Team Member Names*				
Suggests methods or procedures. Suggests ways of doing things; steps to move the discussion forward; use of methods such as brainstorming, circling the group for opinions.					
Seeks information or opinions. Draws out relevant information, opinions, ideas, suggestions, or concerns from team members. Asks questions to invite others' ideas.					
Gives information or opinions. Shares relevant information, opinions, suggestions, and concerns.					
Clarifies and elaborates ideas. Clears up confusion; gives examples; points out issues and alternatives; shares interpretations of what's been said; builds on what others have said.					
Summarizes. Pulls together what's been said; organizes related ideas; integrates different ideas; offers conclusions for the team to consider.					
Checks decisions. Notices when a decision is made and states the decision for the group; checks to be sure the decision method (vote, seek consensus, delegate) is acceptable; checks to be sure decision has been well thought out.					

Meeting Observation Form 3: Patterns of Interaction

Instructions: This method helps you keep track of who talks to whom. However, this method of data collection is very interpretive. Since people rarely name the person to whom they are speaking, the observer usually has to guess at the intended recipient(s) of the comments. This observation method helps uncover interaction patterns such as: the team tends to direct most of its comments to one member, thereby making that member the communication center; or, the women are often interrupted by the men; or, one member had no comments directed to him or her during the meeting.

There are several ways to set up this observation form. If there are six or fewer members, the simplest way is to write the names of team members in a circle, corresponding to where they sit during the meeting. Draw lines connecting each member with every other member. When someone speaks, draw a slash mark near the speaker's name on the line between the speaker and the recipient. If the speaker addresses the whole team, draw a slash mark next to the speaker's name but not on any line (see example below). Before using this form, you will need to operationally define "statement." Does it include murmurs and head nods? If someone speaks for several minutes is that all one statement? If someone starts to speak and then stops, does that count? The choice can be up to the observer. Just be consistent.

Example Sociogram

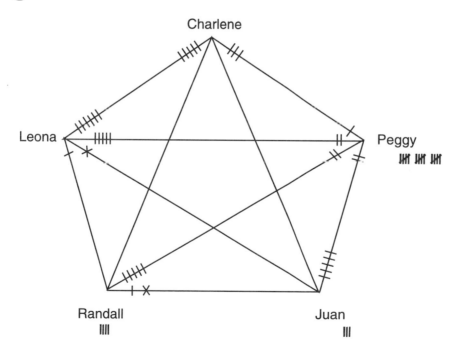

Interpretation of the example sociogram

In this discussion, Peggy was the center of the interaction. She spoke the most, addressed most of her comments to the whole team, and had the most comments directed toward her. Leona and Charlene had side conversations going on during the discussion. The x's show that Juan was interrupted twice.

Meeting Observation Form 4: The Unfolding Discussion

Instructions: Sometimes the best way to notice how team members are working together is to take free-form notes on the unfolding discussion. This can consist of writing down chronologically what team members say. You can also note things such as interruptions, side conversations, tangents, many people talking at once, etc. Review the guidelines for observers on pp. C-19 and C-20. Remember to record what is actually said and done, not your interpretation of comments and behaviors. Keep any notes on your impressions separate from notes of what actually happened. Listen carefully to the participants.

Notes:

Exercise 5
Discussing Your Mission

Time: 1 to 1.5 hours, plus some preparation time

Overview

The primary purpose of this exercise is for the team to explore its charter or mission in depth. This activity can be led by the team leader, sponsor, or coach. However, it could also be led by team members in order to give them experience in planning and facilitating meetings. The instructions below are written for team members in case you choose to have members run this meeting.

This activity involves developing a meeting agenda, applying the Plan–Do–Check–Act strategy (◀see p. 5-37) to the meeting process, and running the meeting (◀see p. 4-4 for how to run a meeting).

Instructions

Task: Your task is to plan and run a meeting with your team to discuss your charter or mission.

1. Plan the meeting.

a. Review meeting skills as discussed in Chapter 4.

b. Decide when and where the meeting will be held (if outside regular meeting time).

c. Clarify roles: You will be the meeting facilitator, the person who runs the meeting, keeps it focused, and moderates discussions. You need to designate someone else to be a scribe, the person who keeps track of time and records notes on flipcharts.

Optional: If you don't want to facilitate the entire meeting, you can switch roles with the scribe or ask someone else to facilitate part of the meeting. Each turn should last at least 30 minutes, however.

Optional: You may ask the team leader or coach to be an observer during the meeting. Observers gather information about the meeting process (◀see p. C-19 for more information about the observer role). You could also ask an observer to give you feedback on your skills as a facilitator.

d. Select a warm-up, either one described earlier in this chapter or one of your own.

e. Decide how to structure the meeting discussion. The procedure on the following page is offered as a guide.

2. "Do" and "Check" the meeting and discussion.
Carry out the plan, which is the "do" step in the Plan-Do-Check-Act cycle. Try to stay close to your agenda. Make sure you evaluate the meeting and review the discussions. This is the "check" step. (◀Refer to meeting evaluation, pp. 4-9 to 4-10.)

3. Act on the team's conclusions.
Record what you learned about the team's mission, the conduct of meetings, and the various roles. File these records with other team documents. Send copies of the conclusions about your mission to the sponsor. Either have the team leader discuss the issues with the sponsor or include this topic on the agenda of a meeting with the sponsor.

Exercise 5: Discussing Your Mission, continued

Suggested meeting format

Instructions: Use these suggestions to create an agenda appropriate for your team. If you base your agenda on the model on p. 4-47, you will need to add more time for this exercise on discussing the mission. Determine what supplies you will need for the meeting. Will you need extra flipchart pads? paper? pens? markers? tape? Who is responsible for getting these supplies?

Instructions

1. Have someone read and explain your team's mission statement (you may ask the team leader or sponsor to do this).

2. Have the team discuss any of the questions listed below. Either write them on flipchart pages before the meeting and post these pages on the wall, or hand out prepared sheets. Ask only one question at a time. After the first three questions, you might divide the team into two smaller groups. Give each small group a different question. Have them discuss the question and then report back to the other small group.

    *   Is it clear what management expects of you?

    *   Does our project cover only part of a larger process or problem? Where do we fit in? Where does our part of the process start and end?

    *   Are the boundaries of the project clear? What will be outside our jurisdiction?

    *   What resources, inside or outside the department, will we need?

    *   Will this project work? Does the mission fit in with our knowledge about the process or problem?

    *   Do we have the right people on this team to accomplish the mission?

    *   What people not on the team will be crucial to our efforts?

    *   Who will support our efforts? Who will be opposed? Who will be neutral? How can we reach all of these people?

    *   Is it clear where this project fits into the organization's priorities?

3. Summarize the team's discussion. List unanswered questions.

4. How will you obtain the information to answer all your questions? Who will get the information? By when?

Exercise 6

Information Hunt—A Preliminary Look at a Process

Time: Each team member will put in 15 to 60 min. for each question;
allow 15 min. per question for team discussion

Overview

A series of questions is presented on the following page. Exploring the process to find the answers will introduce team members to the process you're studying and let you identify key process conditions. The goal is to get the best answers you can in the time allotted. The team may decide to dig further and spread this exercise over several meetings. (Note: The information gathered will be useful background should the team ever use Strategy 8: Describe a Process, p. 5-45.)

Instructions

1. Preparation and start-up.

Copy the list of questions on p. C-30 and hand it out to each team member. Select several questions that seem most relevant to the process you are studying. Don't attempt to answer the whole list of questions the first time around. You can work through them over several weeks. Divide the chosen questions among team members, who will work either individually or in pairs.

2. Investigation.

Have individuals or pairs answer their assigned questions independently. Tell them to seek a balance between carefully gathering objective information and using educated opinions. They should use available data to answer the questions if they are fairly certain the data is reliable; avoid additional data collection unless it can be done easily. They should seek opinions from people involved in the process who are in the best position to know the answers.

3. Discussion.

As members or pairs complete their answers, have them discuss their findings with the entire team. If you are spreading the assignments over several weeks, reserve time at team meetings to review the assignments completed by that meeting.

4. Complete the list.

As members or pairs complete an assignment, give them another question to answer. Continue until all relevant questions have been answered and discussed.

Exercise 6: Information Hunt, continued

Questions to Ask About a Process

Instructions: Give a copy of these questions to each team member.

The process being studied is_____

_____

(All the following questions refer to this process.)

1. Who are its external customers? What individuals, groups, or systems outside our organization rely on or could benefit from this process? Who has (or could have) expectations about this process?

2. How do we know what the external customers like or don't like about this process? What satisfies or dissatisfies them?

3. Who are its internal customers? Describe those within our organization who do (or could) rely on the successful operation of this process or the resulting product or service.

4. How do we determine what the internal customers like or don't like about this process? What satisfies or dissatisfies them?

5. What are the operational definitions of quality in this process? What specifically determines whether the process is working well or poorly?

6. What records are kept regarding quality? Who uses this information? How do they use it? Are these record formats suited to how they are used?

7. What are the most common mistakes or defects that occur? What is the operational definition for each mistake or defect? What proportion of these is commonly assumed to be a worker's fault? What proportion do we usually attribute to the system? How do people arrive at these conclusions?

8. By what process do we inspect, evaluate, and report problems regarding:
   a. Planning required for this process
   b. Incoming materials, supplies, and information critical to this process
   c. The process itself
   d. The final product or service received by the external or internal customer

9. List the critical elements of this process: materials, ingredients, components, parts, information, etc.

10. List the suppliers or vendors of each critical element.

11. Describe the company's procedures for purchasing materials or ingredients brought in from outside the facility (plant office, company, etc.). To what extent is "low bid" a governing factor in our purchasing decisions?

12. Describe the impact of the most common mistakes or defects in this process. What do they cost in time, money, customer loyalty, or employee pride?

13. Who is responsible for quality in this process? Who is responsible for detecting mistakes or defects? Who is responsible for identifying and correcting the causes of mistakes or defects?

Exercise 7
The Living Flowchart

Time: 1.5 to 3 hours

Overview

In this exercise, the people who work with a process meet and talk to each other as customers and suppliers. They discuss issues such as what they want or receive from the steps of a process. This exercise helps participants identify the basic steps and substeps of a process, as well as explore the interdependence of all process steps. It works best, and is most educational, if the participants are asked to "represent" steps which are familiar to them, but which are not their main jobs.

Instructions

1. Preparation.
You may involve anywhere from 5 to 30 people in this exercise. Have several flipcharts and plenty of markers available.

2. Select a process to discuss.
If this activity is done by a team, the process used should be the process targeted for improvement. If you choose to involve a more diverse group of people, pick a process known by most of them.

3. Flowchart the process, Part 1.
Identify the four to five major steps of the process, the steps that would go at the top of a top-down flowchart. If there are fewer than eight people involved in this activity, have the whole group work together. If there are more than eight people, divide them into two or more groups of about four or five members each. Have the small groups report on their versions of the process; then have everyone discuss the different versions until you come up with one version that is best.

4. Assign the major process steps.
Ask one or more people to represent each major step (and substep) you identified. The meeting facilitator may either assign steps to the participants, or let people select a step.

> Note: If participants are allowed to pick the step they want to represent, it cannot be one they work with every day. Rather, have them choose one they think they understand or know something about. This is important so that the participants will begin to see the process—and their own jobs in particular—from different viewpoints.

5. Assemble the flowchart.
Arrange the people or groups in the room so that they represent the general sequence of steps in the actual process (see the cartoon on the next page). That is, the person or people representing the first step will be at one end of the room; the people representing the second step will be next to them; and so forth.

6. Flowchart the process, Part 2.
Each individual or small group takes its step, the one they represent, and divides it into four to six substeps. These substeps would be the same as the columns in a top-down flowchart. If you have small groups, they can assign individual members to represent substeps (the same way the small group represents a major step).

Exercise 7: The Living Flowchart, continued

7. Let the system talk.

The facilitator creates a lively interchange of ideas between participants by working through the process in no particular order. He or she chooses a step or substep and asks the person or group representing it one or two of the following questions:

- What contribution do you make to this overall process?

- Who is your internal customer? What do you believe they expect from you? How do you know?

- How do you keep in touch with what the external customer wants?

- Who is your internal supplier? Pick one or two of your internal suppliers and tell them what you need from them. How could they make your life easier?

The entire group should discuss the answers this person or small group gives. After some discussion, shift the focus to another step or substep, asking its representatives the same kinds of questions. Whenever discussion slows down, ask questions of a different group. Keep shifting the focus unpredictably to keep group members involved and on their toes.

8. Wrap up the discussion.

After the participants have worked through most (if not all) of the substeps, the total assembly discusses the following:

- What did we as a group learn from this activity? What did individuals learn about how their jobs do, or should, operate?

- What inadequacies in the real process came to light?

Appendix D
References

Argyris, Chris. *Integrating the Individual and the Organization.* New York: John Wiley & Sons, Inc., 1964.

Berry, Leonard L. *On Great Service: A Framework for Action.* New York: The Free Press, 1995.

Brassard, Michael. *The Memory Jogger Plus+.* Methuen, MA: GOAL/QPC, 1989.

Brassard, Michael, and Diane Ritter. *The Memory Jogger II.* Methuen, MA: GOAL/QPC, 1994.

Covey, Stephen R. *Principle-Centered Leadership.* New York: Simon & Schuster, 1992.

———. *Seven Habits of Highly Effective People.* New York: Simon & Schuster, 1989.

DeBono, Edward. *Serious Creativity.* New York: HarperCollins, 1993.

———. *Six Thinking Hats.* Toronto: Key Porter Books Limited, 1985.

Deming, W. Edwards. *The New Economics for Industry, Government, Education.* Cambridge, MA: MIT Center for Advanced Engineering Study, 1993.

———. *Out of the Crisis.* Cambridge, MA: MIT Center for Advanced Engineering Study, 1986.

Dyer, William G. *Team Building,* 2nd ed. Reading, PA: Addison-Wesley, 1987.

Filley, Alan C. *Interpersonal Conflict Resolution.* Glenview, IL: Scott Foresman, 1975.

Fisher, Roger, and William Ury. *Getting to Yes: Negotiating Agreement Without Giving In.* New York: Viking Press, 1991.

Gale, Bradley T. *Managing Customer Value.* New York: The Free Press, 1994.

GOAL/QPC, and Joiner Associates. *The Team Memory Jogger™.* Madison, WI: Joiner Associates Inc., 1995.

Harvey, J.B. *The Abilene Paradox and Other Meditations on Management.* Lexington, MA: Heath, 1988.

Ishikawa, Kaoru. *Introduction to Quality Control.* Tokyo: 3A Corporation, 1990.

———. *What Is Total Quality Control? The Japanese Way.* Englewood Cliffs, NJ: Prentice Hall, 1985.

Janis, Irving L. *Groupthink: Psychological Studies of Policy Decisions and Fiascos,* 2nd ed. Boston: Houghton Mifflin, 1982.

Joiner Associates Inc. *Fundamentals of Fourth Generation Management,* an eight-module video-based instructional program. Madison, WI: Joiner Associates Inc., 1993.

———. *Plain & Simple Series.* Madison, WI: Joiner Associates Inc., 1995.
  – *Cause-and-Effect Diagrams: Plain & Simple*
  – *Data Collection: Plain & Simple*
  – *Flowcharts: Plain & Simple*
  – *Frequency Plots: Plain & Simple*
  – *How to Graph: Plain & Simple*
  – *Individuals Charts: Plain & Simple*
  – *Introduction to the Tools: Plain & Simple*
  – *Pareto Charts: Plain & Simple*
  – *Scatter Plots: Plain & Simple*
  – *Time Plots: Plain & Simple*

————. *Running Effective Meetings,* a stand-alone instructional module. Madison, WI: Joiner Associates Inc., 1992.

————. *Joiner 7 Step Method™ Notebook.* Madison, WI: Joiner Associates Inc., 1995.

Joiner, Brian L. *Fourth Generation Management: The New Business Consciousness.* New York: McGraw-Hill, 1994.

Joint Commission on Accreditation of Healthcare Organizations. *Striving Toward Improvement.* Oakbrook Terrace, IL: JCAHO, 1992.

Juran, Joseph M. *Juran on Leadership for Quality: An Executive Handbook.* New York: The Free Press (Macmillan, Inc.), 1989.

Katzenbach, Jon R., and Douglas Smith. *The Wisdom of Teams.* New York: HarperCollins Publishers, Inc., 1993.

Kume, Hitoshi. *Statistical Methods for Quality Improvement.* Tokyo: The Association for Overseas Technical Scholarship, 1985.

Mizuno, Shigeru (ed.). *Management for Quality Improvement: The 7 New QC Tools.* Cambridge, MA: Productivity Press, 1988.

Myers, J. Gordon. "Making Teams Productive." *Pinnacle,* June-July, 1995.

Nadler, Gerald, and Shozo Hibino. *Breakthrough Thinking.* 2nd ed. Rocklin, CA: Primo Publishing, 1994.

Pfeiffer, William, and John E. Jones (eds.). *A Handbook of Structured Experiences for Human Relations Training.* LaJolla, CA: University Associates, Inc., 1972–.

Reddy, Brendan. *Intervention Skills, Process Consultation for Small Groups and Teams.* San Diego, CA: Pfeiffer & Company, 1994.

Rummler, G., and Alan Brache. *Improving Performance.* San Francisco: Jossey-Bass, 1990.

Sampson, Edward, and Marya Marthas. *Group Process for the Health Professions.* Albany, NY: Delmar Publishers, Inc., 1990.

Scholtes, Peter R. "Teams in the Age of Systems," reprinted in *The Handbook of Best Team Practices.* Amherst, MA: HRD Press, 1996. (Order from: Scholtes Seminars and Consulting, PO Box 489, Madison, WI, 53701-0489)

————. "Performing Without Appraisal." *The Total Quality Review.* May/June 1995. (Order from: Scholtes Seminars and Consulting, PO Box 489, Madison, WI, 53701-0489)

Senge, Peter M. *The Fifth Discipline.* New York: Doubleday/Currency, 1990.

Vaill, Peter B. *Managing as a Performing Art.* San Francisco: Jossey-Bass, 1989.

Weisbord, Marvin R. *Productive Workplaces.* San Francisco: Jossey-Bass, 1991.

Weisinger, Hendrie. *The Critical Edge.* New York: Harper & Row, 1989.

Wellins, Richard, William Byham, and G. Dixon. *Inside Teams: How 20 World Class Organizations Are Winning Through Teamwork.* San Francisco: Jossey-Bass, 1994.

Wheeler, Donald J. *Understanding Variation: The Key to Managing Chaos.* Knoxville, TN: SPC Press, Inc., 1986.

Wheeler, Donald J., and David S. Chambers. *Understanding Statistical Process Control,* 2nd ed. Knoxville, TN: SPC Press, Inc., 1992.

Womack, James P., Daniel T. Jones, and Daniel Roos. *The Machine That Changed the World.* New York: Rawson Associates, 1990.

Index

U

Ordering Information

Need additional copies of *The Team Handbook Second Edition*? Now there are four ways to order.

Call Toll Free	**FAX**	**Mail**	**E-Mail**
1-800-669-8326	1-608-238-2908	Joiner Associates Inc.	sales@joiner.com
or 1-608-238-8134	Any day, any time	PO Box 5445 3800 Regent St.	Any day, any time
8 AM - 5 PM Central		Madison, WI 53705-0445	

Price per copy

1-9	$39.00
10-24	35.10
25-99	31.20
100-499	27.30
500-4999	23.40
5000+	Quotation

Shipping charges

Order amount	Shipping/handling
$0–$10	$4.50
$10.01–$50	6.50
$50.01–$100	8.50
$100.01-$200	10.50
$200.01–$400	14.00
$400+	3.5% of sales

(Prices vary for Alaska, Hawaii, and foreign countries.)

Sales tax .

California	7.25%
Illinois	6.25%
Ohio	5%
Wisconsin	5% (5.5% in Dane County)

Payment methods

We accept payment by check, money order, or credit card. Purchase orders are also accepted. If you are paying by purchase order: 1) provide the name and address of the person to be billed, or 2) send a copy of the P.O. when order is payable by an agency of the federal government.

Shipping

Orders are usually shipped in 24-48 hours. We ship UPS ground in the continental U.S. Contact us for shipping charges outside the continental U.S. and for expedited orders.

Order form for *The Team Handbook Second Editio*

1. Shipping address (We cannot ship to a P.O. box.)

Name _____

Organization _____

Address _____

City _____

State _____ Zip _____ Country _____

Phone _____ Fax _____

2. Quantity and price

Code	Quantity	Unit price	Total price
01020			
		Tax CA, IL, OH, WI only	
		Shipping Charge (see left)	
		Total	

3. Payment method

❏ Check enclosed (payable to Joiner Associates Inc.)

❏ VISA ❏ MasterCard ❏ AMEX

Card # _____ Exp. date _____

Signature _____

❏ Purchase order # _____

Bill to name _____

Organization _____

Address _____

City _____

State _____ Zip _____ Country _____

Phone _____ Fax _____

4. Request for other materials

❏ Include me on your newsletter mailing list

❏ Send me a catalog on Joiner products

We'd like your opinion...

Your opinions about *The Team Handbook* are important to us. Please take a few minutes to complete this survey, and return to Joiner Associates by mail (P.O. Box 5445, 3800 Regent St., Madison, WI 53705-0445) or fax (608-238-2908) to the attention of Customer Sales and Service. Thank you.

1. How did you hear about ***The Team Handbook Second Edition***?
   - ❏ Joiner Associates Inc. Product Catalog
   - ❏ Coworker
   - ❏ Magazine advertisement (Please specify) _____
   - ❏ Other (Please specify) _____

2. Did you use the **first edition** of *The Team Handbook* (any copy purchased prior to July 1996)?
   - ❏ Yes   ❏ No

3. What do you like most about the **second edition** of *The Team Handbook*?

4. How could we improve the book?

5. What types of teams do you have in your organization?

6. What are the biggest challenges you face in your work with teams?

If you would like to be added to our newsletter mailing list, please check here ❏ and complete the following:

Name _____   Title _____

Organization _____   Address _____

City _____   State _____   Zip_____   Country _____

Phone _____   Fax _____

Thank you. Your comments will be very helpful to us.

Other Joiner Products and Services

Joiner Associates offers a wide variety of products and services that can help you use your own resources to greater advantage. Call 1-800-669-8326 for more information on the products and services listed below, or to request our catalog.

Books

Fourth Generation Management: The New Business Consciousness by Brian L. Joiner. A book that describes how a new synthesis of management principles is being used to create rapid, sustained improvement. (New York: McGraw-Hill, 1993)

Joiner 7 Step Method™ Notebook. A structured approach to problem solving that provides guidelines on what questions to ask when, how to develop effective solutions, and how to maintain the gains.

Plain & Simple Series. Through this set of 10 learning and application guides, users learn how to decide what tools to use, how to get the right kind of data, and how to create the charts, interpret the information, and put it to use. They can be used for self-study, as a resource, or in training sessions. The set of 10 includes:

> *Introduction to the Tools: Plain & Simple*
> *Data Collection: Plain & Simple*
> *How to Graph: Plain & Simple*
> *Flowcharts: Plain & Simple*
> *Pareto Charts: Plain & Simple*
> *Time Plots: Plain & Simple*
> *Individuals Charts: Plain & Simple*
> *Frequency Plots: Plain & Simple*
> *Scatter Plots: Plain & Simple*
> *Cause-and-Effect Diagrams: Plain & Simple*

The Team Memory Jogger™. An easy-to-use reference guide just for team members—written from their point of view. A handy pocket guide for improving team effectiveness, providing practical action tips on feedback skills, having effective meetings, dealing with common team problems, and more.

Video-based Instruction

Fundamentals of Fourth Generation Management. An eight-module, video-based instructional program that explores the basic principles of a customer focus, a scientific approach, and working together as "all one team." The program mixes video instruction with real-time exercises that emphasize key points and skills.

Training Products

Running Effective Meetings. Learn how to get much more out of meetings. This four-hour instructional program is designed to help any kind of group learn and practice effective meeting skills.

Seminars and Workshops

Joiner Associates also offers public and on-site seminars, workshops, and training programs featuring hands-on learning in core skills such as problem-solving approaches, tools, teams, change, facilitation, and leadership.

Consulting Services

Our experienced consultants specialize in helping customers understand current needs and opportunities, make significant improvement in key business objectives, and implement organization-wide changes. They work with all levels of organizations, from senior executives to shop floor employees, in a breadth of industries encompassing services, manufacturing, education, and government.